KITCHEN COQUETTE

kitchen coquette

KATRINA MEYNINK

ALLEN&UNWIN

Contents

Chapter five — moveable feasts

Chapter six — playing house

Chapter seven — a time for fuss

Chapter eight — what the f*$k should we cook for dinner?

INTRODUCTION

In life, there are a few things everyone agrees are spectacular: Tim Tams. Butter. Summer holidays. True love. Good books. Puppies.

And pulling off a stellar meal.

I don't know about you, but a few killer recipes, an insane assortment of ingredients and a table that has DAZZLE steaming from it when the guests arrive is my version of Narnia. A perfected meal says check out my mad skills in the kitchen. A well-baked cake says to your dear friends that you have culinary prowess up the whazoo.

Well that's my theory and I'm sticking to it. And the very reason why this book lives.

The following pages are filled with recipes that are part tongue-in-cheek, part heart-in-hand, part survival guide for those who like their dinner a little dirtier, a whole lot more exciting, and always in the stellar category. Sometimes we want to cook to impress, sometimes we want to eat to forget, sometimes we just want to gather our friends into the fold, and sometimes we don't want to cook at all.

I'm not professionally trained (I'm on the way) but I am self-taught. I learnt to cook by taste, mistakes, disasters, burnt forearms and sliced fingers, and more than a little advice from my nearest and dearest.

Through it all I have always, always thought that cooking should be fun. An opportunity to reflect who we are or the mood we might be in — smart, funny, whimsical, affectionate, cute, rude, arty, curious or kind. My recipes are a collection to dip into and serve up during all those weird, wonderful, hideous and happy moments in life that require a bite to eat.

I won't tell you to pick from the garden, cook with the seasons, get back to basics or return to Granny's embrace as lovely as all these things might be. I have put forward a whole lot of other suggestions, a few challenges, and some dishes that are super easy — but all of them are what I call damn tasty. I hope you will too.

But recipes, like life, are infinitely nuanced, so what I might like to take to a wake, you might choose to cook for a first date. And good for you (and me). The important thing is to never deny yourself the excitement of not knowing what's ahead when you put a cake in the oven.

Hopefully my little guide will help you create salads that wild animals want to nest in, soufflés that make you fall in love, or a roast that shows someone a little part of who you are. All with a side serving of indiscretion, a liberal seasoning of political incorrectness, and a garnish of come-what-may frippery. (Hold the subtlety.)

Roast it. Bake it. Work it. Love it.

xoxo

Katrina

UNUS TEMPUS

From
dinner dates
TO FIRST ANNIVERSARIES
THERE ARE SOME
monumental first-time
COOKING OCCASIONS IN LIFE
AND PLENTY OF US FLYING BLIND
IN THE KITCHEN.

CHAPTER ONE

LIKE
A
VIRGIN

From dinner dates to first anniversaries there are some monumental first-time cooking occasions in life and plenty of us flying blind in the kitchen.

But there's no need to be nervous about your first time. It is crucial that you maintain your serotonin levels (sans chemicals) and keep your panties out of a twist.

Like great kisses, these meals have the requisite passion, intrigue and reward to make your first time worth remembering.

First dinner date(s)

... the vegetable, animal and mineral kingdoms have been ransacked for the purpose of discovering remedies capable of strengthening the genital apparatus, and exciting it into action.

John Davenport, 'Essay on Aphrodisiacs and Anti-aphrodisiacs', 1859

In my younger, wilder years, I dated a chef. He was an older man with tats in all the right places and he just loved to do it al forno, sous vide, half-baked ... It didn't last. But those midnight nude dinners à deux confirmed how much I love food and cooking. And sex.

Most dates early in a relationship occur over restaurant dinners. Why? The opportunity for date disaster runs deep. The terrain is hostile. It's noisy and crowded. Each of you might meet someone you know (or used to date). Social hazards thrive. Embarrassment and mortification hide behind every incorrect use of cutlery or soufflé that fails to rise to the occasion.

But food and sex are like blood brothers — inextricably linked. And our enjoyment of both will always rest with who shares our table. To avoid any split-the-bill-then-split issues, try cooking at home, where you'll have complete control over the territory and the menu.

With the following dishes you can show off your domestic capabilities with aplomb and find that balance between appetite, consummation and satiation. The key is to not look like a complete fool with wayward tastes, but to create a memorable and intimate meal, leaving your guest wanting to come to your place for dinner again and again ... and again.

Menu 1

Prawns with candied pancetta and gremolata

–

Chorizo Wellington with capsicum salsa and buttered spinach

–

Apple crumble soufflé

Menu 2

Crispy blue cheese ravioli, radicchio and walnut salad with quince dressing

–

Wagyu beef with horseradish butter, parmesan potato rösti and beans

–

Cherry Ripe chocolate pudding

PRAWNS WITH CANDIED PANCETTA AND GREMOLATA
YOU'RE ALL SORTS OF LOVELY

THESE PRAWNS WILL SEE YOUR ROMANTIC INTEREST WONDERING IF THEY HAVE, BY SHEER LUCK, STUMBLED UPON THEIR ONE TRUE SIGNIFICANT OTHER.

INGREDIENTS
4 slices of pancetta, cut into strips
1 tbsp golden syrup (light treacle), or more to taste
1 tbsp grapeseed oil
8 large raw prawns (shrimp), peeled and deveined with tails intact
1 tbsp lemon juice

Gremolata
a small handful of flat-leaf parsley leaves, finely chopped
a small handful of basil leaves, finely chopped
a small handful of watercress leaves, finely chopped
3 lemon thyme sprigs, leaves picked
1 garlic clove, peeled
1 tbsp lemon juice
zest of $1/2$ lemon
60 ml (2 fl oz/$1/4$ cup) olive oil
sea salt and freshly ground black pepper

To serve
micro herbs and edible flowers (optional)

Preheat the oven to 180°C (350°F/Gas 4). Line a baking tray with baking paper and set aside.

For the gremolata, combine the herbs, garlic, lemon juice and half the lemon zest in a food processor. With the motor running, slowly add the oil in a thin steady stream and process until a coarse paste forms.

Season and stir through the remaining lemon zest.

Arrange the pancetta in a single layer on the prepared tray and drizzle over the golden syrup.

Roast in the oven for 5–10 minutes until dark and crispy.

Heat the oil in a large frying pan over medium heat. Cook the prawns on each side for 1 minute and toss with the lemon juice.

Reserve 1 tablespoon of gremolata and spoon the remaining onto the serving plates.

Layer with the micro herbs, prawns and candied pancetta. Drizzle over the remaining gremolata and serve.

Serves 2

CHORIZO WELLINGTON WITH CAPSICUM SALSA AND BUTTERED SPINACH

PILLOW BITER

THERE IS SOMETHING ABOUT TAKING THE TIME TO COOK FOR SOMEONE, THE POSSIBILITY OF TOUCHING AND SMELLING FOOD AND THE CONNECTION WITH APPETITE THAT TURNS WHAT CAN OTHERWISE BE QUITE A TASK INTO A PROFOUNDLY PHYSICAL PLEASURE. MEALS ARE LOADED WITH MESSAGES — SUBLIMINAL AND EXPLICIT — TO WARN YOU OFF OR TURN YOU ON. AND ANTICIPATION IS A SERIOUS TOOL IN FOREPLAY'S BAG OF TRICKS.

THIS WELLINGTON IS NOT THE 1950S YE OLDE COMMON BEEF WELLIE. (COMMON AS IN UNIVERSAL, BUT ALSO COMMON AS IN VULGAR.) THIS NEW TWIST RESPECTS THE CLASSIC, WHILE BEING A LITTLE MORE MODERN AND FAR LESS 'SUNDAY NIGHT COMFORT' FARE IN ITS CONSTRUCTION.

INGREDIENTS

2 tsp olive oil
1 garlic clove, finely chopped
2 chorizo sausages, casings discarded
    and filling finely chopped
zest of 1 lemon
90 g (3¼ oz) freshly shelled peas
60 ml (2 fl oz/¼ cup) thickened cream
½ sheet of puff pastry (approximately
    25 x 27 cm/10 x 10¾ inches)
1 egg, lightly beaten
15 g (½ oz) unsalted butter, softened
200 g (7 oz) English spinach, trimmed

Capsicum salsa

1 tbsp extra virgin olive oil
½ small red onion, finely chopped
1 red capsicum (pepper), diced
1 tbsp balsamic vinegar
1 tbsp chopped basil leaves
1 tbsp chopped coriander (cilantro) leaves
2 tsp soft brown sugar
2½ tbsp red wine
sea salt and freshly ground black pepper

Preheat the oven to 170°C (325°F/Gas 3). Line a baking tray with baking paper and set aside.

For the capsicum salsa, heat the oil in a frying pan over medium-low heat. Add the onion and capsicum and cook for 15 minutes, or until softened. Add the remaining ingredients and season. Turn the heat to low and simmer for 15 minutes until the vegetables are cooked through.

Heat the oil in a large frying pan over medium-low heat. Add the garlic and chorizo, and sauté for 2 minutes. Transfer to a bowl and combine with the lemon zest. Season with salt and pepper.

Cook the peas in boiling water for 3 minutes, or until just tender. Drain, then puree in a food processor with the cream.

Place the pastry on a lightly floured surface and cut into quarters. Spoon half the pea mixture and half the chorizo mixture into the centre of one puff pastry square. Place another square of pastry on top and push down gently around the edges to enclose the filling. Repeat with the remaining pastry squares, and the pea and chorizo mixtures.

Brush the tops of the Wellington parcels with the egg wash, then transfer to the prepared tray and bake for 20 minutes until the pastry looks brown and crisp.

Melt the butter in a large frying pan over medium heat. Add the spinach and stir until just wilted. Season to taste.

Serve the Wellingtons with the capsicum salsa and buttered spinach.

Serves 2

APPLE CRUMBLE SOUFFLÉ

KISSING THE BREASTS OF WOMEN

THE IDEA OF COOKING A SOUFFLÉ USED TO MAKE ME WANT TO LIE DOWN IN A DARK ROOM. THEY ALWAYS SEEMED FAR TOO DIFFICULT AND SOMETHING MORE APPROPRIATE FOR RESTAURANTS WHERE A PROFESSIONAL CHEF (I.E. MICHEL ROUX) IS AT THE HELM. THIS VERSION, HOWEVER, IS SO EASY; FAR EASIER THAN BAKING A CAKE, WITH SIGNIFICANTLY FEWER INGREDIENTS AND LABOUR, AND IS SO MUCH MORE IMPRESSIVE (THINK BREASTS OF A WOMAN HERE).

CONVERSATIONAL BANTER, GREAT FOOD AND THIS APPLE CRUMBLE SOUFFLÉ FINALE WILL HAVE YOU BOTH LONGING TO DO UNSPEAKABLE THINGS BENEATH A SLOWLY REVOLVING FAN.

INGREDIENTS
Soufflé
75 g (2¾ oz/⅓ cup) caster (superfine) sugar, plus 1 tbsp extra for dusting
2 egg whites
125 ml (4 fl oz/½ cup) apple puree
15 g (½ oz) butter
100 g (3½ oz) butter

Crumble
65 g (2½ oz) plain (all-purpose) flour
25 g (1 oz) caster (superfine) sugar
a pinch of ground ginger
50 g (1¾ oz) butter

To serve
vanilla bean ice cream

Preheat the oven to 180°C (350°F/Gas 4).

For the crumble, combine the flour, sugar and ground ginger in a bowl. Rub the butter into the dry ingredients with your fingertips until a breadcrumb consistency has been achieved. Place the crumbs on a baking tray and bake for 10 minutes until golden brown. Continually check the crumble mixture while it is baking to ensure it cooks evenly.

While the crumble is cooking, grease two 250 ml (9 fl oz/1 cup) soufflé dishes or ovenproof coffee cups and dust with the extra caster sugar. Refrigerate for 5 minutes.

Whisk the egg whites and 1 tablespoon of the sugar in a large bowl with electric beaters until soft peaks form. Add the remaining sugar and beat for a further minute until they look thick and glossy and peaks have formed.

Spoon 80 ml (2½ fl oz/⅓ cup) of the apple puree into a large bowl. Fold in one-third of the egg whites, incorporate thoroughly and then fold in the remaining egg whites to lighten the mixture. Place a tablespoon of the remaining apple puree in each of the prepared soufflé dishes or cups and spoon the soufflé mixture on top. Bake for 8 minutes, or until risen.

Top each soufflé with the crumble mixture and serve immediately with ice cream.

Serves 2

Michel Roux, one of the world's most celebrated chefs, once said in an interview about soufflé, 'I love ze soufflé, eet's naughty, but eet reminds me of ze boobs of ze woman.

If it's beautifully cooked I feel like kissing eet!'

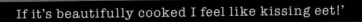

CRISPY BLUE CHEESE RAVIOLI, RADICCHIO AND WALNUT SALAD WITH QUINCE DRESSING

HOLY RAVIOLI

I THINK IT HELPS IF THE ONLY THING YOU SHARE ON A FIRST DINNER DATE AT HOME IS YOUR FORK. IT BUILDS THAT 'FIRST DATE' ANTICIPATION AND EXCITEMENT, AND AVOIDS THAT 'ONE-NIGHT STANDISH' BEHAVIOUR THAT HAS THE POTENTIAL TO HAUNT YOU FOREVER. AND, BEST OF ALL, YOU CAN AVOID ALL THOSE 'IF THESE WALLS COULD TALK YOU'D BE IN DEEP SH$% WITH YOUR MUM' SORT OF MOMENTS.

THIS RAVIOLI WILL DO WONDERS FOR YOUR DATING (AND YOUR DINING) LIFE — WHAT'S NOT TO LOVE ABOUT A BIG FAT-ARSED PLATE OF PASTA? FRIENDS, GATHER IN. THIS IS FIRST-DATE GOLD.

INGREDIENTS

Dressing
2 tbsp quince vino cotto
2 tbsp olive oil
1 tsp lemon juice
sea salt and freshly ground black pepper

Salad
½ radicchio, tough outer leaves discarded,
    finely shredded
½ witlof (Belgian endive), finely shredded
30 g (1 oz/¼ cup) walnuts, toasted and
    roughly chopped
a small handful of flat-leaf parsley,
    roughly chopped
½ red onion, finely sliced

Ravioli
125 ml (4 fl oz/½ cup) buttermilk
60 g (2¼ oz/1 cup) panko crumbs
250 g (9 oz) fresh blue cheese ravioli
grapeseed oil, for deep frying

For the dressing, combine the vino cotto, oil, lemon juice and salt and pepper in a small bowl and whisk until combined.

For the salad, place the radicchio, witlof, walnuts, parsley and onion in a bowl, toss well and set aside.

For the ravioli, place the buttermilk and panko crumbs in separate shallow bowls. Dip the ravioli in the buttermilk, then dip in the crumbs to coat. Fill a large frying pan 4 cm (1½ inches) deep with the oil and heat to 190°C (375°F) or until the oil is hot enough to turn a cube of bread immediately golden. Working in batches of five (less if you are using large ravioli), fry the ravioli for 1–2 minutes until the crumbs are golden and crisp. Remove with a slotted spoon and drain on paper towel.

Add the ravioli to the salad and toss with the dressing just before serving.

Serves 2

WAGYU BEEF WITH HORSERADISH BUTTER, PARMESAN POTATO RÖSTI AND BEANS

CHEWING TIGER

THE WAGYU MAY TAKE VIKING SWINGS AT YOUR BANK ACCOUNT, BUT YOUR FINANCIAL OUTLAY FOR A DATE WITH THE UNKNOWN WILL SEE YOU EATING HAPPY JAPANESE COW REARED ON BOUTIQUE BEERS, CLASSICAL MUSIC, DAILY MASSAGES AND INTENSIVE SPA TREATMENTS. A CREATURE THAT WELL MAINTAINED IS SURELY A SIGN OF THE CALIBRE OF DATES TO COME.

INGREDIENTS

2 x 150–200 g (5½–7 oz) wagyu steaks
2 tsp extra virgin olive oil
sea salt and freshly ground black pepper

Rösti

3 starchy potatoes (such as sebago),
  coarsely grated, rinsed in cold water and
  squeezed of excess moisture
½ brown onion, finely chopped
a small handful of flat-leaf parsley,
  roughly chopped
1 tbsp chives, finely chopped
1 tbsp plain (all-purpose) flour
1 egg, lightly beaten
30 g (1 oz/¼ cup) grated parmesan
2 tbsp olive oil, for shallow frying

Bean salad

180 g (6¼ oz) green beans, topped
40 g (1½ oz/¼ cup) pine nuts, toasted
25 g (1 oz/¼ cup) shaved parmesan

Horseradish cream

2½ tbsp crème fraîche
15 g (½ oz) finely grated fresh horseradish
  (the bottled stuff will do at a pinch)
1 tsp apple cider vinegar
1 tsp dijon mustard

Preheat the oven to 180°C (350°F/Gas 4).

For the rösti, place the potato, onion, parsley, chives, flour, egg and parmesan in a large bowl and stir until well combined. Using wet hands, shape 2 tablespoons of the potato mixture into flat fritters. Heat the oil in a large non-stick frying pan over medium-high heat and cook, in batches, for 3 minutes on each side, or until crisp and cooked through. Drain on paper towel, then keep warm in the oven.

Brush the steaks with the oil, and generously season both sides. Heat a heavy-based ovenproof frying pan over medium-high heat, add the steaks and cook for 2 minutes on each side. Transfer to the oven and cook for 8 minutes for medium-rare, or until cooked to your liking.

Bring a saucepan of water to the boil. Cook the beans for 1–2 minutes, or until just tender. Drain and refresh under cold water. Place the beans in a bowl, season and toss in the pine nuts and parmesan.

For the horseradish cream, combine the crème fraîche, horseradish, vinegar and mustard in a small bowl and season.

Plate each steak with 1 or 2 parmesan röstis, add a dollop of horseradish cream and some green bean salad.

Serves 2

CHERRY RIPE CHOCOLATE PUDDING

THE GREAT PUDDING SCANDAL

THIS IS THE EDIBLE VERSION OF AN ILLICIT AFFAIR — LIKE A NAUGHTY SECRET PHONE CALL FROM A LOVER WHERE YOU HAVE TO CUP YOUR HAND OVER YOUR MOUTH SO NO ONE ELSE CAN HEAR. IT'S ENOUGH TO MAKE YOUR GRANDMOTHER BLUSH — PURELY DELICIOUS, HOPEFULLY A LITTLE BIT SORDID, AND JUST YOURS TO SHARE.

INGREDIENTS

75 g (2¾ oz) dark chocolate (70 per cent cocoa solids), roughly chopped
150 g (5½ oz) butter, softened
2 large eggs
110 g (3¾ oz/½ cup) caster (superfine) sugar
35 g (1¼ oz/¼ cup) self-raising flour
4 large scoops vanilla ice cream
20 g (¾ oz/¼ cup) shredded coconut
1 x 80 g (2¾ oz) Cherry Ripe bar, roughly chopped into bite-sized pieces

Preheat the oven to 200°C (400°F/Gas 6).

Combine the chocolate and half the butter (75 g (2¾ oz)) in a heatproof bowl over a saucepan of gently simmering water and stir until melted and glossy. Set aside to cool, reserving 2 tablespoons of the chocolate.

Beat the remaining butter, eggs and sugar in a large bowl until pale and thick. Gently stir in the flour and melted chocolate mixture. Pour into two 125 ml (4 ½ fl oz/ ½ cup) ramekins until three quarters full. Bake for 20 minutes until firm to the touch.

While the puddings are cooking, take the ice cream out of the freezer to soften. Stir in the coconut, then return the ice cream to the freezer to harden.

To serve, pour the remaining chocolate mixture over the top of the puddings and sprinkle on the Cherry Ripe pieces. Serve immediately with the coconut ice cream.

Serves 2

Birthdays

Whether we're four or forty, there's something about the chaos of birthday rituals — particularly the special luxuries we've come to expect on such occasions — that are excuses for raucousness and overeating.

Birthdays always involve some cocooning and pampering by family and friends; a round of pin-the-tail-on-the-donkey when you're under 10, or a staggering quantity of champagne and hard-kicking cocktails when you're over 16. Whatever the birthday, sinking your teeth into butter-laden cake and feeling hundreds and thousands scratch the back of your throat are sensations that should not be reserved for the young.

When you're a kid, it's about stuffing as many sweets and fizzy drinks as possible into your mouth at once. As you get older, the party food gets boiled down from those many bowls of sugar-frosted havoc to one enormous plate: the cake.

Birthdays at any age aren't birthdays unless there's a cake. A single cupcake, a cake laden with candles or numbers, or a six-level sponge dripping with icing — that cake in its various incarnations represents the pinnacle of the day. It's intensely flavoured, lovingly put together, home baked and decorated with care. It's that mix of mouth-feel and nostalgia, rather than anything to do with flavour, that draws you in — and there's little else in this world, other than a hug from your mum and a strawberry Nesquik, that will so instantly take you back to being five.

When your friends are packed up and gone, it's those last pieces of cake that make your mouth dance until dawn. And then it's the stuffed-full-of-cake stomach-ache that makes you feel lovely and content as you lie prostrate on the couch, feeling that life may prove to be beautiful and surprisingly tolerable after all.

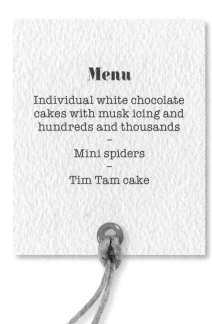

Menu

Individual white chocolate cakes with musk icing and hundreds and thousands

–

Mini spiders

–

Tim Tam cake

INDIVIDUAL WHITE CHOCOLATE CAKES WITH MUSK ICING AND HUNDREDS AND THOUSANDS

PIECE OF CAKE

CAKE IS DIFFICULT TO SHARE. I LEARNT THIS THE HARD WAY. IN YEAR ONE AT SCHOOL, MY BEST FRIEND REFUSED TO SHARE HER PLAYGROUND GOODNESS AND STABBED ME WITH A PENCIL. BITING INTO HER APPLE TEA-CAKE DID NOT A GOOD FRIENDSHIP MAKE. THIS HAPPENED MORE THAN ONCE, AND WHENEVER CAKE WAS INVOLVED I QUICKLY DISCOVERED THAT I COULD PROVOKE THIS KIND OF SENSELESS RAGE. SO AFTER A TEAR OR TWO AND A BIT OF SNOT DOWN MY FRONT, I'D GO BACK TO MY CRAYONS TO LIVE ANOTHER DAY.

THE INDIVIDUAL CAKE IS THE ANSWER TO SUCH WARFARE. THERE IS NEVER ANY DOUBT IT IS MEANT FOR ONE PERSON AND ONE PERSON ONLY. ITS SOLITARY ARCHITECTURAL SPLENDOUR DOES NOT LEND ITSELF TO SHARING; DIFFUSING THOSE WEAPONS-DRAWN-AT-DAWN SCENARIOS.

INGREDIENTS

230 g (8 oz) unsalted butter, chopped
230 g (8 oz) caster (superfine) sugar
230 g (8 oz) self-raising flour, sifted
1 tsp baking powder
4 eggs
1 vanilla bean, split lengthways and
  seeds scraped

Icing

200 g (7 oz) white chocolate, roughly chopped
6 musk sticks, finely chopped
100 g (3½ oz) unsalted butter, roughly
  chopped
100 g (3½ oz) raspberries, pureed
60 g (2¼ oz/½ cup) icing (confectioners')
  sugar, sifted
hundreds and thousands, to decorate

Preheat the oven to 180°C (350°F/Gas 4). Grease a six-cup friand tin and set aside.

Combine the butter, sugar, flour, baking powder, eggs and vanilla seeds in a bowl and beat with electric beaters for 3 minutes until smooth. Divide the batter among the tins until three-quarters full. Bake for 20 minutes, or until light and springy to touch. Turn out and cool on a wire rack.

For the icing, place the chocolate, musk sticks and butter in a heatproof bowl over a saucepan of gently simmering water and stir until the chocolate and musk sticks have melted. Remove from the heat and add the raspberry puree and sugar. Blitz in a food processor or blender until smooth. Allow to cool.

Spread the icing over the cakes and sprinkle on the hundreds and thousands.

Serves 6

INI
PIDERS

I ... DDICTION. A HORRID AND NAUGHTY HABIT. ... TRIED TO GO COLD TURKEY BUT WHENEVER I'M DEPRESSED, HUNG-OVER OR DESPERATE TO GET IN THE PARTY MOOD, I GET AN UNCONTROLLABLE URGE. I KNOW ALL THE GOOD PLACES TO SCORE. PUBLIC PARKS, PLAYGROUNDS AND PRIVATE PARTIES ARE IDEAL. THE RELIEF IS IMMEDIATE. THERE'S A FIZZ. A RUSH, ESPECIALLY IN THOSE INITIAL SECONDS …

MY ADDICTION BEGAN AT AGE THREE, WHEN I DISCOVERED THAT THE PEAK OF ANY PARTY LAY AT THE BOTTOM OF THE GLASS AFTER FINISHING A SPIDER, THAT UNSHAKEABLE COMBINATION OF ICE CREAM AND FIZZY POP. THAT MOMENT WHEN YOU FEEL THE BUTTERFLIES IN YOUR TUMMY, THE SUGAR RUSH TO YOUR HEAD AND THAT INSANE DESIRE TO BURP INAPPROPRIATELY IN FRONT OF YOUR MUM.

THE TRADITIONALIST

Ice cream and fizzy combo is quite simply a match made in heaven. The visual special effects appeal is matched by the sugar-popping waterslide down your throat and that touch of fizz dribbling down your chin.

12 scoops of vanilla ice cream
1.25 litres (44 fl oz/5 cups) Coca Cola

Place two large scoops of ice cream in six tall glasses and pour over the Coca Cola. Drink quickly.

ASIAN MAJOR

6 scoops of lemon sorbet
6 scoops of vanilla ice cream
1.25 litres (44 fl oz/5 cups) ginger beer
3 kaffir lime leaves, thinly sliced

Place a large scoop each of sorbet and ice cream in six tall glasses and pour over the ginger beer. Sprinkle the shredded kaffir lime leaves on top and serve.

AMERICAN BEAUTY

6 scoops of raspberry sorbet
6 scoops of coconut sorbet
1.25 litres (44 fl oz/5 cups) sparkling
   pink grapefruit soft drink
a handful of fresh rose petals

Place a large scoop of the raspberry and coconut sorbets in six tall glasses. Fill the glasses with the pink grapefruit drink. Scatter the rose petals on top and serve.

All recipes serves 6

TIM TAM CAKE
A CHAMPAGNE MOMENT

THIS IS THE SCH-MIZZLE OF BIRTHDAY CAKES. A PARTY BECOMES A BATTLEFIELD OF AWED SILENCES AND STOMACH RUMBLES WHEN THIS BAD BOY IS BROUGHT TO THE TABLE AND YOU FEEL ALL MARIE ANTOINETTE AS YOU MAKE YOUR 'LET THEM EAT ...' PROCLAMATION TO THE MASSES.

WHAT'S MORE, THE TIM TAM CAKE BRINGS OUT DARWINISM AT ITS BEST. JUST WHO WILL GET THE TIM TAMS? WHO'LL FOLD FIRST AND DIVE INTO THE CHOCOLATEY GOODNESS, BIRTHDAY PERSON OR NOT, AS AN EACH-TO-THEIR-OWN MENTALITY ENSUES AND ALL MANNERS AND TABLE ETIQUETTE FLY OUT THE WINDOW?

BUT PERHAPS, BEST OF ALL, IS THE MALT ICING, A SHARD OF TIM TAM AND A CUP OF TEA POST-PARTY.

YEP, I DO BELIEVE THAT'S WHAT DREAMS ARE MADE OF.

INGREDIENTS

220 g (7¾ oz/1 cup) soft brown sugar, firmly packed
165 g (5¾ oz/¾ cup) caster (superfine) sugar
3 large eggs
15 g (½ oz) unsalted butter
175 ml (5¾ fl oz) milk
3 tbsp malted milk powder
185 g (6½ oz/1¼ cups) plain (all-purpose) flour
1 tsp baking powder
25 g (1 oz) unsweetened cocoa powder, sifted
½ tsp bicarbonate of soda
6 Tim Tam biscuits (cookies), crushed
10 Tim Tams, broken into bite-sized chunks

Icing

250 g (9 oz) icing (confectioners') sugar
45 g (1¾ oz) malted milk powder
1 tsp unsweetened cocoa powder
125 g (4½ oz) unsalted butter, softened
2 tbsp boiling water

To serve

extra Tim Tams

Preheat the oven to 170°C (325°F/Gas 3). Butter and line two 20 cm (8 inch) loose-based sandwich cake tins and set aside.

Whisk the sugars and eggs in a large bowl until pale and thick.

Combine the butter, milk and malted milk powder in a saucepan and place over a low–medium heat and cook, being careful not to let it boil, until the butter melts. Set aside to cool for 5 minutes.

Beat the malt mixture into the sugar and eggs, then fold in the flour, baking powder, cocoa powder and bicarbonate of soda. Quickly stir in the crushed Tim Tams and divide the mixture between the prepared tins. Bake for 25 minutes until the cakes are firm to the touch and a skewer inserted comes out clean.

Turn out from the tins and allow to cool on a wire rack.

For the icing, combine the sugar, malted milk powder and cocoa powder in a bowl. Add the butter and, stirring continuously, slowly pour in the boiling water until you have a smooth butter cream.

Spread half the icing over one of the cakes and scatter on half the Tim Tam chunks. Sandwich the cakes together and ice the top of the cake with the remaining icing. Sprinkle the remaining chunks of Tim Tam over the icing.

Serve each piece with an additional Tim Tam to keep the celebration civil.

Serves 8

First anniversary

How good is being in love? After a life lived everywhere else you suddenly feel at home. By the time you reach the celebratory anniversary stakes you are comfortable with nudity in an art world kind of way, you know each other's weird bits, traits and insecurities, and that inescapable touch of oddness that is otherwise kept hidden from the world.

Love is yin and yang. Volatile yet complementary. It's all hand holding, celebrations and sweet tunes being strummed on a ukulele.

But while you've got love oozing from your pores and filling the high ceilings of your bedroom and creases of your doona, it's also worth remembering that love is hard work — you can't space out, lie down and muse about your beating heart while a butterfly carrying cupid's arrow lands on your head. Keeping love alive is also attention, commitment and physical and emotional gestures like love notes. And anniversary-motivated home-cooked meals from the heart.

Menu 1

Spaghettini with zucchini flowers, currants, garlic and chilli
–
Sticky beer 'n' balsamic ribs with crispy sweet potato ribbons and spicy mustard
–
Espresso martini granita

Menu 2

Blood orange duck salad
–
Reef fish curry
–
Chai tea panna cotta with chocolate sauce

SPAGHETTINI WITH ZUCCHINI FLOWERS, CURRANTS, GARLIC AND CHILLI
SUGGESTIVE CONTENT

THE TASTE AND PRETTINESS OF THIS SPAGHETTINI IS YOUR FIRST KISS, YOUR FIRST CRUSH, YOUR FIRST FIGHT AND NOW YOUR FIRST ANNIVERSARY ALL ROLLED INTO ONE — A ROLLERCOASTER TASTE SENSATION.

INGREDIENTS
6 zucchini (courgette) flowers
125 g (4½ oz) spaghettini
80 ml (2½ fl oz/⅓ cup) extra virgin olive oil
1 garlic clove, finely chopped
1 large red chilli, deseeded and thinly sliced
2 tbsp currants
40 g (1½ oz/¼ cup) pine nuts
finely grated zest and juice of 1 lemon
35 g (1¼ oz/¼ cup) grated parmesan,
   plus extra to serve (optional)
a small handful of flat-leaf parsley leaves,
   roughly chopped
sea salt and freshly ground black pepper

Remove the flowers from the zucchini, then gently open the petals and remove the yellow stamens. Tear the flowers into petals and set aside. Cut the zucchini diagonally into 5 mm (¼ inch) thick slices.

Cook the pasta in a large saucepan of boiling water for 6 minutes, or until al dente. Drain well.

Meanwhile, heat the oil in a large saucepan over medium heat. Add the garlic, zucchini flower petals, zucchini slices and chilli and cook, stirring, for 1–2 minutes until slightly softened. Stir in the currants, pine nuts and lemon zest and heat through for 1 minute. Add the pasta, lemon juice, parmesan and parsley and toss to combine. Season to taste, then divide among bowls and serve with the extra parmesan, if desired.

Serves 2

STICKY BEER 'N' BALSAMIC RIBS, WITH CRISPY SWEET POTATO RIBBONS AND SPICY MUSTARD

STICKY ENDINGS

THE KEY TO THESE BABY BACKS IS THE MARINADE, SO YOU NEED TO PLAN AHEAD. THESE ARE AT THEIR STICKY FINGER-LICKING BEST IF MARINATED FOR 24 HOURS AND THEN EATEN IN BED — IDEALLY IN A NAKED STATE OF POST-COITAL BLISS.

INGREDIENTS

1 kg (2 lb 4 oz) baby beef back ribs
125 ml (4 fl oz/½ cup) water

Marinade
4 large garlic cloves, finely chopped
1 tsp salt
1 tsp freshly ground black pepper
1 tbsp finely chopped rosemary
1 tbsp dark brown sugar, firmly packed
1 tbsp honey mustard
1 tbsp balsamic vinegar
1 tsp cayenne pepper
1 tsp sweet paprika
125 ml (4 fl oz/½ cup) beer

Glaze
125 ml (4 fl oz/½ cup) hot water
125 ml (4 fl oz/½ cup) beer
125 ml (4 fl oz/½ cup) balsamic vinegar
60 g (2¼ oz/¼ cup) dark brown sugar,
   firmly packed

Mustard sauce
120 g (4¼ oz/½ cup) ready-made aïoli
1 tsp hot English mustard
1 tsp horseradish paste
1 tbsp lemon juice
sea salt

Crispy sweet potato ribbons
vegetable oil, for deep-frying
400 g (14 oz) sweet potato, peeled and
   thinly sliced lengthways

For the marinade, combine the ingredients in a large bowl. Rub the marinade over the ribs and transfer to a roasting tin. Cover with plastic wrap and place in the fridge to marinate overnight.

Preheat the oven to 210°C (415°F/Gas 6-7).

Pour the water into the roasting tin and tightly cover with foil. Roast the ribs for 1¾ hours, or until the beef is very tender. Remove from the oven and place ribs in a bowl, cover with foil and set aside to rest.

For the glaze, add the hot water to the roasting tin and scrape up the brown caramelised bits from the bottom of the pan. Skim off and discard the fat from the top, then transfer the juices in the tin to a large saucepan. Add the beer, vinegar and sugar and bring to the boil, stirring occasionally. Simmer for 15 minutes, or until the liquid has reduced to about 250 ml (9 fl oz/1 cup).

For the mustard sauce, combine all the ingredients in a small bowl, stir well and set aside.

For the crispy sweet potato ribbons, heat the oil in a large saucepan over medium heat until a small piece of bread thrown in turns brown. Then deep fry the sweet potato, in batches, for 2-3 minutes, or until golden and crisp. Drain on paper towel and keep warm in the oven.

Heat a barbecue or chargrill plate to medium. Brush some of the glaze over both sides of the ribs. Cook, turning occasionally, for 5 minutes until the ribs are hot.

Brush the ribs with some more glaze and serve with the mustard sauce and crispy sweet potato ribbons.

Serves 2

ESPRESSO MARTINI GRANITA

MIX IT UP

I DON'T KNOW ABOUT YOU BUT I AM INCREDIBLY WITTY AFTER A FEW COCKTAILS. MY FIRST COCKTAIL WAS MY WORST: AT AGE 15, IT INVOLVED AN OLD WATER BOTTLE AND WHATEVER I COULD GET MY HANDS ON FROM MY PARENTS' LIQUOR CABINET. I HAD MY FIRST REAL COCKTAIL — A MOJITO, MADE BY A PROFESSIONAL — A FEW YEARS LATER AND WISHED I'D HAD THE PATIENCE TO WAIT. IT MADE ME FEEL SOPHISTICATED, COOL AS A CUCUMBER, LIKE I BELONGED IN A BLACK-AND-WHITE PHOTOGRAPH IN THE COMPANY OF, YOU KNOW, COOL PEOPLE.

THE KEY TO A GOOD COCKTAIL, ACCORDING TO MY MIXOLOGIST FRIENDS, IS THE QUALITY OF INGREDIENTS, SPEED OF ASSEMBLY AND THE RIGHT GEAR TO ENSURE ADEQUATE CONSTRUCTION. I CAN'T PROMISE ANYTHING OTHER THAN THE QUALITY COMBINATION OF THE INGREDIENTS, WHICH MAKES THIS DESSERT A SERIOUSLY SCRUMPTIOUS, ALCOHOLIC ICE-LOLLY. THE ESPRESSO ELEMENT MAKES YOU FEEL LIKE YOU ARE INSIDE YOUR FAVOURITE COFFEE SHOP, ONLY WITH LOTS OF LOVELY, SLIGHTLY WICKED, WIT-INDUCING ALCOHOL.

Combine the water and sugar in a saucepan and bring to the boil, stirring until the sugar is completely dissolved and a syrupy consistency is achieved. Remove from the heat and allow to cool.

Stir in the espresso and Kahlua and pour into a 10 x 20 cm (4 x 8 inch) tray, cover and place in the freezer for 4 hours, or until frozen.

Remove the granita from the freezer and scrape with a fork to create fine shards of ice. Place some granita in the base of two bowls or glasses. Top with a scoop of ice cream, sprinkle on the chocolate shavings and serve.

Serves 2

INGREDIENTS
110 ml (3½ fl oz) water
60 g (2¼ oz) caster (superfine) sugar
60 ml (2 fl oz/¼ cup) espresso
60 ml (2 fl oz/¼ cup) Kahlua liqueur

To serve
3 almond biscotti, broken into chunks
  (optional)
vanilla bean ice cream or marscapone
40 g (1½ oz) dark chocolate
  (70 per cent cocoa solids), shaved

BLOOD ORANGE
DUCK SALAD

THE DUCK STOPS HERE

DUCK IS SO INDULGENT — RICH AND GAMEY, WITH CRISPY PAPER-THIN SKIN — PERFECT FOR AN INTIMATE CELEBRATION À DEUX. JUST MAKE SURE YOUR PAN IS HEATED THROUGH SO YOU CAN SEAR THE DUCK TO PERFECTION, THEN LET IT REST, COVERED, SO THE JUICES STAY IN THE MEAT INSTEAD OF EMBARRASSING THEMSELVES ALL OVER YOUR CHOPPING BOARD.

INGREDIENTS

2 x 150 g (5½ oz) boneless duck breasts,
   skin on
125 g (4½ oz/2½ cups) baby English
   spinach leaves
1 blood orange, peeled and segmented
1 small red chilli, deseeded and
   finely chopped

Dressing

1 tsp finely grated fresh ginger
2 garlic cloves, finely chopped
60 ml (2 fl oz/¼ cup) lime juice
1 tsp sesame oil
1 tsp grated palm sugar
1 tsp fish sauce

Heat a large non-stick frying pan over medium heat. Add the duck, skin side down, and cook for 3 minutes on each side, for medium, or until the skin is brown and crispy and the duck is cooked to your liking. Remove from the heat and transfer to a plate. Cover with foil and set aside for 10 minutes to rest.

For the dressing, combine the ginger, garlic, lime juice, oil, sugar and fish sauce in a bowl and set aside.

Toss the spinach with the blood orange segments and chilli in a large bowl.

Thinly slice the duck across the grain. Add to the salad mixture and toss to loosely combine. Divide between two plates, drizzle with the dressing and serve.

Serves 2

REEF FISH CURRY

THE GOLDEN TICKET

THIS DELIGHT IS A BIT CHEFFY IN
CONSTRUCTION; IT IS, AFTER ALL, AN
ADAPTATION OF A RECIPE FROM CHEF DAVID
MOYLE. SO THERE ARE A FEW INGREDIENTS, A
FEW PROCESSES, AND A TASTE THAT WILL HAVE
YOU WEARING ROSE-TINTED GLASSES FOR DAYS.
COOK IT AND GOOD THINGS WILL COME.

IF YOU WANT TO MINIMISE YOUR TIME IN THE
KITCHEN, YOU CAN PREPARE THE CURRY PASTE
DAYS IN ADVANCE. SEAL IT UP AND KEEP IT
IN THE FRIDGE.

INGREDIENTS

150 g (5½ oz/¾ cup) jasmine rice
2 x 160 g (5¾ oz) blue eye or other firm
   white fish fillets

Curry paste
Step 1
3 dried long red chillies
3 red Asian shallots, finely chopped
4 garlic cloves, roughly smashed
3 lemongrass stems, white part only,
   finely chopped
2 tbsp finely chopped galangal
¼ cup finely chopped coriander (cilantro) root
25 g (1 oz/¼ cup) grachai (wild pickled ginger)

Step 2
100 g (3½ oz) red curry paste (above)
3 tbsp shrimp paste
20 g (¾ oz) grated palm sugar
1 tbsp fish sauce
200 ml (2¼ fl oz) coconut milk
2½ tbsp grapeseed oil

Salad
25 g (1 oz) cuttlefish, cleaned
½ Lebanese cucumber, cut into matchsticks
1 tbsp sorrel leaves, finely chopped
1 red Asian shallot, thinly sliced
1 tbsp finely chopped fresh young ginger

Salad dressing
100 ml (3½ fl oz) white vinegar
80 g (2¾ oz) sugar
185 ml (6 fl oz/¾ cup) fish sauce

To serve
lime juice to taste
2 tbsp ready-made fried shallots

For the first stage of the red curry paste, soak the chillies in warm water for 30 minutes. Remove and scrape out the excess seeds. Roughly chop chillies then add to a blender with the shallots, garlic, lemongrass, galangal, coriander and grachai and blend to a fine paste. Spoon into a bowl and set aside.

For the second stage of the red curry paste, heat a large frying pan over medium heat, add the oil, half the coconut milk and the shrimp paste and fry until the shrimp paste dissolves and turns brown and the coconut milk starts to brown. Add the red curry paste, made in the first stage, and stir, making sure you scrape the base of the pan to mix any caramelised bits back into the paste. Once the paste begins to foam white around the edges of the pan, add the sugar and cook for 2 minutes. Scrape to the side of the frying pan and deglaze the pan with the fish sauce.

Reduce and stir the paste into the fish sauce, being careful not to burn the paste or it will taste bitter.

Add the remaining 100 ml (3½ fl oz) of coconut milk, bring to the boil and simmer until the mixture is the consistency of toothpaste.

For the salad, slice the cuttlefish lengthways as thinly as possible. Bring a saucepan of salted water to the boil, take it off the heat, then plunge the cuttlefish in, stir quickly and drain. Combine the vinegar, sugar, fish sauce, cucumber, sorrel, shallot and ginger in a bowl and mix well. Toss the cuttlefish in the dressing just before serving.

Cook the jasmine rice according to packet instructions.

Sear the fish fillets for approximately 5 seconds in a non-stick hot frying pan and place on a baking tray lined with silicon paper. Smear the curry paste evenly over the top of the flesh and place under a medium-low grill (broiler) for 6–8 minutes, depending on the thickness of the fish, or until the paste starts to lightly colour.

Spoon the rice onto two plates, add the fish, squeeze on some lime juice and scatter on a thin layer of fried shallots. Finish with a jumble of the salad on top.

Serves 2 (with some extra red curry paste for other dishes)

CHAI TEA PANNA COTTA WITH CHOCOLATE SAUCE

FOOLS FOR LOVE

MOST THINGS IN LIFE COME WITH TERMS AND CONDITIONS. WITH TWO EXCEPTIONS — LOVE AND SURRENDER. THEY DON'T WORK WITHOUT THE OTHER. AND BOTH WORK BEST WHEN UNCONDITIONAL. (PANNA COTTA IS BOTH.)

IT'S FRAGILE. IT'S DELICATE. AND IT REQUIRES CAREFUL NURTURING, GIVEN IT CAN SOMETIMES BE ANGST-RIDDEN IN ALL ITS GELATINE-BASED CONSTRUCTION. BUT BEST OF ALL, WHEN YOU TASTE IT, YOU SURRENDER YOURSELF, YOUR POSSESSIONS AND YOUR SANITY TO ITS DELICATE CREAMY GOODNESS.

INGREDIENTS

1–2 heaped tsp chai tea leaves
100 ml (3½ fl oz) hot water
150 ml (5 fl oz) cream
50 g (1¾ oz) caster (superfine) sugar
1 tsp ground cinnamon
1½ sheets of gold-strength gelatine

Chocolate sauce

25 g (1 oz) dark chocolate (70 per cent
    cocoa solids), roughly chopped
1 tbsp honey
75 ml (2¼ fl oz) cream
1 teaspoon ground cinnamon

Combine the tea leaves and water in a small bowl and set aside for 2 minutes until infused.

Heat the cream and sugar in a saucepan over medium heat, stirring until the sugar dissolves. Bring to the boil, then remove from the heat.

Strain the tea through a fine sieve into the pan and add the cinnamon. Return the pan to a low heat and simmer for 5 minutes until slightly reduced.

Soak the gelatine in a bowl of cold water for 5 minutes or so, then squeeze out the excess water. Add the gelatine to the cream mixture and stir until dissolved.

For the chocolate sauce, melt the chocolate and honey in a heatproof bowl over a saucepan of gently simmering water. Gradually add the cream and stir until smooth. Add the cinnamon and stir to combine.

Pour the chocolate sauce into two 125 ml (4 fl oz/½ cup) capacity serving glasses. Pour the cream mixture over the chocolate and refrigerate for 2 hours, or until set.

Serves 2

Meeting the mates

Cooking for a large group is tough, but it's also a wonderful thing. It teaches you how to delegate and how to sell (yourself). It requires performance, charm, humbleness and a capacity to adapt ... basically everything you need to survive.

So cooking for the mates, the gay mates, the 'too close' of the opposite-sex mates, and mates that are more family than friends should all be considered an opportunity.

Life's short. Anything could happen and it usually does, so there's no point thinking about all the 'what will they think of this and that' scenarios. As long as you are taking the French onion dip and crackers up a notch or two then all will be impressed. As far as they're concerned, it beats having to cook at home, so they'll be receptive to pretty much anything you put on the table, and if they are any kind of decent friends, appreciative of the effort you've gone to.

Menu 1

Grilled haloumi with
salsa verde

–

Roast tarragon chicken
with sun-dried
tomato butter

–

Duck-fat roast potatoes
with chorizo and
preserved lemon

–

Chocolate and peanut
butter semifreddo

Menu 2

Asian oyster po' boys

–

Mustard risotto with
peppered eye fillet and
balsamic rocket

–

Chocolate Turkish delight
self-saucing pudding

GRILLED HALOUMI WITH SALSA VERDE

GREEK TO ME

THE MELTED CHEESE, THE BITE OF LEMON AND THE SWEET TOUCH OF MINT IN THIS DISH IS A PARTY OF TASTES SLIDING DOWN YOUR THROAT, PROVOKING THAT 'I'M GLAD TO BE ALIVE' REACTION. HALOUMI IS A CHEESE YOU WILL FIND IN EVERY SUPERMARKET, SAVING YOURSELF THAT EMBARRASSING TRIP TO A SNOBBY DELI OR CHEESE-MONGER WHERE YOU HAVE TO PUT ON AIRS AND GRACES, ORDER DÉLICE DE BOURGOGNE AS IF YOU KNOW WHAT IT IS, ONLY TO DISCOVER THEY WON'T SELL IT TO YOU UNLESS YOU SAY IT IN LILTING ENGLISH LIKE YOU'VE SPENT HALF YOUR LIFE IN FRANCE.

For the salsa, place the garlic, lemon zest, pomegranate seeds, pistachio nuts, parsley, mint and salt and pepper in a bowl and stir to combine.

Heat the oil in a large non-stick frying pan over medium-high heat and fry the haloumi for 2–3 minutes on each side, or until golden. Squeeze on the lemon juice and sprinkle on the sumac. Top the haloumi with the salsa and serve immediately with the lemon wedges and warm toasted sourdough.

Serves 8–10

INGREDIENTS

2 tsp olive oil
640 g (1 lb 6½ oz) haloumi cheese,
    cut into 16 slices (2–3 slices per person)
juice of 1 lemon
2 heaped tsp sumac

Salsa verde

2 garlic cloves, finely chopped
2 tbsp finely grated lemon zest
2 tbsp fresh pomegranate seeds
100 g (3½ oz/ ¾ cup) pistachio nuts
a handful of flat-leaf parsley, roughly chopped
a handful of mint leaves, roughly chopped
sea salt and freshly ground black pepper

To serve

8 lemon wedges
8 slices of toasted sourdough bread

ROAST TARRAGON CHICKEN
WITH SUN-DRIED TOMATO BUTTER

YOU'RE THE BREAST

YOU NEVER GET A SECOND CHANCE TO MAKE A FIRST IMPRESSION. THIS CHICKEN
IS FLAVOURSOME AND DEMONSTRATIVE OF EFFORT WITHOUT BEING PRETENTIOUS,
AND WILL HAVE THE MATES SIGHING IN EQUAL PARTS CULINARY CONTENTMENT
AND APPROVAL OF YOUR PERFECT PAIRING. IT'S LADY GODIVA IN FOOD FORM:
CONFIDENT WITH THE OCCASIONAL FLASH OF BRILLIANCE TO KEEP
THE PEEPING TOMS IN CHECK, SO TO SPEAK.

INGREDIENTS
Tomato butter
1 garlic clove, roughly chopped
40 g (1^1/$_2$ oz/^{1}/$_4$ cup) chopped
    sun-dried tomatoes packed in oil, drained
80 g (2^3/$_4$ oz/^{1}/$_2$ cup) pine nuts, toasted
^{1}/$_4$ tsp ground coriander
^{1}/$_4$ tsp cayenne pepper
1 tbsp chopped flat-leaf parsley
sea salt and freshly ground black pepper
60 g (^{1}/$_4$ oz) unsalted butter, softened
1 tsp lemon juice
8 x 200 g (7 oz) chicken breasts on the bone,
    skin on
80 ml (2^1/$_2$ fl oz/^{1}/$_3$ cup) olive oil, extra

Marinade
juice of 1 large lemon or more to taste
zest of 1 lemon
75 ml (4 fl oz/^{1}/$_4$ cup) olive oil
2 tbsp chopped tarragon leaves

To serve
green salad
chorizo taters **(recipe follows)**

Preheat the oven to 180°C (350°F/Gas 4). Line a baking tray with baking paper and set aside.

Combine the garlic, sun-dried tomatoes, pine nuts, ground coriander, cayenne pepper, parsley and salt and pepper in a food processor and blitz until finely chopped. Blend in the butter and lemon juice.

Gently loosen the skin on the chicken with your fingertips, Carefully slide about 1 heaped teaspoon of the tomato butter under the skin until the flesh is evenly coated. Roll the remaining tomato butter into a sausage shape, cover with plastic wrap and refrigerate until required.

For the marinade, place the lemon juice and zest, oil, tarragon and salt in a large bowl and mix well. Add the chicken, cover with plastic wrap and marinate in the fridge for 30 minutes.

Heat a large non-stick frying pan over high heat. Cook the chicken skin side down, for 5–8 minutes until golden and crispy. Turn and cook for another 3 minutes. Transfer to the prepared tray and roast, skin side up, for 10 minutes, or until the chicken is cooked through.

Serve the chicken with slices of the reserved tomato butter, a simple green salad and chorizo taters.

Serves 8

…K-FAT ROAST POTATOES
…H CHORIZO AND
…ESERVED LEMON
…OCK 'EM OUT TATERS

THE BRUTAL TRUTH ABOUT 'ROASTED TATERS'
IS THAT ANYTHING LESS THAN PERFECTION IS
TOTAL DISAPPOINTMENT.

INGREDIENTS

6 large (about 2 kg/4 lb 8 oz) starchy potatoes
   (such as sebago), peeled and chopped
250 ml (9 fl oz/1 cup) duck fat
1 tsp saffron threads
2 tbsp warm water
4 garlic cloves, smashed
sea salt and freshly ground black pepper
2 chorizo sausages, thinly sliced
4 preserved lemon quarters, thinly sliced
a large handful of coriander (cilantro) leaves,
   roughly torn
a large handful of basil leaves, roughly torn
70 g (2½ oz/½ cup) Persian feta
1 red onion, thinly sliced

Preheat the oven to 180°C (350°F/Gas 4).

Place the potatoes in a saucepan and
cover with cold water. Bring to the boil
and cook for 4 minutes. The potatoes will
still be quite firm. Drain and tip back
into the saucepan until ready to roast.

Put the duck fat into a roasting tin
large enough to hold the potatoes in a
single layer. Place the tin in the oven
for 5 minutes to melt and render the fat.

While the fat is melting, combine the
saffron threads and water in a small bowl
and set aside.

Remove the tin from the oven (carefully,
that fat is damn hot) and add the potatoes,
turning to coat evenly. Add the saffron
water and garlic, turn to combine and
generously season with the salt and
pepper. Return the tin to the oven and
roast for 40 minutes, turning the potatoes
after 20 minutes. When you turn the
potatoes, stir in the chorizo sausage
and preserved lemon.

Once the potatoes are brown and crisp, tip
them into a large salad bowl and add the
coriander, basil, feta and onion. Toss and
serve.

Serves 8–10 (as a side)

CHOCOLATE AND PEANUT BUTTER SEMIFREDDO

A FRIENDLY REMINDER

NOTHING PUTS THE KIBOSH ON GOOD TIMES FASTER THAN A WANNA-BE MASTERCHEF HEADY FROM THE FUMES OF FOOD-BUZZ INFLATION. IT'S THE FOOD EQUIVALENT OF THAT TOSSER WHO SPENDS THEIR TIME NAMEDROPPING FRIENDS THEY DON'T HAVE AND DESCRIBING PLACES THEY'VE NEVER BEEN. DON'T GET ME WRONG, THIS DESSERT ISN'T HOMESTEADER CHIC — FAR FROM IT — BUT THE SUBTLE EXECUTION OF YOUR CULINARY FLAIR WILL SOON SEE YOU BASKING IN THE LIMELIGHT OF ADORATION IN YOUR NEW CIRCLE OF FRIENDS.

START THIS RECIPE THE DAY BEFORE.

INGREDIENTS

6 egg yolks
90 g (3¼ oz/¼ cup) golden syrup
    (light treacle)
250 ml (9 fl oz/1 cup) thickened cream
100 g (3½ oz) milk chocolate, roughly
    chopped
100 g (3½ oz) dark chocolate (70 per cent
    cocoa solids), roughly chopped
140 g (5 oz/½ cup) smooth peanut butter,
    warmed in the microwave for 30 seconds
    or in a saucepan over low heat until soft
    and pliable

To serve

10 g (¼ oz) crushed peanuts or enough
    to taste
150 g (5½ oz) raspberries

Line a 1 litre (35 fl oz/4 cup) freezer-proof mould with plastic wrap and set aside.

Whisk the egg yolks and golden syrup in a large bowl for 5 minutes or until pale and thick. You should be able to hold up your whisk and see ribbons form.

In a separate bowl, whip the cream until soft peaks form. Fold the cream into the egg yolk mixture.

Melt the chocolates and peanut butter in a heatproof bowl over a saucepan of gently simmering water and stir until smooth. Allow to cool slightly, then fold into the cream and egg yolk mixture. Spoon into the prepared mould, cover with plastic wrap and freeze until firm (about 6 hours but best overnight).

When ready to serve, remove the semifreddo from the freezer and allow to soften slightly. Slice or scoop the semifreddo, top with a sprinkle of peanuts and some raspberries.

**Serves 8–10, plus a few blissful slices
for leftovers once friends have gone**

ASIAN
OYSTER
PO' BOYS
THE WORLD IS YOUR OYSTER

SERVE THESE WITH A FEW BOUTIQUE PALE ALES
OR A CRISP WHITE AND THE MATES WILL BE
PUTTY IN YOUR HANDS.

INGREDIENTS
235 g (8½ oz/1 cup) whole-egg mayonnaise
1 garlic clove, finely chopped
1 tbsp wasabi mustard
8 small French baguettes
30 pacific oysters, shucked and removed
   from shell
4 eggs
sea salt and freshly ground black pepper
75 g (2¾ oz/1¼ cups) panko crumbs
sesame oil, for deep-frying

Dressing
2 garlic cloves, finely chopped
1 long red chilli, deseeded and finely chopped
2 tbsp caster (superfine) sugar
60 ml (2 fl oz/¼ cup) fish sauce
2 tbsp lime juice
2 tbsp rice vinegar

Salad
225 g (8 oz/3 cups) shredded white cabbage
3 carrots, cut into matchsticks
1 Lebanese cucumber, thinly sliced
   into ribbons
2 large handfuls of Vietnamese mint leaves
2 large handfuls of coriander (cilantro) leaves
1 red onion, thinly sliced
50 g (1¾ oz/⅓ cup) roughly chopped
   toasted peanuts

Combine the mayonnaise, garlic and wasabi mustard in a bowl and mix well.

Halve the baguettes and smear the inside of each with a healthy dollop of the wasabi mayonnaise. Set aside.

For the dressing, place the garlic, chilli, sugar, fish sauce, lime juice and vinegar in a bowl and stir until well combined.

For the salad, gently toss the cabbage, carrot, cucumber, mint, coriander, onion and peanuts together in a large bowl. Add just enough dressing to moisten the salad, then reserve the remaining dressing to serve in a separate bowl.

Pat the oysters dry with paper towel.

Lightly beat the eggs in a shallow bowl, season with the salt and pepper. Place the panko crumbs on a plate. Dip the oysters in the egg, then coat with the panko crumbs.

Heat the oil in a large saucepan to 180°C (350°F) or until the oil is hot enough to turn a cube of bread immediately golden. Fry the oysters, in batches, for 3–4 minutes, or until golden. Remove with a slotted spoon and drain on a plate lined with paper towel.

Fill the baguettes with the salad and oysters. Serve with extra wasabi mayo and salad dressing on the side.

Serves 8–10

MUSTARD RISOTTO WITH
PEPPERED EYE FILLET
AND BALSAMIC ROCKET

THESE GRAINS
OF TRUTH

MEETING THE MATES MEANS THERE IS NO OPPORTUNITY TO PLAY DOOR BITCH AT YOUR OWN DOOR. WHICH IS A SAD AND SOMETIMES TRULY FRIGHTENING CONCEPT. WOULDN'T THE MEET 'N' GREET (AND COOK) GO FAR MORE SMOOTHLY IF YOU COULD HANG A LITTLE SHINGLE WITH SOME *FIGHT CLUB* STYLE RULES ON YOUR DOOR BEFORE THE FRIENDS ARRIVED. THEN YOU'D BE SAFE: NO BORING PEOPLE. NO WORK SUITS. NO WANKERS.

AT LEAST, THIS RISOTTO WILL SEE THE FRIENDS UNANIMOUS IN THEIR APPROVAL, EVERY GRAIN BRINGING WITH IT COMPLIMENTS TO MAKE YOU BLUSH. WARM, CARING, EXOTIC AND INTERESTING; A BEACON OF CERTAINTY IN A RANDOM WORLD. THAT'S YOU TO A TEE. OBVIOUSLY, PERFECTION IS NO ACCIDENT.

INGREDIENTS

3 x 150 g (5^1/$_2$ oz) beef eye fillet steaks
sea salt and freshly ground black pepper
1 tsp olive oil

Risotto

75 g (2^3/$_4$ oz) unsalted butter
1 tsp olive oil
1 onion, finely chopped
250 g (9 oz) carnaroli rice
375 ml (13 fl oz/1^1/$_2$ cups) dry white wine
1 litre (35 fl oz/4 cups) chicken stock
2 heaped tbsp dijon mustard
30 g (1 oz/^{1}/$_4$ cup) grated parmesan

Salad

90 g (3^1/$_4$ oz/2 cups) baby rocket (arugula)
3 tsp extra virgin olive oil
2 tbsp caramelised balsamic vinegar

For the risotto, melt the butter and oil in a saucepan over medium heat, add the onion and cook gently for 5 minutes until softened. Stir in the rice and turn in the oil until evenly coated. Turn the heat to high and pour in the wine, stirring constantly for even absorption. Reduce the heat to medium and ladle in the chicken stock, letting each ladleful be absorbed before adding the next. Cook, stirring constantly, until the rice is soft (18–20 minutes). Remove the pan from the heat. Stir in the mustard and parmesan, cover with the lid and set aside.

Season the steaks with the salt and pepper. Heat the olive oil in a frying pan over high heat and sear the steaks on each side for 3^1/$_2$ minutes for medium rare, or until cooked to your liking. Remove the steaks from the pan, wrap in a layer of foil and allow to rest for 5 minutes.

Return the risotto to a low heat and stir until warmed through.

Toss the rocket with the extra virgin olive oil and vinegar and carve the steak into thin diagonal slices.

Spoon the risotto onto serving plates and serve topped with the dressed rocket and sliced steak.

Serves 4–6 (8 if you serve with other dishes)

CHOCOLATE
TURKISH DELIGHT
SELF-SAUCING PUDDING

TOUT DE SWEET

REMEMBER IN *THE LION, THE WITCH AND THE WARDROBE* WHEN EDMUND COULDN'T SAY NO TO A TURKISH DELIGHT TREAT FROM THE WHITE WITCH? MESSAGES OF STRANGER-DANGER AND GLUTTONY ASIDE, THIS CAKE WILL SEE YOUR GUESTS 'GO EDMUND', EATING BAKED GOODS THE WAY THEY SHOULD BE EATEN: WITH GUSTO, RELISH AND CALLS FOR MORE — AND NO DOUBT FEELING LIKE THEY'VE JUST EMERGED FROM A MAGIC WARDROBE INTO ANOTHER WARM BUT FAR MORE DELIGHTFUL WORLD. YOURS.

INGREDIENTS

200 g (7 oz/1⅓ cups) self-raising flour
30 g (1 oz/¼ cup) unsweetened
  cocoa powder
220 g (7¾ oz/1 cup) caster (superfine) sugar
125 g (4½ oz) butter, melted
250 ml (9 fl oz/1 cup) milk
200 g (7 oz) Turkish delight, chopped into
  5 cm (2 inch) pieces and frozen for at least
  20 minutes
100 g (3½ oz) dark chocolate (70 per cent
  cocoa solids), broken into pieces and
  frozen for at least 20 minutes
110 g (3¾ oz/½ cup) soft brown sugar,
  firmly packed
250 ml (9 fl oz/1 cup) boiling water

To serve

150 g (5½ oz) raspberries
80 g (2¾ oz/¼ cup) crushed pistachio nuts
icing (confectioners') sugar, sifted, for dusting
vanilla bean ice cream

Preheat the oven to 180°C (350°F/Gas 4).
Grease a 19 x 30 cm (7½ x 12 inch) baking tin.

Sift the flour and cocoa into a bowl.

Add the caster sugar, butter and milk and whisk until smooth.

Spread the batter into the prepared tin, then gently push in the pieces of Turkish delight and dark chocolate.

Using the back of a spoon, gently smooth the top.

Sprinkle on the brown sugar and very carefully pour the boiling water over the pudding. Bake for 40 minutes, or until the top is just set. Stand for 5 minutes.

Scatter the raspberries and crushed pistachios over the pudding, sprinkle on the icing sugar and serve with the ice cream.

Serves 4–6 (8 if you serve with other dishes)

the 'bring a plate'

CONCEPT, LIKE A RECIPE
SHOULD BE TREATED AS A LIVING THING

–

an ever-changing concept
MOULDED TO SUIT OUR
INGREDIENTS, OUR MOOD
& OUR DESIRES.

CHAPTER TWO

BRING A PLATE

My heart sinks when I hear someone utter the words 'bring a plate'. I don't love it when people ask, I get particularly irritable if I'm told what that plate must entail, and I get sensationally pissed off when I'm told to bring the salad. A salad takes five minutes and is something, I dare say, you could do yourself. If you are going to burden your kitchen tasks on others, you may as well make them sing for their supper.

Yes, I do believe next time I have a dinner party, I'll make the salad and you, my dear friend, can prepare the seafood bisque for entrée, Joe Bloggs can do the gateau and Tom, Dick and Harry can prepare the cocktails.

The 'bring a plate' concept, like a recipe, should be treated as a living thing — an ever-changing concept that can be moulded to suit our ingredients, our effort level, our mood and our desires. I have never believed in the foolproof recipe to suit each and every occasion, so the recipes that follow are mere suggestions. I cannot take into account the variables — the type of occasion, the location, the cooking facilities on site and the level of commitment (on your behalf) the situation requires.

Next time you're asked to bring a plate, you'll be prepared. And don't be afraid to say no to the salad. It may be their party but it's your meal.

Work do

I used to hate the work do — what to take, how much and, god forbid, what if people find a hair or remnant of egg shell and then remember me from then on as the grubby girl who no doubt has the grubby house, grubby work ethic and grubby life to match. It was just one more pressure, until I realised it was actually an opportunity. Preparing food shows dexterity, an interest and skill outside of work. You're a hero. After all, you feed people. And, quite simply, it's a damn nice thing to do.

I've worked as anything and everything from dish bitch in restaurant kitchens, the office girl Friday, internet sales; hell, I've even travelled the yellow brick road with the corporate hoi polloi and, just like Dorothy, endured countless forests of wild beasts. But despite my inconsistency in employment, the one decent thing I learnt from all of those jobs was to show whatever skills I had, even if they weren't work related.

My advice? Go forth and cook like your next promotion depended on it. Besides, it never hurts to prepare something that receives a few under-the-breath 'wows' from your ever-charming colleagues, now does it?

Menu

Spiced doughnut muffins
with rhubarb jam

—

Chicken and caper
tramezzini

—

White chocolate
and rosemary brownie
biscuits

SPICED DOUGHNUT MUFFINS
WITH RHUBARB JAM

CONFESSIONS
OF A DANGEROUS KIND

THESE MUFFINS ARE THE EQUIVALENT OF IRON MAN'S LATEX-ARMOURED POWER SUIT;
THEY ARE FOOD'S SUPERHERO. PUT THESE ON THE TABLE AND ON FIRST BITE THEY
WILL TAKE YOU FROM SOCIALLY AWKWARD NOWHERE MAN IN THE COPY ROOM
TO CAPTAIN COOKING SENSATION — BREATHTAKING AND ALLURING WORK
COLLEAGUE AND GENERAL ALL-ROUND HUMAN SPECTACULAR.

INGREDIENTS

55 g (2 oz/¼ cup) caster (superfine) sugar
2 tsp ground cinnamon

Muffins

45 g (1¾ oz) butter, melted for brushing
450 g (1 lb/3 cups) plain (all purpose) flour,
   plus extra for dusting
2½ tsp baking powder
¾ tsp fine salt
1 tsp freshly grated nutmeg
1 tsp ground cinnamon
1 tsp mixed spice
¼ tsp baking powder
180 g (6¼ oz) butter softened
165 g (5¾ oz/¾ cup) caster
   (superfine) sugar
2 large eggs
185 ml (6 fl oz/¾ cup) buttermilk,
   at room temperature

Rhubarb jam

500 g (1 lb 2 oz) rhubarb, roughly chopped
400 g (14 oz) caster (superfine) sugar,
   or jam sugar if available
2 tsp ground cumin
1 tsp lemon juice
1 tsp natural vanilla extract

Combine the sugar and cinnamon in a small bowl
and set aside.

Preheat the oven to 200°C (400°F/Gas 6). Lightly brush
a six-hole giant muffin tin with a little melted butter, then
coat the base and side with flour, tapping out any excess.

Sift the flour, baking powder, salt, nutmeg, cinnamon,
mixed spice and baking powder into a large bowl. In a
separate bowl, beat the butter and sugar until pale and
fluffy. Beat in the eggs, one at a time, until just combined.

Mix in half the flour mixture, then half the buttermilk,
alternating until all the ingredients are incorporated.
Be careful not to overwork the mixture. Fill the muffin
moulds to the rim with the batter and bake for 20 minutes,
or until golden on top and firm to touch. Turn the muffins out
onto a wire rack set over a baking tray.

While the muffins are cooking, prepare the rhubarb jam.
Place the rhubarb, sugar, cumin, lemon juice and vanilla
in a saucepan over medium–high heat. Bring to the boil,
stirring occasionally until the sugar has dissolved. Boil
rapidly, without stirring, until the jam coats the back of a
spoon and the fruit appears to have sunk to the bottom
of the pan. Transfer to a food processor and blitz to ensure
all the lumps are removed and a smooth consistency is
achieved. Pour the jam into a piping bag and fit the bag with
a small plain nozzle.

Brush each muffin generously with the remaining melted
butter and generously dust with the cinnamon sugar. Poke a
small hole in the top of each doughnut muffin and pipe the
jam inside. Serve warm.

Makes 6 jumbo or 12 small muffins

CHICKEN AND CAPER TRAMEZZINI

NICE GIRLS DON'T WANT THE CORNER OFFICE

WE OWE A MINUTE'S SILENCE TO THE EARL OF SANDWICH — THAT GENIUS OF A MAN WHO DISCOVERED THAT A PIECE OF MEAT, A SLAB OF CHEESE, OR AN INCARNATION OF THE TWO, SLIPPED BETWEEN TWO PIECES OF BREAD IS TRULY MAGNIFICENT. MANGLE BUSINESS RIVALS AND CEMENT ALLIES WITH A CLASSIC CHICKEN AND MAYO COMBO — YOUR NOD TO THE CLASSIC SHOWS CLASS, THE POACHED CHICKEN MEANS YOU ARE HEALTH CONSCIOUS, WHILE THE CAPERS HINT AT YOUR ALLURING CONTINENTAL EUROPEAN ROOTS.

INGREDIENTS

2 large chicken breasts, about 150–180 g (5$\frac{1}{2}$–6$\frac{1}{4}$ oz) each
750 ml (26 fl oz/3 cups) chicken stock
sea salt and freshly ground black pepper
295 g (10$\frac{1}{4}$ oz/1$\frac{1}{4}$ cups) whole-egg mayonnaise
1 celery stalk, finely chopped
2 tsp salted baby capers, rinsed
3 garlic cloves, finely chopped
2 tbsp finely snipped chives
3 tbsp finely chopped flat-leaf parsley
16 slices of good-quality ciabatta bread

Place the chicken breasts in a large saucepan, cover with chicken stock and bring to the boil over medium heat. Simmer for 10 minutes, turn off the heat and leave for 5 minutes until the chicken is just cooked. Remove the chicken and set aside to cool.

Using your fingers, finely shred the chicken into a large bowl. Add the mayonnaise, celery, capers, garlic and herbs, season to taste and mix well.

Spread the chicken mixture over eight slices of the bread, top with the remaining slices of bread, cut each tramezzino into quarters and serve.

Serves 10–12 as part of a selection

WHITE CHOCOLATE AND
ROSEMARY BROWNIE BISCUITS

MONICA LEWINSKY

'HOW'S WORK?' IT'S A SEEMINGLY HARMLESS QUESTION TO ASK DURING AN AWKWARD-CONVERSATION-WITH-A-BORING-COLLEAGUE PAUSE, BUT ONE THAT'S LIKELY TO INVOKE FURTHER AWKWARD PAUSES, JEALOUSY, RAGE AND SENSELESS INSECURITY AS IT GOES DOWN THE WHY-DO-YOU-ASK, AM-I-GOING-TO-LOSE-MY-JOB, UNREALISED-DREAMS-AND-AMBITIONS TANGENT. THE MONICA-LEWINSKY-STUFF-YOUR-FACE-WITH-SOMETHING-LARGE-AND-CHEWY (SNAPS TO YOU BILLY BOY)-AND-SMILE APPROACH SAVES THE CONVERSATION FOR THOSE WHO ACTUALLY HAVE SOMETHING WORTHWHILE TO SAY.

INGREDIENTS
1 tbsp canola oil
10 g (¼ oz) unsalted butter
280 g (10 oz/2 cups) chopped
    white chocolate
2 large eggs
165 g (5¾ oz/¾ cup) soft brown sugar,
    firmly packed
½ tsp natural vanilla extract
75 g (2¾ oz/½ cup) plain
    (all-purpose) flour
¼ tsp baking powder
¼ tsp salt
4 rosemary sprigs, leaves picked and
    very finely chopped

Preheat the oven to 180°C (350°F/Gas 4). Line two baking trays with baking paper and set aside.

Melt the oil, butter and 140 g (5 oz/1 cup) of the chocolate in a heatproof bowl over a saucepan of gently simmering water, stirring continuously until smooth. Allow to cool.

In another bowl, whisk together the eggs, sugar and vanilla. Fold into the melted chocolate.

Combine the dry ingredients in a large bowl. Add the chocolate and egg mixture and stir to combine. Mix in the remaining chopped chocolate and the rosemary and place the bowl in the freezer for 5–10 minutes for the mixture to become firm.

Dollop dessertspoons of the batter onto the prepared trays, about 10 per tray. Bake for 10–12 minutes until the tops are cracked. Cool completely on the tray and transfer to a wire rack once cooled.

Makes about 20

Hens' night

If there is one thing I have learnt it is that brides are fragile creatures. They are easy prey for the dark side, kryptonite, full moons and rabid-creature behaviour. Welcome Bridezilla, who cometh with her wedding day wrath and fury.

Your witty friend, gone. Your shoot-the-breeze-over-cups-of-tea buddy, abducted. Your touchstone of normalcy, stolen. All sadly replaced by an alias who has French tulle in her blood, Hollywood tape in her handbag, and the Devil himself spouting wedding filth from her tongue. And God have mercy on your soul if the hens' night isn't 'just so'. Leave no cupcake unfrosted, no place card misspelt and have your Excel spreadsheet at the ready.

Don't bother planning a well-cooked feast for her hens' night. Just rip the chapter dedicated to the celebration from her scrapbook, follow it like your life depends on it, and face the fact that you'll be staring deep into the barrel of fiscal misery as you buy shoes, hair pieces, spray tans and outfits that you really won't 'wear again'. And bide carefully or be sucked into the vortex. Your inbox is full of wedding dress photos, your weekends turn into trips to feather suppliers and bridal expos, and before you know it you're welcoming sunrise after a heavy night tying gift bags for the guests, your fingers clawed by some sugar-almond-induced palsy.

Menu

Lime and coconut pancakes
with chicken, crab and mint

–

Truffle cheese toasties

–

Zucchini whoopie pies with goat's
curd and candied pancetta

–

Apple tea macaroons
with apple shooters

LIME AND COCONUT PANCAKES WITH CHICKEN, CRAB AND MINT

LAST HURRAH

THERE NEEDS TO BE BALANCE. ENERGETIC DANCE BY STRIPPER SHOULD BE TEMPERED BY EQUALLY ENERGETIC CANAPÉ — ONE INVOLVING TASTE, PRECISION AND SIZE.

INGREDIENTS

170 ml (5½ fl oz/⅔ cup) lime juice
2 tsp sesame oil
2 tbsp grated palm sugar
2 tsp fish sauce
1 small red chilli, deseeded and
    finely chopped
300 g (10½ oz) skinless chicken breast,
    poached and shredded
100 g (3½ oz) picked fresh crabmeat
125 g (4½ oz) plain (all-purpose) flour
¼ tsp salt
1 egg, lightly beaten
finely grated zest and juice of 1 lime
250 ml (9 fl oz/1 cup) coconut milk
2–3 tsp grapeseed oil
a large handful of mint leaves
a large handful of coriander (cilantro) leaves

Combine the lime juice, sesame oil, sugar, fish sauce and chilli in a bowl and stir to dissolve the sugar. Add the chicken and crabmeat and set aside.

Sift the flour and salt into a bowl. Whisk in the egg, lime zest and juice and coconut milk to form a smooth batter.

Heat the oil in a large non-stick frying pan over low heat. Drizzle in the batter to make a 10 cm (4 inch) round pancake. Cook for 2 minutes, then flip and cook for a further minute, or until golden. Transfer to a plate and repeat with the remaining pancake batter.

To assemble, mix the fresh coriander through the chicken mixture. Plate the pancakes and place a dollop of the mixture in the centre of each pancake.

Makes 20

TRUFFLE CHEESE TOASTIES
TRUFFLES IN PARADISE

WHILE THE TRUFFLE PASTE IS VERY CHEFFY AND CIRCA EARLY NAUGHTIES, THIS FAIL-SAFE TOASTIE IS MAGIC WITH A GLASS OF CHAMPAGNE, AND REQUIRES NO MANUAL EFFORT WHATSOEVER IN ITS CONSTRUCTION.

INGREDIENTS
10 small brioche buns or good quality
   sourdough, thickly sliced
10 slices of gruyere
4 tbsp truffle salsa

Preheat the oven to 180°C (350°F/Gas 4).

Halve the brioche buns and place in the oven to toast for 1 minute or until just warmed through. Place a slice of gruyere over half of the buns and leave under the grill for an additional minute or until cheese has melted. Smear the truffle salsa over the remaining buns and allow to warm through slightly. Remove from heat, sandwich bun halves and serve immediately.

Alternatively you can cook these in a flat sandwich grill, just pop a slice of cheese and dollop of truffle salsa in each brioche and toast for 2 minutes or until cheese has melted.

Serve immediately. And with Champagne.

Makes 10

ZUCCHINI WHOOPIE PIES WITH GOAT'S CURD AND CANDIED PANCETTA

NOT THAT KIND OF GIRL

ONE OF THE MORE MEMORABLE HENS' DOS I'VE ATTENDED INVOLVED THE BRIDE SPENDING A SIGNIFICANT PORTION OF THE DAY/NIGHT THROWING UP IN VARIOUS LOCATIONS ACROSS THE CITY. THE MISTAKE: A WHOLE LOTTA BOOZE, A STRESSED-OUT BRIDE-TO-BE, AND NO FOOD.

THESE WHOOPIE PIES HELP STAVE OFF THE AFOREMENTIONED 'BEEN THERE, DONE THAT, GOT THE TEAM T-SHIRT' MOMENTS. UNLESS, OF COURSE, YOU WANT THEM.

INGREDIENTS
Cakes

270 g (9$^{1}/_{2}$ oz/2 cups) coarsely grated
  zucchini (courgette)
375 g (13 oz/2$^{1}/_{2}$ cups) plain
  (all-purpose) flour
1$^{1}/_{4}$ tsp bicarbonate of soda
sea salt and freshly ground black pepper
125 g (4$^{1}/_{2}$ oz) unsalted butter, chopped
  and softened
1 large egg
185 ml (6 fl oz/$^{3}/_{4}$ cup) well-shaken
  buttermilk
a handful of basil leaves, finely chopped
155 g (5$^{1}/_{2}$ oz/1 cup) pine nuts, toasted
  and chopped

Filling

20 slices of pancetta
60 ml (2 fl oz /$^{1}/_{4}$ cup) golden syrup
  or more to taste
150 g (5$^{1}/_{2}$ oz) goat's curd
a handful of basil leaves

Preheat the oven to 180°C (350°F/Gas 4). Line two baking trays with baking paper and set aside.

For the cakes, wrap handfuls of the grated zucchini in paper towel and squeeze to remove as much moisture as possible. Whisk the flour, bicarbonate of soda and salt and pepper in a bowl until combined.

Beat the butter and egg in a large bowl with electric beaters for 5 minutes, or until pale and fluffy. Alternately add the flour and buttermilk in batches, beginning and ending with the flour mixture, and mix until smooth. Stir in the zucchini, basil and pine nuts until just incorporated.

Spoon 60 ml (2 fl oz/$^{1}/_{4}$ cup) mounds of batter about 5 cm (2 inches) apart on the prepared trays. Bake, switching the position of the trays halfway through cooking, for 18–22 minutes, or until the tops are puffed and golden and spring back when touched. Transfer to a wire rack to cool completely.

Lay out the slices of pancetta on another baking tray lined with baking paper. Lightly drizzle on the golden syrup and bake for 15 minutes until crispy. Allow to cool.

Just prior to serving, spread about 1 tablespoon of goat's curd on the flat side of half the cakes. Top each with a piece of candied pancetta and a basil leaf then sandwich closed with a remaining cake. Repeat with the remaining cakes, pancetta, curd and basil.

Makes 20 cakes

APPLE TEA MACAROONS WITH APPLE SHOOTERS
THE APPLE OF HER EYE

I AM PARTICULARLY OBSESSED WITH APPLE TEA — AND I THINK IF 'AWESOME' HAD A FLAVOUR IT WOULD BE APPLE TEA MACAROONS.

INGREDIENTS
Macaroons
90 g (3¹/₄ oz /³/₄ cup) icing
   (confectioners') sugar
40 g (1¹/₂ oz) apple tea leaves
100 g (3¹/₂ oz/1 cup) ground almonds
2 egg whites, at room temperature
1 tbsp caster (superfine) sugar
3 drops of green food colouring

Ganache
2¹/₂ tbsp cream
100 g (3¹/₂ oz) white chocolate,
   roughly chopped
1 tbsp apple puree

Apple shooters
3 granny smith apples, cored
1.5 litres (52 fl oz/6 cups) sake
crushed ice
3.75 litres (130 fl oz/15 cups) lemonade
8 lime wedges
8 tsp apple tea
apple tea to sprinkle

Line two baking trays with baking paper.

For the apple tea macaroons, combine the icing sugar, apple tea and ground almonds in a food processor and process until finely ground. Triple sift into a large bowl and set aside. Whisk the egg whites in a large bowl with electric beaters for 1–2 minutes until soft peaks form. Add the caster sugar and whisk for 2–3 minutes until thick and glossy. Fold in the food colouring, then stir in the almond mixture, in batches, until incorporated. Spoon into a piping bag and pipe 3 cm (1¼ inch) rounds onto the prepared trays. Let stand for 1 hour.

Preheat the oven to 140°C (275°F/Gas 1).

Bake the macaroons, swapping the trays halfway through cooking, for 10–12 minutes until firm but not coloured. Set aside to cool completely on the trays.

Meanwhile, for the ganache, bring the cream just to the boil in a small saucepan. Remove from the heat, add the chocolate and stand for 5 minutes. Stir until melted and glossy. Refrigerate for 45 minutes or until firm yet still pliable, then stir until smooth.

Smear the ganache on half the macaroons and sandwich with the remaining macaroons. Refrigerate until served.

For the apple shooters, cut the apples into matchsticks or fine slices, then place in a jug and stir in the sake. Cover and chill for at least 30 minutes. Fill glasses with ice cubes, strain about 60 ml (2 fl oz/¼ cup) of the apple sake into each glass, then add some apple and apple tea. Top the drinks with the lemonade and serve each apple shooter with an apple tea macaroon.

Makes 30 macaroons and drink quantity is for 8

Baby shower

She's fat, her hormones are raging, and let's face it, a baby changes everything.

So when there are tears about the room-temperature chicken-ribbon sandwiches she couldn't possibly eat for fear of poisoned foetus, tell miss melodramatic Lady Bracknell to get a grip. Some docs say you can do everything except bungee jump and smoke crack when you are up the duff.

Hormonal wench-like behaviour aside, she needs you. Right now it's to host the shower — which will be her last social, child-free outing in aeons — and in five years' time, when you'll be sitting on the floor amidst toys, pipe cleaners, Elmer's glue and Styrofoam while 'Mum' has a lie down.

Why? Because you are a wonderful friend and there is nothing wrong with a little extra mothering.

Menu

Dukka-dipped eggs

—

Mini apricot 'n' cream éclairs

—

Beetroot vacherins

—

Cinnamon bun cake

HELLO BABY

DUKKA-DIPPED EGGS
PEAS IN A POD

MENSTRUATION. PREGNANCY. LABOUR. LIFE THROWS WOMEN SOME CRUEL BLOWS.

THIS EGG AND DUKKA COMBO MAY VERY WELL BE THE LAST TASTE OF THE SIMPLE LIFE FOR THE MOTHER-TO-BE.

INGREDIENTS
24 quail eggs

To serve
150 g (5$^1/_2$ oz/1$^1/_2$ cups) dukka
fresh sourdough bread, thickly sliced
butter

Bring a large saucepan of salted water to the boil over high heat, add the quail eggs and cook for 3 minutes.

Drain and cool under cold running water. Peel 12 of the eggs.

To serve, place the unpeeled quail eggs in a bowl. Place the 12 peeled quail eggs on a plate and serve with the dukka and bread and butter.

Makes 24

MINI APRICOT 'N' CREAM ÉCLAIRS
BUN IN THE OVEN

OVERNIGHT YOUR FRIENDSHIP GROUP MORPHED INTO PEOPLE BIRTHING TWINS, TRIPLETS, EVEN A PICK-UP IN CHINA. AND THE MOST SHOCKING PART IS THEIR SUDDEN AND VERY VOCAL NEED TO GIVE YOU THE EXTRA PUSH. THESE BITE-SIZED DELIGHTS WILL HELP FOCUS THE CONVERSATION ON THE PARTY AT HAND AND HOPEFULLY DIMINISH THE PLETHORA OF POOP, PEE AND PLAYGROUND POLITICS TO A DULL ROAR.

INGREDIENTS
125 g (4$^1/_2$ oz) butter
2$^1/_2$ tbsp caster (superfine) sugar
1 egg yolk
1 tsp natural vanilla extract
150 g (5$^1/_2$ oz/1$^1/_2$ cups) ground almonds
225 g (8 oz/1$^1/_2$ cups) plain
  (all-purpose) flour
185 g (6$^1/_2$ oz/$^3/_4$ cup) mascarpone
4 tbsp icing (confectioners') sugar
80 ml (2$^1/_2$ fl oz/$^1/_3$ cup) apricot nectar
12 glazed apricots

Preheat the oven to 180°C (350°F/Gas 4). Line a baking tray with baking paper.

Cream the butter and caster sugar in a bowl until pale and fluffy. Beat in the egg yolk and vanilla, then sift in the ground almonds and flour and mix to form a smooth dough.

Roll the dough into 24 small balls with your hands and place on the prepared tray. Bake for 35 minutes, or until lightly golden and firm to the touch. Transfer to a wire rack to cool.

Combine the mascarpone, icing sugar and apricot nectar in a bowl. Smear a little of the sweetened mascarpone over the base of a biscuit. Top with a glazed apricot and sandwich closed with one of the remaining biscuits.

Repeat with the remaining biscuits, sweetened mascarpone and glazed apricots.

Makes 12

24 quail eggs

BEETROOT VACHERINS

SWEET DELIVERY

A PREGNANT FRIEND OF MINE WANTS A NATURAL BIRTH — SHE HAS THIS IDEA SHE WILL BECOME A WAFTING EARTH MOTHER, OPENING UP LIKE A BEAUTIFUL FLOWER TO GIVE BIRTH, AND THAT AROMATHERAPY, WAVE MUSIC AND ACUPUNCTURE WILL SEE HER THOUGH. WHY WOULD YOU CHOOSE NOT TO HAVE PAIN RELIEF? THAT'S LIKE CHOOSING TO HAVE FOOD POISONING. WE OWE OUR MOTHERS PAST, WHO WISHED DESPERATELY FOR MEDICAL MIRACLES TO AVOID BITING DOWN ON A STICK AND HEAVING ONTO THE KITCHEN TILES, TO TAKE THE LABOUR OUT OF LABOUR.

INGREDIENTS
300 g (10$\frac{1}{2}$ oz) mascarpone
2 tsp unsweetened cocoa powder
2 tbsp icing (confectioners') sugar, sifted
250 g (9 oz) strawberries, hulled and sliced
25 g (1 oz/$\frac{1}{4}$ cup) grated dark chocolate
   (70 per cent cocoa solids)

Meringues
3 egg whites
125 g (4$\frac{1}{2}$ oz) caster (superfine) sugar
100 g (3$\frac{1}{2}$ oz) icing (confectioners') sugar
2 tbsp cornflour (cornstarch)
1 tbsp beetroot powder

Preheat the oven to 120°C (235°F/Gas $\frac{1}{2}$). Line two baking trays with baking paper and draw fifteen 6 cm (2$\frac{1}{2}$ inch) circles on the paper.

For the meringues, whisk the egg whites in a large bowl with electric beaters until soft peaks form. Gradually add the caster sugar, whisking until stiff peaks form. Sift together the icing sugar, cornflour and beetroot powder and fold into the egg whites.

Spoon the meringue mixture into a piping bag fitted with a plain piping nozzle and pipe spirals within the circles drawn on the paper.

Bake for 1 hour, or until dry and crisp. Cool in the oven with the door slightly ajar.

Combine the mascarpone, cocoa and icing sugar in a bowl.

To serve, top half the meringues with the sweetened mascarpone, the strawberries and grated chocolate and finish with another meringue.

Makes 15

CINNAMON BUN CAKE

PARENT TRAP

An essential consideration when planning a baby shower is the gastronomic opportunities it may provide. The food needs to play happy medium between those with and without child, providing distraction, energy and entertainment. This sweet cinnamon bun cake meets these lofty expectations, making a simple shower seem like Broadway. One bite and it's as if the world has gone from monochrome to Technicolor, with Joseph himself on the couch feeding you by hand, resting your sugar-filled head on his amazing coat.

Yeah, that's just the sort of food needed for a baby shower.

INGREDIENTS
250 g (9 oz) butter, softened
220 g (7¾ oz/1½ cups) brown sugar, firmly packed
2 tbsp ground cinnamon
2 tsp salt
4 green apples, peeled, cored and chopped

Dough
2½ tsp dried yeast
185 ml (6 fl oz/¾ cup) warm water
375 ml (13 fl oz/1½ cups) warm milk
900 g (2 lb/6 cups) bread flour
2 tbsp salt
220 g (7¾ oz/1 cup) sugar
30 g (1 oz) butter, softened

Cream cheese frosting
125 g (4½ oz) butter, softened
350 g (12 oz/1½ cups) cream cheese, softened
1 tsp natural vanilla extract
250 g (9 oz/2 cups) icing (confectioners') sugar

Preheat the oven to 190°C (375°F/Gas 5). Grease a 23 x 33 cm (9 x 13 inch) baking tin or two 25 cm (10 inch) pie tins.

For the dough, dissolve the yeast in the warm water and milk and wait for 5 minutes until bubbles appear on the surface. Knead in the dry ingredients. Add the butter and rub in with your fingertips until a loose dough has formed. Knead until smooth and let stand for 45 minutes, covered in a large bowl.

On a lightly floured surface, roll out the pastry to form a rectangle a little larger than a piece of A4 paper.

Spread the butter over the top, sprinkle on the sugar, cinnamon, and salt and scatter the apple chunks down the middle. Roll up the rectangle into a long cylinder. Cut into fourteen 5 cm (2 inch) pieces. Place in the prepared tin/s and cover with plastic wrap. Let stand for 45 minutes, until they have puffed up in size. Bake in the oven for 20–25 minutes until the buns spring back to the touch and are brown on top.

For the frosting, combine the butter, cream cheese, vanilla and sugar in a bowl and stir well. While the buns are still slightly warm, spread the cream cheese frosting over the top.

Makes 14

Divorce party

Usually far more entertaining than the wedding, the divorce party is a guest list of your true friends. Now the real party can begin; no more irrational demands, bitchy remarks about the bride's dress, or overbearing aunts with a taste for peach satin.

The mother of the bride will be silenced, the maid of dishonour can show her true colours, and there'll be no boring in-laws, picky matron of honour, or food-obsessed third cousins from the planet 'Gourmatron' complaining about the food.

There you have it. Everyone's happy.

Menu

Meat 'n' mushroom tartlets
–
Da nang dagwood dogs
–
Blue cheese grissini sticks

MEAT 'N' MUSHROOM TARTLETS

BITTERSWEET

IT'S ODD THAT NOWADAYS MANY OF US SPEND OUR LIVES BEING CONSUMED AND EMBITTERED BY DIVORCE. WE'RE REALLY GOOD AT IT — DIVORCERS WITH SKILL. AS THIRD-GENERATION DIVORCERS AND THE OFFSPRING TWICE OVER OF DIVORCEES, WE HAVE THE GROUNDING, AND THE HISTORY. WE'RE SUPERB AT IT — THE STATS TELL US EXACTLY THIS.

SO WHEN DIVORCE IS A REALITY AND NOT AN ODDITY, WE SHOULD CELEBRATE THE NEW BEGINNINGS IT PRESENTS. AND IF FOOD IS THE PATHWAY TO THE SOUL, MAYBE, JUST MAYBE, A WELL-COOKED TREAT WILL TAKE AWAY THAT EPIC, GRACELESS STRUGGLE IN THE SETTLEMENT STAKES.

INGREDIENTS

80 ml (2½ fl oz/⅓ cup) extra virgin olive oil
200 g (7 oz) button mushrooms, stalks
    removed and finely chopped
1 onion, thinly sliced
300 g (10½ oz) minced (ground) pork
300 g (10½ oz) minced (ground) chicken
2 garlic cloves, finely chopped
1 tbsp finely chopped rosemary
zest of 1 lemon, finely grated
2 tbsp plain (all-purpose) flour
250 g (9 oz) crème fraîche, plus
    50 g (1¾ oz) extra to garnish
sea salt and freshly ground black pepper
24 savoury tartlet cases (roughly 5 cm
    or 2 inches in diameter)
a small handful of flat-leaf parsley leaves,
    to garnish

Preheat the oven to 180°C (350°F/Gas 4).

Heat a saucepan over medium heat, add 2 tablespoons of the oil and sauté the mushrooms for 3–5 minutes until brown and softened. Remove from the pan and set aside.

Pour the remaining oil into the pan and sauté the onion until softened. Add the pork and chicken and cook until the meat is browning at the edges. Stir in the garlic, rosemary and lemon zest and cook for 2 minutes. Return the mushrooms to the pan, sprinkle in the flour and stir well.

Add the crème fraîche, season and stir for 1 minute or until slightly thickened and the mixture appears creamy.

Spoon the meat 'n' mushroom mixture into the tartlet cases and transfer to a baking tray. Bake for 15–20 minutes until the pastry is crisp and the tops are golden.

Serve warm with a small dab of the extra crème fraîche and garnish with the parsley.

Makes 24

ANG
OOD DOGS

IFE GIVES YOU LEMONS

CANAPÉS SHOULD BE MINIATURES OF BEAUTIFULLY PREPARED FOOD. THE AFTERSHOCK OF THE PINEAPPLE AND CHEESE, AND THE DEVIL ON HORSEBACK COMBOS HAS FADED, REPLACED BY EXCITING TASTES SUCH AS THESE UPSCALE TAKES ON THE OLD AGRICULTURAL SHOW FAVOURITE, WHICH WILL LEAVE GUESTS WISHING THEY HAD JUST ONE MORE MOUTHFUL.

INGREDIENTS

24 lemongrass stems
500 g (1 lb 2 oz) minced
    (ground) chicken
2 garlic cloves, finely chopped
1 tbsp Vietnamese mint, chopped
1 tbsp Thai basil, chopped
1 kaffir lime leaf, finely shredded
3 tsp fish sauce
2 tsp soft brown sugar
½ red onion, thinly sliced
1 small red chilli, deseeded
    and finely chopped
60 ml (2 fl oz/¼ cup) coconut milk
2 eggs
120g (4¼ oz/2 cups) panko crumbs

To serve

sweet chilli sauce, for dipping

Preheat the oven to 220°C (425°F/Gas 7). Line a baking tray with baking paper and set aside.

For the lemongrass skewers, slice the lemongrass stems into 10 cm (4 inch) pieces.

Combine the chicken, garlic, mint, basil, kaffir lime leaf, fish sauce, sugar, onion, chilli and coconut milk in a large bowl and mix well. Moisten your hands with a little vegetable oil, gather up some of the mixture and mould into a walnut-sized ball.

Press the ball into the cup of your hand to create a small disc and wrap it around one end of a lemongrass skewer. Repeat with the remaining mixture and skewers.

Place the eggs in a shallow bowl and lightly beat. Spread the panko crumbs on a plate.

Dip the chicken covered part of each skewer into the egg, then roll in the panko crumbs. Place the skewers on the prepared tray and roast, turning twice, for 20 minutes, or until cooked through and slightly crisp and brown on the outside.

Serve with the sweet chilli dipping sauce.

Makes 24

BLUE CHEESE GRISSINI STICKS

PICKED THE WRONG GUY. GAVE HIM THE WRONG FINGER

STEPHEN KING CAPTURES THE MISTAKE PERFECTLY IN HIS NOVELLA *A GOOD MARRIAGE*:

HE ASKED HER OUT ON A DATE. 'WOULD YOU LIKE TO COME TO …' SHE CAME. AND SHE CAME ON THEIR WEDDING NIGHT, TOO. NOT TERRIBLY OFTEN AFTER THAT, BUT NOW AND THEN. OFTEN ENOUGH TO CONSIDER HERSELF NORMAL AND FULFILLED.

UNTIL SHE DECIDED TO GO ELSEWHERE.

INGREDIENTS
300 g (10½ oz/2 cups) plain
   (all-purpose) flour
2 tsp salt
2 tsp dried yeast
75 g (2¾ oz) unsalted butter, chopped
   and chilled
75 g (2¾ oz) creamy soft blue cheese
150 ml (5 fl oz) warm milk

Place the flour, salt and yeast in a bowl. Rub in the butter with your fingertips.

In a separate bowl, crumble the cheese into small pieces and mix with the milk. Pour into the flour mixture and briefly knead to form a soft, sticky dough. Cover and leave to stand for an hour.

On a floured worktop, lightly knead the dough for 20 seconds. Return to the bowl and let stand for another hour.

Preheat the oven to 160°C (315°F/Gas 2–3). Line a baking tray with baking paper.

Roll out the dough to about 1 cm (½ inch) thick. Cut into strips about 3 cm (1½ inch) wide and, using your hands, roll into pencil shapes, pressing firmly on the ends so they don't unroll in the oven. Gently transfer to the prepared tray and bake for 40 minutes, or until crisp.

Makes 8

+ +

AWKWARD MOMENTS

+ +

Good social situations and good questions should be unexpected. Oblique rather than direct, offering participants the opportunity for unrehearsed wit. Sadly life is not a constant stream of pithy one-liners delivered by beautiful people. More often than not it involves social blunders and silences that move from awkward to oppressive in the blink of an eye.

Human relationships are difficult, complicated things and so many of them involve variants of the same scenario — something you don't like, involving pain and awkwardness.

But easily the most funny, fascinating and cringe-worthy times in anyone's life happen in such moments; those times when you get lumped with people without any filter, and you experience first hand the visual and physical spectacular of small talk grinding along like a knife through concrete.

There are too many scenes about the cruelty, self-consciousness and forced spontaneity of social situations to mention here. Life's full of them — from tattooing incidents at school and much anxiety about kissing and physical

contact, to weddings, cocktail parties and other situations involving ... much anxiety about kissing and physical contact.

Truly awkward moments don't even need words to obliterate small gatherings. A look, a misplaced touch and boom — the awkward bomb explodes, triggering a nebula of shifting looks and mumbled excuses as the crowd diffuses, leaving the front line to pick water crackers and French onion dip from their limbs and hair, like shrapnel.

These moments generally occur when people are gathered in a small room for reasons that have nothing to do with skills or interests — just age, association, bad luck and, quite often, a lack of social judgment and foresight. Good food tends to help smooth these scenarios, and it is a mindful and caring host who provides in this hour of need.

I have no doubt that many a sliced devon and pickled onion have played their part in keeping world peace, almost as much as the humble sausage roll when discussions over priests, politics and little boys have come to the fore.

Meeting the ex

The new girlfriend/wife/lover does not, on the whole, enjoy an outstanding reputation. Misguided opinions often paint her as young and predatory — a person who is all about the sex rather than responsibility, and to the jilted partner the equivalent of kill zones she didn't see coming: dangerous dead spots, deceit and 'perilous risk' personified.

This makes the meet-and-greet, coupled with eating, a steadfastly ordinary situation to find yourself in, and socially awkward for all concerned. Unfortunately, the responsibilities and expectations for this bizarre ménage a trois are not clearly laid down or generally accepted. All too often petty chafings can turn into gaping wounds, with resentment tangled up with bitterness about the past, and anxieties about the future.

The trick is to find a balance. You can't cook anything too amazing or fiddly (think homemade ganache), nor too imposing. No, what you cook needs to be understated yet impressive. It has to say enough to ensure you fly under the social-etiquette-plausibility radar, while quietly making sure she well and truly pees her pants when you reveal the true extent of your awesomeness.

Visions of her doubled over with food poisoning are tempting, but this is a time to let social subtlety reign, to toe the line and trust the magic. And it can work in your favour — food is the perfect social-tension diffuser. Conversation lags? Stuff mouth. Have nothing to say? Talk about the food. Her posse of bitches is death staring you straight to hell? Be a gracious host and distribute food.

The following dishes are the gold, frankincense and myrrh of the food world. You'll arrive like the Star of Bethlehem, home-baked goods in hand to herald your own season of goodwill (and upper-hand) on the proceedings.

I have made the quantities fairly large, so if you are feeling particularly beatific you can prepare enough to leave her leftovers, so the memory of you lingers long after you have gone.

Yep, that's right. You live to give.

Menu

Chocolate and
raspberry nougat

–

Rosewater madeleines

–

Moussaka cupcakes

–

Green chicken
curry biryani

CHOCOLATE AND RASPBERRY NOUGAT
EXCESS MODERATION

WITH THIS NOUGAT, YOU CAN NEVER STOP AT ONE PIECE, SO BEFORE LONG SHE'LL STRUGGLE TO HAVE ANY BLOOD LEFT IN HER GLUCOSE STREAM. AND LATER THAT NIGHT, WHEN YOU'RE BUSY BURNING KILOJOULES HAVING BOISTEROUS SEX WITH HER EX, SHE'LL BE LYING IN BED IN A FRUCTOSE-DEPENDENT STATE, MUNCHING ANGRILY ON YOUR NOUGAT. AND PROBABLY READING *CHARLIE AND THE CHOCOLATE FACTORY.*

INGREDIENTS
2–3 sheets of edible rice paper
440 g (15 1/2 oz/2 cups) caster
 (superfine) sugar
350 g (12 oz/1 cup) glucose syrup
175 g (6 oz/1/2 cup) honey
1 tsp natural vanilla extract
2 egg whites
1 x 250 g (9 oz) packet of Allen's Ripe
 Raspberries sweets (candy), cut into halves
160 g (5 3/4 oz/1 cup) whole almonds,
 coarsely crushed
150 g (5 1/2 oz) milk chocolate, roughly chopped
 into bite-sized pieces
150 g (5 1/2 oz) white chocolate, roughly
 chopped into bite-sized pieces

Lightly grease a 22 x 30 cm (8 1/2 x 12 inch) baking tin and line with a sheet of the edible rice paper.

Place the sugar, glucose, honey and vanilla in a saucepan and cook, stirring onstantly, over high heat for 8–10 minutes, or until the temperature reaches 143°C (290°F) on a sugar (candy) thermometer.

Alternatively, you can test if the syrup is ready by dropping a teaspoonful into a bowl of cold water: it should form a pliable ball.

Beat the egg whites in a large bowl until firm peaks form. Then, while constantly beating, slowly pour in the glucose syrup until the mixture is thick and holds its shape. Gently and quickly fold in the raspberries, almonds and chocolate pieces.

Pour the mixture into the tin and gently press a layer of rice paper over the top. Leave to set for a few hours in the fridge (best overnight), then cut into squares or bars with a hot, wet knife.

Remember to watch the sugar thermometer like you would his ex-wife. If the temp is over or under, the nougat won't work.

Makes 30 pieces

ROSEWATER MADELEINES
TWO-FACED BISCUIT

COOKING SOMETHING TO TAKE TO THE EX IS FRAUGHT, BRINGING ON THAT STOMACH-CHURNING ANXIETY AS YOU DO YOUR BEST IMPRESSION OF CAREER WOMAN MEETS DOMESTIC GODDESS COME SEX KITTEN WITH LIFE BALANCE.

YOU DON'T HAVE TO BE PROUST TO BE WHISKED AWAY BY THESE LITTLE SHELL-SHAPED SPONGES. A CUP OF TEA AND A MADELEINE NEVER FAIL TO PROVIDE INSTANT CALM … AND IT NEVER HURTS TO DEMONSTRATE YOUR KNOWLEDGE OF, AND COMFORT IN HANDLING, FRENCH CUISINE. ON FIRST BITE SHE'LL REALISE, WITH AWKWARD SUDDENNESS, THAT AMIDST ALL YOUR OTHER POSITIVE TRAITS YOU ARE ALSO TRULY BEAUTIFUL. BEAUTIFUL IN A WAY THAT'S SURE TO SAP HER WILL TO LIVE.

PERFECT.

INGREDIENTS

----

100 g (3$^1/_2$ oz) unsalted butter

2 eggs

a pinch of salt

55 g (2 oz/$^1/_4$ cup) caster (superfine) sugar

2 tbsp rosewater

75 g (2$^3/_4$ oz/$^1/_2$ cup) plain (all-purpose) flour, sifted, plus extra for dusting

1 tsp baking powder

icing (confectioners') sugar, sifted, for dusting

Preheat the oven to 170°C (325°F/Gas 3). Grease a standard or small madeleine tin and dust with flour, shaking off any excess. You might think not to bother with this, especially if you have a non-stick tin but it really does affect the end result — giving an even crust to the outside of the madeleines.

Melt the butter in a small saucepan over medium heat until brown. Set aside to cool.

03

Whisk the eggs and salt in a bowl until pale and thick. Gradually beat in the sugar in a steady stream. Gently fold in the rosewater. Add the flour, baking powder and melted butter and fold in until just combined. Be careful not to overwork the mixture.

Spoon into the prepared tin until three-quarters full and bake for 8–10 minutes until golden. Turn out onto a wire rack, allow to cool then dust with the icing sugar.

Makes 20

ROSEWATER
MADELEINES

AKA CUPCAKES

FFED

AKA IS COMFORTING. EVERY FLAVOURFUL
REAMY LAYER IS A TRUE PEACE OFFERING
OF GRACE, FORTITUDE AND GOODWILL. IT'S
A MUFFIN-SIZED EQUIVALENT OF THE YA YA
SISTERHOOD, GLASS HALF FULL, AND ALL OF
THAT. IF SHE TURNS UP HER NOSE RATHER THAN
GOBBLING THESE UP, DON'T WORRY, SHE'LL GET
HER COMEUPPANCE.

AND COME TO LOVE MOUSSAKA CUPCAKES AND
PERHAPS EVEN THOSE WHO MAKE THEM.

INGREDIENTS
Filling
4 tbsp olive oil

1 Lebanese eggplant (aubergine), sliced

1 onion, thinly sliced

1 garlic clove, finely chopped

400 g (14 oz) minced (ground) lamb

1 x 400 g tinned tomatoes, chopped
   (or use fresh passata)

125 ml (4 fl oz/$\frac{1}{2}$ cup) red wine

1 tsp ground cinnamon

1 tsp freshly grated nutmeg

1 tsp dried oregano

1 tsp allspice

1 bay leaf

Layers
24 square wonton wrappers

60 g (2$\frac{1}{4}$ oz/$\frac{1}{2}$ cup) grated parmesan

65 g (2$\frac{1}{2}$ oz/$\frac{1}{2}$cup) grated mozzarella

115 g (4 oz/$\frac{1}{2}$ cup) ricotta

Preheat the oven to 180°C (350°F/Gas 4).
Grease a six-hole jumbo muffin tin and
set aside.

Heat 2 tablespoons of the oil in a large
frying pan over medium heat. Add one-
quarter of the eggplant slices and cook for
1-2 minutes each side or until golden
brown and tender. Transfer to a plate.
Repeat in batches with remaining
eggplant, adding more oil when necessary.

Heat any remaining oil in the pan over
medium heat. Add the onion and garlic
and cook, stirring, for 5 minutes or until
soft. Add the mince and cook, stirring with
a wooden spoon to break up any lumps, for
5 minutes or until cooked through. Add the
tomatoes, wine, herbs and spices and cook,
stirring occasionally, for 15 minutes or
until sauce thickens slightly. Remove from
the heat and season with salt and pepper.
Remove the bay leaf.

For the layers, line each muffin mould with
four wonton wrappers. You need to encase
the filling, so each wrapper should overlap
the next and there should be some
overhang at the top to prevent any spillage.

Put a little parmesan, a little mozzarella
and a little ricotta into each mould. Top
with a little of the filling and a slice of
grilled eggplant. Repeat with the cheeses,
filling and eggplant until each mould is
full (usually about three layers). Sprinkle
each moussaka with any left-over
parmesan and mozzarella.

Bake for 20 minutes until the cheese is
melted and the tops are nicely browned.
Cool in the tin for 5 minutes, then run a
knife around the inner edge and gently
remove. These can be eaten hot or cold.

Makes 6 jumbo cupcakes

+ +

LAMB KOFTE
CIGARS
SMOKE AND MIRRORS

RUMOUR HAS IT THAT WHEN HITLER BOMBED BRITAIN'S LAST-STANDING DUNHILL STORE, SIR WINSTON CHURCHILL'S FIRST CALL WAS TO CONFIRM THAT HIS STOCK OF CUBAN CIGARS HAD SURVIVED THE BLAST. NOW I'M NOT SAYING THESE LAMB KOFTE CIGARS ARE WORTHY OF HAVANA FOLKLORE, BUT THEY ARE DANGEROUSLY CLOSE. I LIKE TO THINK CIGARS SAVED BRITAIN AND THAT THE VERY CONSTRUCTION OF THIS CIGAR-INSPIRED MEAL WILL BODE YOU EQUALLY SAFE PASSAGE THROUGH YOUR OWN DINNERTIME WARFARE.

INGREDIENTS

80 ml (2½ fl oz/⅓ cup) olive oil
2 small red onions, finely chopped
2 garlic cloves, finely chopped
500 g (1 lb 2 oz) minced (ground) lamb
1 heaped tsp ground cumin
1 heaped tsp ground allspice
1 heaped tsp ground coriander
1 heaped tsp ras el hanout
125 g (4½ oz/½ cup) diced tinned tomatoes
2 tbsp currants
2 tbsp pine nuts, toasted
a handful of coriander (cilantro) leaves,
   finely chopped
12 sheets of filo pastry
40 g (1½ oz) butter, melted

Dipping sauce

200 g (7 oz/¾ cup) Greek yoghurt
1 tbsp ground coriander
1 tbsp ground cumin
juice of 1 lemon

Preheat the oven to 190°C (375°F/Gas 5). Line a baking tray with baking paper and set aside.

Heat the oil in a large frying pan over medium heat, add the onion and garlic and cook for 10 minutes, or until soft. Remove from the heat and mix in the lamb and spices. Return the pan to the heat and cook until the lamb is lightly browned. Stir in the tomatoes and currants and cook for 10 minutes. Stir in the pine nuts and coriander, and remove from the heat.

Place one sheet of filo pastry on a work surface, lightly brush with the butter and fold in half crossways. Pile a little filling mixture along the folded edge, leaving a 3 cm (1¼ inch) border at each side. Roll up to enclose the filling and make a cigar shape. Repeat with the remaining pastry and filling.

Place on the prepared tray and bake for 25 minutes until lightly golden. (It helps to keep the remaining filo sheets under a clean damp tea towel while you work.)

Combine the yoghurt, spices and lemon juice in a small bowl.

Serve the cigars warm with the dipping sauce.

Makes 12

+ +

DUCK RAGU
HONEYCOMB CANNELLONI

UNFIT TO MOTHER

SOMETIMES I SORT OF WISH I HAD A SUPER CRAZY FAMILY FULL OF QUIRK, HARMLESS MADNESS AND DYSFUNCTIONALLY FRAUGHT EXISTENCES.

THIS DUCK RAGU HONEYCOMB CANNELLONI IS A LITTLE TWISTED AND DEFINITELY INTRIGUING — THE ROYAL TENENBAUMS IN FOOD FORM.

INGREDIENTS

800 g (1 lb 12 oz) boneless duck breasts, skin on
sea salt and freshly ground black pepper
20 g (¾ oz) butter
1½ tsp olive oil
1 onion, finely chopped
2 garlic cloves, smashed
2 tsp chopped rosemary leaves
185 ml (6 fl oz/¾ cup) red wine
750 ml (26 fl oz/3 cups) chicken stock
800 g (1 lb 12 oz) tinned cherry tomatoes
500 g (1 lb 2 oz) cannelloni tubes
120 g (4½ oz/1 cup) parmesan, grated

Preheat the oven to 220°C (425°F/Gas 7).

Season the duck with the salt and pepper.

Heat the butter and oil in a frying pan over medium heat until the foam subsides. Sear the duck, skin side down, for 5 minutes until golden brown. Turn and cook on the other side for 2 minutes. Transfer the duck to a plate, reserving the juices in the pan.

Add the onion, garlic and chopped rosemary to the pan and cook until the onion has softened. Pour in the wine, turn the heat to low and reduce for 3 minutes. Add the duck, skin side up, the stock and tomatoes. Season generously with salt and pepper and simmer, covered, for an hour. Gently remove the duck from the pan and, when cool enough to handle, shred the meat and skin.

Spoon the sauce into a shallow ovenproof saucepan or baking dish that will fit the cannelloni in snugly to a depth of 2 cm (¾ inch). Stand the cannelloni tubes upright in the dish, making sure they are nice and snug, and press down with the palm of your hand so they are touching the base.

Return the shredded meat to the sauce in the pan and mix well. Spoon the ragu into the cannelloni, don't worry if the mixture spills out and around the tubes. Sprinkle on the parmesan and bake in the oven for 35–40 minutes until golden brown.

Serve hot.

Serves 8–10

CHOCOLATE CRUMPETS WITH VANILLA RICOTTA AND ESPRESSO CARAMEL
THE FAMILIAL TOUCH

MOST OF US ARE LUCKY ENOUGH TO AGREE THAT WE HAVE GREAT FAMILIES, GIVE OR TAKE A FEW MEMBERS, AND THAT TIME TOGETHER IS TREASURED RATHER THAN ABHORRED. BUT EVEN IN THE BEST FAMILIES, RELATIONSHIPS CAN WEAR MIGHTY THIN AT WARP SPEED. WHETHER IT'S COUSIN BETTY FEEDING THE DOG HER ZUCCHINI UNDER THE TABLE, NANNA DROPPING THE C-BOMB, YOUR UNCLE RUNNING OFF AFTER RAMONA HIS INTERNET WIFE, OR SOME RANDOM INDIVIDUAL BANGING ON ABOUT POLITICS, THERE ARE MOMENTS OF FEELING WELL AND TRULY TRAPPED INSIDE A WORLD CALLED 'I JUST COULDN'T GIVE A TOSS'. AS A SENSORY RETARD NOT PARTICULARLY SKILLED IN FAKING SOCIAL NICETIES AT SUCH TIMES, I ESCAPE TO THE KITCHEN AND I SUGGEST YOU DO THE SAME. THE RELLIES MIGHT FLIT IN AND OUT, ASKING WITHOUT A SKERRICK OF SINCERITY 'CAN I DO ANYTHING TO HELP?', BUT MOSTLY YOU'LL BE LEFT IN PEACE.

IF ONLY THAT RAMONA WOULD STOP RUMMAGING THROUGH YOUR SILVERWARE.

INGREDIENTS
170 ml (5½ fl oz/⅔ cup) milk
1 tsp dried yeast
1½ tsp caster (superfine) sugar
200 g (7 oz) plain (all-purpose) flour
1 tsp unsweetened cocoa powder
a small pinch of salt
¼ tsp bicarbonate of soda
200 ml (7 fl oz) water

Vanilla ricotta
240 g (8¾ oz/1 cup) ricotta
1 vanilla bean, split lengthways and
    seeds scraped
2 tbsp icing (confectioners') sugar

Espresso caramel
125 ml (4 fl oz/½ cup) water
1½ tbsp espresso coffee
110 g (3¾ oz/½ cup) soft brown sugar,
    firmly packed

Lightly grease two 10 cm (4 inch) diameter metal rings with butter and set aside.

Heat the milk in a small saucepan until tepid. Pour into a jug and stir in the yeast and sugar. Leave for 10 minutes, or until frothy.

Sift the flour, cocoa and salt into a large bowl. Pour in the milk and yeast mixture and whisk until smooth. Cover and stand in a warm place for 2 hours, or until doubled in size. Beat in the bicarbonate of soda and water and set aside to rest for 10 minutes.

While the mixture is resting, make the vanilla ricotta. Combine the ricotta, vanilla seeds and sugar in a bowl and set aside.

Heat a heavy-based frying pan over low-medium heat and place the prepared rings in the pan. Spoon 2 tablespoons of the batter inside each ring and cook for 6–8 minutes, or until the top is set and filled with tiny holes. Turn and cook the crumpets on the other side for a further 2–3 minutes until firm to the touch.

For the espresso caramel, pour 60 ml (2 fl oz/¼ cup) of the water and the espresso into a small glass and stir well. Bring the sugar and the remaining water to the boil in a saucepan over medium heat, stirring until the sugar has dissolved. Continue to simmer, without stirring, until the syrup is a deep golden caramel. Remove from the heat and carefully stir in the espresso, being careful as the caramel will be very hot and is likely to spit.

Serve the warm crumpets with the vanilla ricotta and drizzle over the espresso caramel.

Serves 8–10

+ +

BEER-BATTERED ONION HALVES WITH CHORIZO, FETA AND OLIVES
SPICE, LIES AND FAMILY TIES

THIS IS SO EASY AND ALMOST SHOCKINGLY ADDICTIVE; A RECIPE TO THREATEN FAMILY TRADITIONS.

THE VERY BEST KIND.

INGREDIENTS
95 g (3½ oz/½ cup) smoked
   kalamata olives
1 red onion, thinly sliced
70 g (2½ oz/½ cup) crumbled Persian feta
210 g (7½ oz/1 cup) smoked semi-dried
   tomatoes
2 chorizo sausages, sliced
2 small handfuls flat-leaf parsley,
   roughly chopped
3 pita breads, toasted and coarsely torn

Dressing
juice of 1 lemon
60 ml (2 fl oz/¼ cup) olive oil
salt and pepper to season

Onion halves
150 g (5½ oz/1 cup) plain
   (all-purpose) flour
125 g (4½ oz/1 cup) cornflour (cornstarch)
1 tsp baking powder
1 tsp sea salt
330 ml (11¼ fl oz/1⅓ cups) pale ale
vegetable oil, for deep-frying
12 pickled onions, halved

For the dressing, combine the lemon juice and olive oil and season with salt and pepper.

Combine the olives, onion, feta and semi-dried tomatoes in a large bowl. Drizzle on the dressing and set aside.

Heat a frying pan over medium heat, add the chorizo slices and cook for 3 minutes, or until browned and cooked through. Cover with foil and set aside until ready to serve.

For the onion halves, combine the flour, cornflour, baking powder and salt in a bowl. Use a whisk to gradually mix in the ale until smooth.

Heat the oil in a large saucepan over high heat to 180°C (350°F) or until the oil is hot enough to turn a cube of bread immediately golden.

Dip the onion halves in the batter and shake off the excess. Cook the battered onion halves, in batches, for 4–5 minutes, or until golden. Remove with a slotted spoon and place on paper towel to drain. Season with salt and pepper.

Add the onion halves, chorizo, parsley and pitta breads to the olive and onion salad and toss to combine. Serve immediately.

Serves 8–10

ROASTED LAMB RACK WITH SMOKY EGGPLANT PUREE AND THREE-TOMATO SALAD
MARY HAD A LITTLE LAMB

IT'S IMPORTANT TO REMEMBER AT TIMES LIKE THESE THAT NATURAL SELECTION IS NOT A PROCESS THAT ALWAYS OFFERS HAPPY ENDINGS. AS DARWINISM UNFOLDS ACROSS THE KITCHEN TABLE, DRAW COMFORT FROM IT — AFTER ALL, IT IS THE MECHANISM BY WHICH ONLY THE FITTEST SURVIVE.

IF YOU ARE PINCHED FOR TIME AND/OR INCLINATION, YOU CAN SUBSTITUTE THE HOMEMADE BABA GHANOUSH WITH A GOOD QUALITY STORE-BOUGHT VERSION.

INGREDIENTS
2 x 8-cutlet lamb racks, French trimmed
60 ml (2 fl oz/¼ cup) olive oil
10 cherry tomatoes on the vine
10 smoked semi-dried tomatoes
2 large balls of buffalo mozzarella,
  torn into 4 pieces
1 tbsp extra virgin olive oil
1 tbsp lemon juice
1 tbsp sumac
salt and freshly ground black pepper

Roast tomatoes
3 roma (plum) tomatoes, halved lengthways
olive oil, to drizzle
1 tbsp balsamic vinegar
1 tbsp sugar
1 tsp salt
freshly ground black pepper

Eggplant puree
2 x 550 g (1 lb 4 oz) eggplants (aubergines)
60 ml (2 fl oz/¼ cup) olive oil
1 garlic clove, finely chopped
2 tbsp lemon juice

For the roast tomatoes, spread the roma tomatoes, cut side up, on a baking tray, drizzle on the oil and vinegar and sprinkle with the sugar, salt and pepper. Roast for 20 minutes, or until the skin is starting to blister. Set aside.

For the eggplant puree, prick the eggplants all over with a fork. Place on a chargrill pan and cook, turning occasionally, over medium heat for 20–25 minutes, or until the flesh is very soft and the skin is charred. Cool, then cut the eggplants in half and scoop out the flesh. Combine the flesh, oil, garlic and lemon juice in a bowl and, using a fork, mash until quite smooth. Season to taste.

Preheat the oven to 180°C (350°F/Gas 4).

Cut the lamb racks in half to give four 4-cutlet racks, then brush with a little olive oil and season. Heat a large ovenproof frying pan over high heat and sear the lamb, fat-side down, for 1–2 minutes. Turn, then transfer the pan to the oven and roast the lamb for 5 minutes. Turn the racks again and roast, fat side up, for a further 5 minutes for medium-rare.

While the lamb is cooking, combine the cherry, semi-dried and roast tomatoes in a large bowl and mix gently.

Smear a large dollop of eggplant puree on each plate. Cut the lamb racks into double cutlets and place two on each plate. Divide the tomatoes evenly between the plates and scatter the mozzarella over the top. Combine the extra virgin olive oil, lemon juice and sumac in a bowl and season. Drizzle the sumac dressing over the tomatoes and mozzarella and serve immediately.

Serves 4

CHOCOLATE AND KAHLUA MERINGUE

PASS THE VALIUM

DESSERT IS A FAMILY REUNION'S BEST FRIEND.
IT'S LIKE INTERVAL AT A SHIT PLAY — AN
IMPORTANT SIGNPOST TO GAUGE HOW MUCH
LONGER YOU HAVE TO ENDURE THE PROCEEDINGS
BEFORE MAKING GOOD YOUR ESCAPE. A SWEET
FIX AND A TIME-OUT BELL ALL IN ONE, THIS
IS QUICK TO SERVE AND QUICKER TO EAT.

INGREDIENTS

100 g (3½ oz) milk chocolate, broken into
    bite-sized pieces
100 g (3½ oz) white chocolate, broken
    into bite-sized pieces
250 g (9 oz) Maltesers, smashed
1 x 72 g (2½ oz) Mars Bar,
    finely chopped
150 g (5½ oz) raspberries
150 g (5½ oz) strawberries, hulled and
    sliced
300 ml (10½ fl oz) thickened cream
icing (confectioners') sugar, sifted,
    to serve

Meringue

4 egg whites
a pinch of salt
330 g (11½ oz/1½ cups) caster
    (superfine) sugar
1 tbsp unsweetened cocoa powder,
    sifted
1½ tsp white vinegar
1½ tsp natural vanilla extract
1½ tsp Kahlua liqueur

Preheat the oven to 180°C (350°F/Gas 4). Line the bases of three 22 cm (8½ inch) loose-bottom baking pans with baking paper.

For the meringue layers, beat the egg whites and salt in a large bowl with electric beaters until soft peaks form. Gradually add the sugar and cocoa and beat until thick and glossy. Fold in the vinegar, vanilla and Kahlua.

Spoon the meringue mixture onto the prepared baking bases, ensuring the mixture is slightly smaller than the diameter of the pan base as the meringue will spread in the oven. Smooth the top and sides with a spatula and place in the oven. Immediately reduce the oven temperature to 150°C (300°F/Gas 2) and bake for 1½ hours. Turn off the oven and leave the door slightly ajar to allow the meringues to cool for 3 hours.

Loosely combine the chopped chocolates, Maltesers and Mars Bar with the raspberries and strawberries in a bowl.

Whip the cream in a large bowl until soft peaks form.

Place a meringue layer on a serving plate, spread one-third of the whipped cream over the top and sprinkle with one-third of the chocolate and fruit mixture.

Repeat with the remaining meringue layers, cream and chocolate and fruit mixture. Dust with the icing sugar and serve immediately.

Serves 8–10

CHOCOLATE
& KAHLUA
Meringue

The token comes home to roost

We all like to think of ourselves as good people with good hearts, completely qualified for the human race Hall of Fame. Maybe that's why it's difficult for so many of us to admit that we just don't like someone. Particularly those people who bear us no ill will, and have done nothing to us per se; we just don't seem to click.

So we throw out the token dinner invite and presume said social suicide-bomber will follow that unspoken social order, and decline. We don't really want them to know where we live, let alone have them sitting at our table, pushing our favourite cutlery into personal orifices and taking note of what sort of toilet paper we use.

Remember this. People don't choose to be social suicide-bombers — they are born that way, so tread carefully. If you make a throwaway line to those carrying 'the mark' about catching up for dinner in an attempt to be social and pleasant, they will kamikaze-dive their way into your home, run a few victory laps around your dinner table and obliterate any otherwise carefully orchestrated social gathering. Make it quick, dirty, easy and above all, time efficient.

Or scare the pants off them with your culinary prowess.

Menu

Spiced carrot and labne baked cheesecakes with speck and dukka crumble

–

Turkish chicken with eggs and flat breads

–

Banoffee pots

CHAPTER THREE **AWKWARD MOMENTS**

+ +

BANOFFEE POTS
BAKE OFF

THIS IS SERIOUSLY TASTY — A DESSERT THAT WILL SEE YOUR PLATES LOOKING LIKE A BATTLE SCENE. AS THEY LICK THE PLATE, YOUR DINING FRIEND-FOE WILL BE UNCONSCIOUSLY MAKING FUNNY FACES AS THEY GO — MOUTH AGAPE, EYES SQUINTING OR STARING TO THE HEAVENS, TONGUES WAGGING … PERHAPS A NERVOUS TWITCH. IT WON'T BE A PRETTY SIGHT. BUT THE IRONY AND COMIC TIMING OF SOMEONE WHO SPEAKS A VERY DIFFERENT SOCIAL LANGUAGE WILL FURNISH YOU WITH THE EVENING'S ENTERTAINMENT.

YOU MAY THINK THE NEED FOR A SPECIAL TIN — A SIX-CAVITY DESSERT SHELL TIN — ABSURD FOR DINNER GUESTS YOU PREFER YOU DIDN'T HAVE, BUT I PROMISE YOU'LL FIND SO MANY USES FOR IT. AND AT LEAST YOU'LL KNOW YOUR DESSERT IS SPECTACULAR.

INGREDIENTS
Bases
125 g (4½ oz) unsalted butter
110 g (3½ oz/½ cup) caster (superfine) sugar
60 ml (2 fl oz/¼ cup) golden syrup
　(light treacle)
125 ml (4 fl oz/½ cup) buttermilk
1 egg
1 tsp natural vanilla extract
150 g (5½ oz/1 cup) plain (all-purpose) flour
1 tbsp hazelnut meal
1 tbsp ground cinnamon
½ tsp baking powder

Topping
4 scoops of vanilla bean ice cream
30 ml (1 fl oz) dark rum
4 tbsp dulce de leche (caramel)
　at room temperature
2 small bananas, sliced
40 g (1½ oz/¼ cup) hazelnuts,
　roughly chopped
50 g (1¾ oz/½ cup) dark chocolate
　(70 per cent cocoa solids)

To serve
hazelnuts, roughly chopped to scatter

Preheat the oven to 200°C (400°F/Gas 6). Grease a six-cavity dessert shell tin and set aside.

For the bases, melt the butter in a saucepan over low heat and add the sugar, stirring until completely dissolved. Remove from the heat, allow to cool slightly, then stir in the golden syrup. Add the buttermilk, egg and vanilla, stirring to combine. Sift the flour, ground hazelnuts, cinnamon and baking powder into a large bowl. Stir in the butter mixture until combined, being careful not to overwork the mixture. Fill the prepared dessert tin three-quarters full and bake for 12 minutes, or until slightly bouncy to touch. Allow to cool for 5 minutes in the tin before turning out onto a wire rack.

While the bases are cooking, remove the ice cream from the freezer, allow to soften a little and stir in the rum. Return to the freezer.

Just prior to serving, on each slightly warm base, place a scoop of vanilla ice cream, scatter on the banana and chopped hazelnuts and drizzle over the dulce de leche. Grate on some chocolate and serve immediately.

Serves 6

Friendship divorce

De-friending non-friends is an awkward, disconcerting process. There is something noble in honouring a relationship with another, but not when it drags you down to Dang Town. Most friendships are situational, though we don't like to admit it.

They spring up in the ground of common interests and/or common circumstances, meaning it's not necessary to follow through with them. Consider dinner your trump card, an opportunity to lay it out on the table, or at least confirm that intimate social scenarios (with them) are not for you.

Menu

Smoked chicken terrine
with mustard apple cider

–

Pork schnitzel
with caponata and
cauliflower mash

–

Honeycomb cannoli

SMOKED CHICKEN TERRINE WITH MUSTARD APPLE CIDER
BORDERLINE PERSONALITIES

I USED TO STAY AWAY FROM THE TERRINE BUT THEY ARE SO EASY, A QUICK DUMP OF INGREDIENTS, SOME SETTER AND VOILÀ.

YOU'LL NEED TO **BEGIN THIS A DAY AHEAD.**

INGREDIENTS

----

500 g (1 lb 2 oz) smoked chicken meat

1 garlic clove, finely chopped

zest of 1 lemon

2 small handfuls of flat-leaf parsley, finely chopped

1 large red onion, finely chopped

sea salt and freshly ground black pepper

500 ml (1 fl oz/2 cups) apple cider

2 heaped tbsp dijon mustard

2 tsp powdered gelatine

To serve

slices of sourdough bread, toasted

Line a 8 x 25 cm (3 x 10 inch) terrine mould (or a loaf pan will do) with plastic wrap.

Coarsely shred the chicken meat into a bowl (discarding the carcass). Add the garlic, lemon zest, parsley and onion and season.

In a separate bowl, combine the apple cider, mustard and gelatine. Stir well then pour over the chicken mixture. Spoon the chicken mixture into the prepared terrine tin, press down firmly and smooth the top with the back of a spoon. Cover with plastic wrap and refrigerate until firm (preferably overnight).

04

Unmould the terrine, thickly slice and serve with toasted sourdough.

Serves 4–6

PORK SCHNITZEL WITH CAPONATA AND CAULIFLOWER MASH
DOOR POLICY

SOCIAL GATECRASHERS ARE A FAST-EVOLVING SPECIES — WHICH IS BAFFLING WHEN MOST PEOPLE SPEND THEIR LIVES TRYING TO GET OUT OF PARTIES AND DINNERS AND THINGS THEY DON'T WANT TO GO TO, LEAVING CROAKY VOICEMAIL OR TEXTING 'SOOO SORRY, THOUGHT IT WAS NEXT FRIDAY'.

WHAT KIND OF CRAZED SOCIAL ANIMALS INVITE THEMSELVES, UNINVITED? MAYBE IT'S THE FACT WE DON'T WANT THEM THERE THAT APPEALS TO THEM; IT'S NO FUN OTHERWISE. WHEN YOU THINK ABOUT IT, EVERYBODY IS WELCOME AT CHURCH, AND THAT'S PROBABLY WHY NOBODY GOES.

THE COMFORT FACTOR OF A GOOD PORK SCHNITZEL PROVIDES THE NECESSARY PROTECTION AGAINST FEAR OF THE UNINVITED, SOCIALLY BLIGHTED.

INGREDIENTS

Schnitzel

600 g (1 lb 5 oz) pork topside, cut into 4 slices

50 g (1¾ oz/½ cup) finely grated parmesan

120 g (4¼ oz/2 cups) fresh sourdough breadcrumbs, toasted

2 eggs

sea salt and freshly ground black pepper

2 tbsp grapeseed oil

Caponata

1 kg (2 lb 4 oz) eggplants (aubergines), cut into cubes

100 ml (3½ fl oz) olive oil

1 onion, thinly sliced

5 celery stalks, thickly sliced

200 g (7 oz) green olives, halved and pitted

2 tbsp drained capers

375 g (13 oz/1½ cups) tomato passata

2 tsp caster (superfine) sugar

80 ml (2½ fl oz/⅓ cup) red wine vinegar

70 g (2½ oz) slivered almonds

Mash

600 g (1 lb 5 oz) cauliflower, cut into florets

6 starchy potatoes (such as sebago), peeled and roughly chopped

1 tbsp lemon juice

125 ml (4 fl oz/½ cup) thickened cream

100 g (3½ oz/1 cup) shredded parmesan

125 ml (4 fl oz/½ cup) milk

50 g (1¾ oz) butter

01

Preheat the oven to 200°C (400°F/Gas 6). Line a baking tray with baking paper and set aside.

02

For the schnitzel, place the pork steaks between two sheets of plastic wrap. Using a rolling pin or the flat side of a meat mallet, beat the steaks until flattened. Combine the parmesan and breadcrumbs in a shallow bowl. Place the eggs in a separate bowl, lightly beat and season with salt and pepper. Coat the steaks in the egg mixture, then dip in the parmesan crumbs. Heat the oil in a frying pan over medium heat. Lightly fry the pork for 1 minute on each side then transfer to the prepared tray. Bake for 20 minutes, or until the crumbs are crisp.

03

For the caponata, heat half the oil in a large frying pan, add the eggplant and cook until golden. Drain on paper towel. Heat the remaining oil in the same pan and cook the onion over low-medium for 5 minutes, then add the celery and cook for another 2 minutes. Add the olives, capers, passata, sugar and vinegar and simmer over medium heat for 10 minutes. Add the eggplant, reduce the heat to low and simmer for 20 minutes. Season to taste.

04

For the mash, bring a large saucepan of water to the boil over high heat. Add the cauliflower and potato and cook for 10–15 minutes, or until tender. Drain, return to the pan and mash until almost smooth. Place over low heat, add the lemon juice, cream, parmesan, milk and butter and cook, stirring with a wooden spoon, for 2–3 minutes, or until the butter melts and the mash is well combined. Taste and season with salt and pepper.

05

Serve the caponata topped with the pork and a side of potato and cauliflower mash. Sprinkle on the almonds just prior to serving.

Serves 4

HONEYCOMB CANNOLI
SWEET RELEASE

AHHH, THERE YOU ARE WITH YOUR UNINVITED GUEST — CLOTHED IN A DRESS, SHOES AND PRETENCE.

INGREDIENTS

- -

500 g (1 lb 2 oz) ricotta

3 tbsp icing (confectioners') sugar, or more to taste

12 cannoli shells

200 g (7 oz) dark chocolate (70 per cent cocoa solids), melted

110 g (3¾ oz) honeycomb, broken into rough chunks

- -

To serve
melted chocolate

Combine the ricotta and sugar in a bowl and mix well.

Using a teaspoon or a piping bag, gently fill the cannoli shells with the ricotta mixture. Layer the filled shells on a plate and drizzle on the melted chocolate.

03

Drizzle over the melted chocolate, top with the honeycomb chunks and serve.

Serves 4

PMS

PMS, the clinical definition being a few days a month where the hormonal cycle causes an imbalance of serotonin in the brain.

Thank god for the medical clarification.

Normally I am a moderately mild-mannered, relatively balanced individual until those few days of rage commence, turning me into a senseless wildebeest. My breasts turn into rocks, random sobbing erupts, god him/herself couldn't get me to the gym and I can't park my car to save myself. And the possibility of forgetting to turn off the iron or lock the house as I am leaving for work rises exponentially, the longer it takes me to source a block of Dairy Milk the size of my head. It's not a question of my puny female mind being flooded with irrational mood-altering hormones. Phooey to that, I'm really not that bad ... it's just that sometimes I'm sort of angry at the world, you know, a bit upset.

The last thing you want to do is cook, but the opportunity to eat whatever comforts you and calms you is very healing. We're meant to reduce our saturated fats and sugar consumption to a minimum. Why can't the whole world just feck off and let us eat our king-sized Mars Bars in peace? With these dishes you can get as weary, moody, hungry, spotty and irrational as you like.

Menu

Chimichangas
–
Soy salmon and rice
–
Mexican smoky
pork cheesies
–
Pear and quince walnut
crumble with custard
–
Chocolate and salted
caramel brownies

Dairy Milk

(Phewww)

CHIMICHANGAS
BREAKING THE CYCLE

THIS IS A TIME WHEN YOU GET TO BE SOUR, INTROVERTED AND ANGSTY. A BRIEF — AND USUALLY UNEXPECTED — TIME WHEN YOU FIND YOURSELF GOING ALL JUDY BLUME ON YOUR SHIZ:

> ARE YOU THERE GOD? IT'S ME MARGARET.
>
> THIS SUCKS.
>
> THAT'S ALL. PERIOD.

INGREDIENTS

100 g (3½ oz) skinless chicken
1 tbsp extra virgin olive oil
1 tsp curry powder
1 tsp cumin powder
sea salt
100 ml (3½ fl oz) sour cream
50 g (1¾ oz/½ cup) grated cheddar
a small handful of coriander (cilantro) leaves, roughly chopped
1 jumbo tortilla wrap (or 2 small)

Preheat the oven to 200°C (400°F/Gas 6).

Combine the chicken, oil, curry powder, cumin and salt in a bowl and toss to ensure the chicken is evenly coated. Lightly sear the chicken in a frying pan over medium heat until browned but not completely cooked through.

Combine the sour cream, cheddar and coriander in a bowl. Add the chicken and mix well. Place the chicken mixture in the middle of the tortilla. Wrap the tortilla around the filling and place on a baking tray. Bake in the oven for 15 minutes.

Serve with an oversized glass of wine. Eat quickly and then lie very flat on the couch.

Serves 1

SOY SALMON AND RICE
I CAN FEEL IT IN MY WATERS

THERE ARE BUT A HANDFUL OF MOMENTS IN OUR LIFETIME WHEN WE CAN TRULY SAY WE FEEL AT ONE WITH OURSELVES AND THE WORLD. LYING ON THE COUCH IN NOTHING BUT YOUR UNDIES AND A SLOUCHY JUMPER, WITH A HOT WATER BOTTLE ON YOUR BELLY AND A STEAMING BOWL OF THIS IN YOUR HANDS, IS ONE OF THE FEW.

INGREDIENTS

50 g (1¾ oz/¼ cup) basmati rice
125 ml (4 fl oz/½ cup) water
125 ml (4 fl oz/½ cup) soy sauce
1 tsp wasabi
squeeze of lime juice
150 g (5½ oz) salmon steak, cut into bite-sized pieces
150 g (5½ oz) snow peas
1 tbsp pickled ginger

Bring a small saucepan of water to the boil. Add the rice and cook over high heat for 10 minutes or until cooked through. While the rice is cooking, combine the soy sauce, wasabi and lime juice in a bowl. Add the salmon and toss to coat.

Brown the salmon in a frying pan over medium–high heat for 5 minutes until just cooked through.

Add the snow peas and wasabi marinade and cook for a further minute.

Remove from the heat, stir in the pickled ginger and serve with the rice.

Serves 1

MEXICAN SMOKY
PORK CHEESIES
WOMB SERVICE

THIS BURGER, AN ADAPTATION OF US *GOURMET* MAGAZINE'S RECIPE, IS THE PERFECT ANTIDOTE TO MENSTRUAL ANARCHY. THE SMOKINESS BRINGS A TEAR TO YOUR EYE, THE SPICE A RUMBLE TO YOUR BELLY, AND THE AVOCADO AND AŸOLI A PLACATING SENSE OF ZEN FOR YOUR OVERALL WELLBEING.

INGREDIENTS

250 g (9 oz) minced (ground) pork
1 dried chipotle chilli, finely chopped
1 garlic clove, finely chopped
a small handful of coriander (cilantro)
   leaves, chopped
sea salt and freshly ground black pepper
1 tsp vegetable oil
3 slices of smoked cheddar
1 tsp paprika
125 ml (4 fl oz/½ cup) ready-made aïoli
3 burger buns
1 avocado, sliced
3 tbsp ready-made Mexican salsa
50 g (1¾ oz/1 cup) baby English spinach

Preheat the oven to 180°C (350°F/Gas 4).

Combine the pork, chipotle, garlic, coriander and salt and pepper in a bowl and mix well with your hands. Shape into three burger patties.

Place a large frying pan over medium heat, add the vegetable oil and fry the patties for 4 minutes. Flip the burgers, top with a slice of cheese and cook for another 4 minutes.

Combine the paprika and aïoli in a small bowl and stir well.

Split the burger buns in half. Smear the base bun with the aïoli and add the burger pattie and some avocado, salsa and spinach. Top with the other half of the burger bun and eat immediately.

Serves 3

PEAR AND QUINCE WALNUT CRUMBLE WITH CUSTARD
SLOW BURN

I SUGGEST THIS ONE FOR THOSE WEEKEND DAYS WHEN YOU HAVE THE HOUSE TO YOURSELF AND YOU ARE IN THE MOOD TO POTTER AROUND IN YOUR PYJAMAS WITH YOUR 'BLOAT' OUT, YOUR HAIR UNWASHED AND YOUR 'THE WORLD CAN GET STUFFED' GAME ON.

NOTE THAT WHILE MINIMAL EFFORT IS REQUIRED, THIS IS NOT AN INSTANT FIX AS THE QUINCES TAKE TIME TO COOK AND YOU NEED TO HAVE A FEW INGREDIENTS ON HAND.

INGREDIENTS

330 g (11½ oz/1½ cups) caster (superfine) sugar
200 ml (7 fl oz) dessert wine
200 ml (7 fl oz) verjuice
zest and juice of 1 lemon
1 vanilla bean, split lengthways and seeds scraped
250 ml (9 fl oz/1 cup) water
1 quince (about 200 g/7 oz), peeled, cored and cut into thick slices
3 beurre bosc pears, peeled, cored, halved and cut into slices
75 g (2¾ oz) soft brown sugar

Crumble

100 g (3½ oz/⅔ cup) plain (all-purpose) flour
65 g (2½ oz) soft brown sugar
50 g (1¾ oz) ground walnuts
30 g (1 oz) walnuts, roughly chopped
75 g (2¾ oz) butter, roughly chopped
1 tsp finely grated lemon zest

To serve

vanilla custard or vanilla bean ice cream

Preheat the oven to 150°C (300°F/Gas 2). Grease two 250 ml (9 fl oz/1 cup) ramekins.

Combine the caster sugar, wine, verjuice, lemon juice, vanilla and water in a casserole dish and stir over medium-high heat until the sugar has dissolved. Add the quince, cover with a sheet of baking paper and a sheet of foil and bake in the oven for 2 hours, or until quince is tender and dark pink. Add the pear, cover and bake for another hour. Transfer the fruit and juices to a bowl and macerate with a fork until bite-sized lumps are achieved. Add the brown sugar and toss to coat. Place the quince mixture in the prepared ramekins and set aside.

For the crumble, combine the flour, sugar, ground and chopped walnuts in a bowl. Rub in the butter and lemon zest with your fingertips until the mixture resembles coarse breadcrumbs.

Scatter the crumble over the quince mixture, place the ramekins on a baking tray and bake for 20 minutes or until golden on top.

Serve with vanilla custard or ice cream.

Serves 1 (with some leftovers at the ready for when the need hits)

CHOCOLATE AND SALTED CARAMEL BROWNIES

THE ONE-TWO PUNCH

THIS LEGENDARY RECIPE REALLY IS THE CRACK COCAINE OF THE PMS WORLD — PLENTY OF SUGAR, FAT AND SALT FOR THAT SLIGHT BITTERSWEET TANG OF HORMONAL RESENTMENT.

IF THE IDEA OF MAKING THE CARAMEL APPEALS ABOUT AS MUCH AS ANOTHER VISIT FROM AUNTY FLOW, WAIT UNTIL THE BROWNIE COOLS, THEN SMEAR A JAR OF DULCE DE LECHE (CARAMEL) OVER THE TOP AND SPRINKLE WITH THE SALT.

INGREDIENTS

175 g (6 oz) dark chocolate (70 per cent cocoa solids), chopped
185 g (6½ oz) unsalted butter, cubed (hate to sound like a Francophile but French butter is best)
440 g (15½ oz/2 cups) caster (superfine) sugar
3 large eggs
1 tsp vanilla extract
150 g (5½ oz/1 cup) plain (all-purpose) flour

Caramel glaze

125 ml (4 fl oz/½ cup) thickened cream
440 g (15½ oz/2 cups) caster (superfine) sugar
125 ml (4 fl oz/½ cup) water
60 g (2¼ oz) unsalted butter, cubed
2 tsp sea salt flakes
2 tsp powdered gelatine combined with 60 ml (2 fl oz/¼ cup) cold water (sprinkle over the water to make it easier to blend)

Preheat the oven to 170°C (325°F/Gas 3). Grease a 22 x 30 cm (8½ x 12 inch) baking tin and set aside.

For the brownies, melt the chocolate and butter in a heatproof bowl over a saucepan of gently simmering water. Add the sugar and stir until smooth. Remove from the heat. In a separate bowl, lightly whisk the eggs and vanilla, then stir in the chocolate mixture. Add the flour and stir gently until well combined. Pour the batter into the prepared tin and bake for 30 minutes until crisp on top. Allow to cool in the tin.

Prepare the caramel glaze by warming the cream in a small saucepan over low heat until hot, not boiling. In a separate saucepan combine the sugar and water, place over medium-high heat and cook, without stirring, until the sugar reaches a dark amber colour. Carefully add the cream and butter and stir until smooth. Remove from the heat and mix in the gelatine liquid.

Pour the caramel glaze over the brownies and cool until the caramel just sets. Sprinkle over the sea salt flakes and slice into bars or dive straight in with a spoon.

Makes 24 brownies

Hangover food

The evening started out innocently enough. A cute but sexy sundress. Witty, intelligent conversation. Chilled Champagne.

The clock strikes 'nothing good happens at 2 a.m.' Suddenly, gutter jokes. Make-out sessions in dark corners. Questionable new dance moves or a drink 'n' dial to an ex of yesteryear. Sunrise. Filthy kebab on the street corner.

Walk of shame.

But there is no need for shame. There is something empowering about wandering home, mascara down your face, panties in your handbag, feeling every bit the gorgeous, feckless, drunken It girl.

A silly night on the piss can heighten the sense of smell, the appetite, the trifecta desire for grease, carbs and comfort. And the food you choose in that delicious moment between nuit blanche and hangover is uniquely significant. For this reason alone I am not bored with being drunk or hung-over. Far from it. Every new drink-fuelled episode is dear to me, as is the discovery of the dish that will take the 'day after' pain away.

Menu

Omelette sandwich with bacon and tomato aïoli

–

Spaghetti carbonara

–

One-pan chorizo hash brown

I don't feel too good...

OMELETTE SANDWICH WITH BACON AND TOMATO AÏOLI

LADETTE TO LADY

YOUR HOUDINI-LIKE ATTEMPTS AT ESCAPE EARLY IN THE EVENING. THWARTED.

A NOT-SO-SUBTLE TRANSITION TO SIPPING WATER SHOUTED DOWN BY YOUR COCKTAIL OF FRIENDS.

THE GUT-CHURNING, EAR-BLEEDING PAIN THE NEXT DAY SEES YOUR DRAMA CONTINUE TO PLAY OUT IN DETAIL — YOU THE CENTRAL PROTAGONIST, AND YOUR FRIENDS THE SINISTER DRINK-BUYING SUPPORTING CAST.

PREVENT AN ENCORE WITH THIS SANDWICH OF COMFORT, GREASE, SALT AND SERENITY.

INGREDIENTS

Spicy tomato aïoli

2 roma (plum) tomatoes, halved
60 ml (2 fl oz/¼ cup) olive oil
120 g (4¼ oz/½ cup) whole-egg mayonnaise
1 garlic clove, finely chopped
1 tsp hot Spanish paprika
sea salt and freshly ground black pepper
4 eggs
60 ml (2 fl oz/¼ cup) milk
2 tbsp finely chopped flat-leaf parsley
4 slices of bacon
2 baguettes, cut in half lengthways

Preheat the oven to 190°C (375°F/Gas 5). Line the base of a 26 x 32 cm (10 ½ x 12 ¾ inch) Swiss roll tin (jelly roll tin) with baking paper.

Brush the tomatoes with oil and season with salt and pepper. Place the tomatoes on a baking tray and roast in the oven for 20 minutes. Place the roasted tomatoes, mayonnaise, garlic and paprika in a food processor and process until smooth. Season with salt and pepper and set aside.

For the omelette, combine the eggs and milk in a bowl, season and whisk well. Pour into the prepared tin, sprinkle over the parsley and bake for 10-12 minutes, or until puffed and golden.

While the eggs are cooking, place the bacon in a frying pan and cook over medium-high heat, turning occasionally, for 3 minutes, or to your liking.

Run a small knife around the inner edge of the tin, turn the omelette out onto a chopping board and peel away the paper. Cut the omelette into strips.

In each baguette, layer strips of the bacon and the omelette, then drizzle with the spicy tomato aïoli.

Serves 2

SPAGHETTI CARBONARA
MORNING-AFTER THRILL

IF YOU DON'T WAKE UNTIL THE AFTERNOON, THIS IS THE ANSWER TO THE 3 P.M. WALL OF PAIN. TRUST ME: A BOWL OF CARBONARA AND A BIG GLASS OF BLACK ASPIRIN (COKE) WITH ICE WILL WORK ABSOLUTE WONDERS.

INGREDIENTS
2½ tbsp extra virgin olive oil
200 g (7 oz) mild pancetta, finely chopped
1 small brown onion, finely chopped
6 egg yolks
3 egg whites
50 g (1¾ oz/⅓ cup) parmesan, finely grated
35 g (1¼ oz/⅓ cup) pecorino, finely grated
sea salt and freshly ground black pepper
500 g (1 lb 2 oz) spaghetti

Heat the oil in a frying pan over medium heat. Add the pancetta and onion and sauté until crisp and set aside.

Whisk the egg yolks and egg whites in a large bowl. Add the parmesan and pecorino and season with salt and pepper.

Cook the spaghetti in a large saucepan of boiling salted water until al dente. Drain, reserving about a tablespoon of the cooking water. Add the spaghetti, pancetta and onion to the egg mixture and quickly mix to combine, adding some reserved cooking water if it seems a little dry. Season and serve.

Serves 3–4

ONE-PAN CHORIZO HASH BROWN

PRETEND LIKE IT NEVER HAPPENED

I HATE THE POUNDING HEADACHE POST PISS-UP; THE THROBBING SO VIOLENT YOU FEEL AS IF A TEEN-FLICK SLASHER MOVIE IS BEING SHOT INSIDE YOUR HEAD. THESE HASHIES WON'T TAKE IT AWAY COMPLETELY, BUT WILL TURN IT INTO A BEARABLE DULL THUD.

IF YOU FEEL LIKE YOU HAVEN'T EATEN SINCE A PREVIOUS LIFE, ADD SOME FRESHLY SLICED AVOCADO, A POACHED EGG, A FEW SLICES OF SMOKED SALMON, A SQUEEZE OF LEMON JUICE AND A DOLLOP OF CRÈME FRAÎCHE. GET THROUGH THAT COMBO AND YOUR STOMACH WILL BE THANKING YOU SO LOUDLY IT WILL DISTRACT YOU FROM THE PAIN IN YOUR HEAD.

INGREDIENTS

2 potatoes
1 large egg, lightly beaten
2 tsp olive oil
1 small red onion, finely chopped
1 garlic clove, finely chopped
1 tsp paprika
1 tsp ground coriander
2 chorizo sausages, casings discarded and
    filling finely chopped
2 thick slices of haloumi cheese, chopped into
    small pieces
a small handful of flat-leaf parsley,
    finely chopped
sea salt and freshly ground black pepper
a dollop of butter

Peel and coarsely grate the potatoes and wrap in a clean tea towel to squeeze out any excess water. Place in a bowl, add the egg and toss to coat.

Heat the oil in a frying pan over medium heat and sweat the onions and garlic until soft. Remove from the heat and transfer to a bowl. Add the paprika, ground coriander, sausage meat, haloumi and parsley, stir in the potato mixture and season generously with the salt and pepper.

Return the frying pan to the heat and melt the butter over medium heat, swilling it around the base of the pan. Add the hash brown mixture, pressing down gently with a spatula to flatten, and cook for 8–10 minutes. Place a plate over the pan, flip the hash brown over and slide it, uncooked side down, back into the pan. Cook for another 8–10 minutes, or until both sides appear crisp and golden and the potato has cooked through.

Get stuck into it with a fork or, if you have more than one to feed, cut into slices and serve.

Serves 2–4

Wake

The first funeral I attended was my grandfather's. His name was Chisholm. He was a regal man, just over six feet tall. He had fought in wars and was a butterfly catcher. I was too young to know him as a person. I adored him, but I didn't 'know' him. To this day, I desperately wish I could have asked him questions instead of just watching him tend to his hibiscus trees. And what I wouldn't give to have him teach me how to catch a butterfly, and all the patience and gentleness of touch that accompanies it.

I want to know the little things. I know he loved his rum; I just wish I knew what he liked to eat when he drank it. I remember that he could fillet a fish at lightning speed, but have absolutely no idea how he cooked it. And that makes me very sad.

At the wake, I ate until I was fit to burst. It was as if those stale crumbs of comfort would help the suddenness of his passing and hold the warmth of his words and the memory of our last conversation.

My grandmother could not eat. A foreign concept to me, but some people suffering from grief do not find solace in food. In fact they abhor it. This aside, I think offering a dish, whether it ends up eaten by others, in the bin, or forgotten in the back of the freezer, is a way of expressing genuine sadness and demonstrating your support. It can eliminate the awkwardness of not knowing what to say, or how long you should stay, and most importantly, it lets people who are hurting know that you care.

Menu

Pork and rhubarb pies

–

Blood orange and pistachio
frangipane galette

–

Pastitsio

PORK AND RHUBARB PIES

IT'S A PLEASURE TO DISCOVER A WORLD-BEATING PORK PIE — ONE THAT FORTIFIES, COMFORTS AND NOURISHES. SADLY, MANY MISS THE MARK — SOGGY BOTTOMS, NOT ENOUGH MEAT, TOO MUCH FAT, AND SO ON. WHEN IT COMES TO A PORK PIE, IF YOU AREN'T DELIVERING THE GOODS YOU'RE IN TROUBLE.

IN THESE PIES, THE RHUBARB SITS NESTLED ON THE PORK, WHICH HUMBLY ACKNOWLEDGES AND APPRECIATES ITS BRIGHT FLAVOUR. IT PROVIDES THAT TART SHOCK, AS SHARP AND AS FRESH AS A HARSH WINTER'S MORNING ON WHAT CAN OTHERWISE BE A VERY DARK TIME FULL OF PAIN AND SUFFERING.

INGREDIENTS

5 garlic cloves, smashed
2 tbsp rosemary leaves
1 tsp black peppercorns
60 ml (2 fl oz/¼ cup) olive oil, plus extra
  for brushing
sea salt and freshly ground black pepper
1 x 1 kg (2 lb 4 oz) pork loin, rolled, tied,
  skin scored (ask your butcher to do this)
3 rhubarb stalks, thinly sliced
80 ml (2½ fl oz/⅓ cup) apple juice
3 tbsp brown sugar
1 tbsp dijon mustard
2 tbsp finely chopped flat-leaf parsley
4 x 375 g (13 oz) ready-made puff
  pastry sheets
1 egg, lightly whisked for egg wash

Preheat the oven to 220°C (425°F/Gas 7). Grease two six-hole jumbo muffin tins.

Combine the garlic, rosemary, peppercorns, half the oil and 2 teaspoons of salt in a mortar and pestle and pound to create a smooth paste.

Rub the paste into the scored pork skin and place in a small roasting tin. Roast for 15 minutes, then reduce the oven temperature to 180°C (350°F/Gas 4) and roast for a further 40 minutes, or until the pork is cooked through, but still a touch pink. Remove the pork from the tin, cover and set aside to rest in a warm place for 10 minutes. When the pork is cool enough to handle, pull the meat from the bone.

Add the rhubarb to the pan, drizzle on the apple juice and the remaining oil, sprinkle on the sugar and finely chopped rosemary. Coarsely mash the rhubarb and pan juices together with a fork and add the mustard and parsley. Season to taste.

Roll out each sheet of puff pastry to 3 mm (⅓ inch) thick and cut into even-sized squares for a total of 24 squares. Brush half these squares with the extra oil and press into the prepared tins.

Bake for 5 minutes, or until slightly crisp. Remove from the oven and working carefully, spoon the pork and rhubarb mix into the pastry cases and top with the remaining pastry squares. Brush over with the egg wash, then make a small slit in the centre of each pie. Return to the oven for 20 minutes or until the tops are golden brown.

Makes 12

BLOOD ORANGE AND PISTACHIO
FRANGIPANE GALETTE

LOVE, DEATH
AND FRANGIPANIS

THIS BLOOD ORANGE TART IS PERFECT WHEN PEOPLE NEED FEEDING. NOT IN THE
USUAL SUSTAINING-LIFE WAY, BUT WHEN A DAMAGED SOUL NEEDS HEALING. THIS IS
THE DISH WHEN THE CHOICE OF WHAT TO EAT TRULY MATTERS. IT IS EASY ON THE
STOMACH, ITS CONSTRUCTION BELIES A TENDERNESS OF TOUCH AND INTENT, AND
IT IS JUST THE SORT OF THING TO NIBBLE ON WHEN THERE IS AN IMPERATIVE
ATTACHED TO EATING.

INGREDIENTS

2 blood oranges
375 g (13 oz) puff pastry
1 egg yolk, beaten
melted butter, for brushing
75 g (2¾ oz) marzipan, grated
1 tbsp soft brown sugar
1 tbsp lavender honey

Frangipane

40 g (1½ oz) unsalted butter, softened
3 tbsp caster (superfine) sugar
1 egg yolk
¼ tsp natural vanilla extract
3 tbsp pistachio nuts, shelled and unsalted,
    roughly chopped
3 tbsp ground almonds

Preheat the oven to 220°C (425°F/Gas 7). Line a baking tray with baking paper and set aside.

Peel the blood oranges, then cut the flesh into 5 mm (¼ inch) thick slices, ensuring no white pith remains and set aside.

On a lightly floured surface, roll out the pastry to 3 mm (⅛ inch) thick and trim the edges (to help the pastry rise evenly) to form a 22 x 30 cm (8½ x 12 inch) rectangle. Place on the prepared tray. Use the point of a sharp knife to score a 1 cm (½ inch) border around the edge of the pastry, being careful not to cut all the way through. Prick the centre all over with a fork and brush with the egg yolk.

For the frangipane, cream the butter and sugar until pale and fluffy. Add the egg yolk and vanilla and stir in the pistachios and ground almonds.

Spread the frangipane evenly over the pastry within the scored area. Layer the orange slices over the top, brush lightly with the melted butter and sprinkle on the marzipan and sugar. Bake for 15 minutes, drizzle on the honey, reduce the oven temperature to 180°C (350°F/Gas 4) and bake for another 15 minutes, or until golden and the blood oranges have caramelised.

Serves 6

WAKE

+ +

PASTITSIO

GRIEF

WARMTH AND COMFORT. SPEAKS FOR ITSELF REALLY.

INGREDIENTS

500 g (1 lb 2 oz) risoni
2 eggs, lightly beaten
50 g (1³/₄ oz) parmesan, grated
10 g (¹/₄ oz) panko crumbs

Meat sauce

80 ml (2¹/₂ fl oz/¹/₃ cup) olive oil
1 onion, finely chopped
4 garlic cloves, finely chopped
1 kg (2 lb 4 oz) lean minced (ground) beef
200 ml (7 fl oz) red wine
400 g (14 oz) tinned chopped tomatoes
2 tbsp tomato puree
1 cinnamon stick
¹/₄ tsp ground cloves
1 tbsp dried oregano
2 tbsp oregano, chopped
3 bay leaves
100 ml (3¹/₂ fl oz) water
sea salt and freshly ground black pepper

White sauce

115 g (4 oz) butter
115 g (4 oz) plain (all-purpose) flour
1.25 litres (44 fl oz/5 cups) milk, plus a little
    extra if necessary
¹/₂ tsp freshly grated nutmeg

For the meat sauce, heat the oil in a saucepan over medium heat, add the onion and garlic and sweat until the onion is translucent. Stir in the beef and fry over high heat for 5 minutes, or until browned. Add the red wine, tomatoes, tomato puree, cinnamon stick, ground cloves, oregano, bay leaves, water and salt and pepper and simmer for an hour, or until reduced. Remove from the heat, discard the cinnamon stick and bay leaves, and set aside.

Preheat the oven to 180°C (350°F/Gas 4). Grease a 23 x 33 cm (9 x 13 inch) shallow ovenproof dish.

Bring a large saucepan of water to the boil. Add the risoni and cook until just al dente. Drain well, transfer to a large bowl and leave to cool slightly.

For the white sauce, melt the butter in a saucepan over medium heat, add the flour and cook, stirring, for 1 minute. Gradually stir in the milk and bring to the boil. Reduce the heat to low and leave to simmer for 5–7 minutes, stirring occasionally. Season with the nutmeg and salt and pepper and keep warm over low heat, stirring now and then and adding more milk if the sauce begins to get a little too thick.

Stir 250 ml (9 fl oz/1 cup) of the white sauce, the beaten eggs and half the parmesan into the warm risoni. Spread one-third of the pasta over the base of the prepared dish and cover with half the meat sauce. Repeat the layering with the remaining pasta and meat sauce, finishing with a layer of pasta. Spoon on the remaining white sauce, top with the parmesan and sprinkle on the panko crumbs. Bake for 40 minutes until bubbling and golden brown.

Serves 6–8

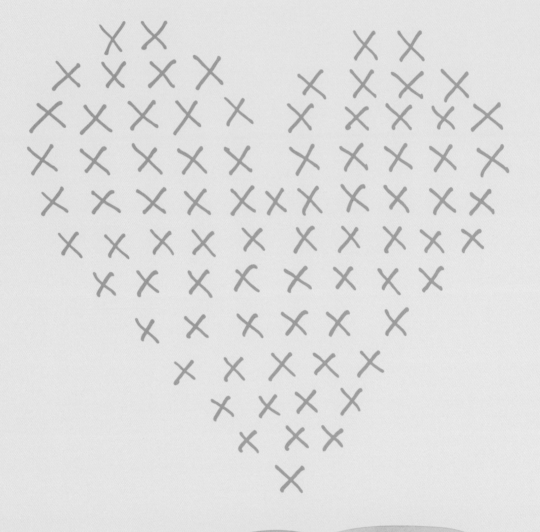

**To love and lose is
a brave thing.**
IT IS TAKING LIFE IN ITS OWN HANDS
AND CREATING A 'MOMENT'.
*There aren't many times that we get
to choose our moments but*
LIFE
IS FULL OF THEM.

CHAPTER FOUR

XXXXXXXXXXXXXXXXXXXXXXXXXXXXXXXXXXXXXXXXXXXXXXXXXXXXXXXXX

LOVE
AND OTHER
BRUISES

XXXXXXXXXXXXXXXXXXXXXXXXXXXXXXXXXXXXXXXXXXXXXXXXXXXXXXXXX

To love and lose is a brave thing. It is taking life into your own hands and creating 'a moment'. There aren't many times that we get to choose our moments, but life is full of them, good and bad. My first kiss was awful. I broke my arm when my mother pushed me down a grassy hill in a cardboard-box race and in a moment of loving motherly concern, grabbed my arm to pull me back from certain grass-stained death. I also stole my neighbour's kitten and hid it under my bed for three days. I've never been more ashamed. And that's just the formative years.

Then the past decade — university, changed careers, family, friends, travel, success, failure, credit card debt and broken hearts. It is these moments, all of them — be they forced, chosen or otherwise — that make us who we are.

I've had my heart truly broken twice. I'm either lucky, meeting hoards of hopeless men not worth my tears, or I'm as guarded as hell. Either way I am proud to say I've cried my guts out lying in the foetal position on the kitchen floor and lived to tell the tale. The scars, invisible to the world, are my war wounds and I wear them with pride.

So if you've risked, won, lost, cheated, stole, fucked, dared, subjugated, failed, and loved, and want it all again, I salute you.

I also think you should eat. Food is often the missing ingredient in most seemingly perfect unions. Well-cooked dishes can cater to your every emotional need and provide perfect harmony, perfect understanding and, well, a perfect moment, really.

Heartbreak

Heartbreak is one of the most agonisingly beautiful and painful things that can happen to a person. Amidst the tears you rediscover the love of your family and your besties — those people who gather round you like a protective shield in your hour(s) of need. But the most profound discovery is finding friends you didn't know you had. Heartbreak binds people. If you've suffered it, you feel a mortal obligation to help someone else. To pass on survival tips in the hope you can take away that awful feeling akin to being smashed in the solar plexus.

I know too well the difficulty in eating without thinking of his soulful eyes and perfect nose ... the effort of masticating solids is just too much for a tortured and broken heart. The key is consistent and slightly destructive drinking, puffy eyes, raging headaches and dehydrated skin. All heartbreak-associated meals must be made in a blender and come with ice and so the following menu of inebriation will help tend to those key, well-known heartbroken phases and send you on your way to recovery.

Phase 1 – Devastation
At this point you are painful to everyone around you. Needy, sniffy, desperate. And boring. Time to drink one too many alcopops, crash through glass objects and raise a few sheets to the wind. The sooner you realise the only thing you'll be getting for the next little while is some liquid relations, the better for all concerned.

Phase 2 – Anger
Singledom can be a hard melody to find your groove to. Anger, on the other hand, is heatbreak's Prozac. It's the most productive phase of the lovesick cycle, involving random outbreaks of violence and some spirited drinking, with only the jug and your glass complicit in the madness

Phase 3 – Introspection
Time to enjoy the fact that sperm can now be cloned from stem cells, providing the perfect opportunity to breed out all the 'killer' genes that ruin the world, and all the 'mindless shagging' genes that screw up relationships.

Phase 4 – Breaking even
As the horror and pain of the rupture recedes, and as other things, really lovely things slowly start to snowball, you realise that the situation is no longer bringing you to your knees. It dawns on you that you have not thought about him, or indeed 'it', for weeks. It is then that you acknowledge, with a thankful glance towards heaven, that you are cured. You're all paper umbrellas, swizzle sticks and sunshine.

Phase 5 – Recovery and rebound
After relationship drain, it's time for you. Selfish freedom. Dream of garden parties and stirring your Pimm's with a cucumber. Collect frippery. Start a lamington run just because, and know wounds heal, the pain fades and life really does return to a state of blissful equilibrium.

Menu

Rose vodka

Tequila red

Beer margaritas

Brandy sour

Rum honey Champagne

Limoncello vodka sunrise

Cranberrry cosmopolitan

Blue martini ice pops

Cinnamon caipirinha

Elderflower and
gin soda

ROSE VODKA
BLEEDING HEART

THIS PRETTY DRINK IS EASY ON THE EYE AND THE STOMACH. BETTER YET, IT'S COMFORTING, LIKE A BIG, WELCOMING HUG FROM A CHUBBY-ARMED ITALIAN MAMMA.

OH, AND EACH SWEET SIP IS AS GOOD AS KICKING HIM IN THE NUTS AND CALLING HIM A DOUCHEBAG.

INGREDIENTS
½ lime
45 ml (1½ fl oz) vodka
15 ml (½ fl oz) Aperol
15 ml (½ fl oz) rose syrup
ice cubes
soda water (club soda)
edible rose petals, to decorate

Rub the rim of your drinking glass with the lime. Combine the vodka, Aperol and rose syrup in a cocktail shaker with some ice. Shake and strain into glasses. Top with a dash of soda water and garnish with the rose petals.

Serves 1

TEQUILA RED
TEQUILA MOCKING BIRD

THIS IS TO HEARTBREAK WHAT ROAST CHICKEN IS TO FRENCH BISTROS. IT'S ALL ABOUT SOME QUALITY TIME WITH SHARP KNIVES AND A BOTTLE OF HARD LIQUOR, AND AN AFTER-BURN THAT FEELS AS IF SOME RECKLESS BOGAN HAS LEFT TYRE MARKS DOWN THE INSIDE OF YOUR THROAT.

INGREDIENTS
juice of ½ lime
1 tsp sugar
4 dashes of grenadine
60 ml (2 fl oz/¼ cup) tequila
soda water (club soda) (optional)

Pour the ingredients into a cocktail shaker, shake well and serve in a cocktail glass.

Serves 1

BEER MARGARITA
BITTER? MOI?

UNDERNEATH YOUR SEEMING INABILITY TO ENJOY ANYTHING AT YOUR TIME OF TRAGEDY LURKS THE OPPOSITE IMPULSE: TO FIND IN DAILY PLEASURES — PARTICULARLY A DRINK — SOMETHING THAT WILL KEEP YOU GOING. IT IS THE ONE THING THAT LINKS YOU TO THE REST OF HUMANITY AT A TIME WHEN THAT LINK SEEMS FAR TOO FRAGILE.

INGREDIENTS
1 lime, cut into 8 wedges
80 g (2¾ oz/¼ cup) coarse sea salt
2 x 355 ml (12 fl oz) bottles of beer (not dark, make sure it is a light-style lager), chilled
125 ml (½ cup) frozen limeade concentrate
125 ml (4 fl oz/½ cup) tequila
ice cubes

Rub the lime wedges around the rims of four margarita glasses. Dip the rims in the salt to coat lightly.

Combine the beer, limeade and tequila in a jug. Fill the prepared glasses with the ice, then with the margarita mixture. Garnish with the remaining lime wedges. Drink quickly or stick a straw straight into the jug and ditch the niceties of glass.

Serves 1

BRANDY SOUR
UP YOURS PAMELA PLOWDEN

TURNS OUT WINSTON CHURCHILL SUFFERED HEARTBREAK WHEN HIS HOPES OF MARRYING THE FIRST GREAT LOVE OF HIS LIFE WERE DASHED. CHURCHILL PROPOSED TO PAMELA PLOWDEN, A RENOWNED SOCIETY BEAUTY, WHEN HE WAS IN HIS EARLY TWENTIES. WRITING FROM CALCUTTA, NO DOUBT BY CANDLELIGHT WITH A QUILL, IN MARCH 1899, HE BEGAN:

MY DEAR MISS PAMELA, I HAVE LIVED ALL MY LIFE SEEING THE MOST BEAUTIFUL WOMEN LONDON PRODUCES ... NEVER HAVE I SEEN ONE FOR WHOM I WOULD FOREGO THE BUSINESS OF LIFE. THEN I MET YOU ... WERE I A DREAMER OF DREAMS, I WOULD SAY ... 'MARRY ME — AND I WILL CONQUER THE WORLD AND LAY IT AT YOUR FEET.'

SHE MARRIED SOME IMP CALLED VICTOR, EARL OF LYTTON, THE SON OF A VICEROY OF INDIA.

WTF PAMMY? I WOULD MARRY WRITING LIKE THAT. I WOULD WEAR LIPSTICK, COOK IT DINNER AND THEN FRAME IT FOR THE WORLD TO SEE.

INGREDIENTS
crushed ice
110 ml (3¾ fl oz) Pisco brandy
45 ml (1½ fl oz) lime juice
3 heaped tsp sugar
2 egg whites

Half-fill a cocktail shaker with the crushed iced and pour in the brandy, lime juice, sugar and egg whites. Shake well and strain into three cocktail glasses (or one glass x 3).

Serves 1

XXX

RUM HONEY CHAMPAGNE

WHERE DO WE GO NOW
BUT NOWHERE

THIS DRINK IS LIKE A SILVER-TONGUED DEVIL IN A WELL-TAILORED SUIT. COMPLETELY IRRESISTIBLE. AND THE HEALTHY DOSE OF RUM ADDS TO ALL THE INTERNALISED TORTURE OF THE MOMENT.

INGREDIENTS
60 ml (2 fl oz/¼ cup) white rum
40 ml (1¼ fl oz) lemon juice
Champagne

Honey syrup
100 g (3½ oz/⅔ cup) honey
100 ml (3½ fl oz) water

For honey syrup, combine honey and boiling water in a jug and stir until dissolved. Combine the rum, 2 tablespoons of the honey syrup and the lemon juice in a jug, cover and shake. Pour into a flute glass and top up with the Champagne. Garnish with whatever takes your fancy.

Makes 2

LIMONCELLO
VODKA SUNRISE

THE ONLY WAY IS UP

SEE, YOU FEEL BETTER ALREADY.

INGREDIENTS
30 ml (1 fl oz) vodka
30 ml (1 fl oz) Campari
dash of limoncello
juice of 2 blood oranges
ice cubes
dash of soda water (club soda)

Combine the vodka, Campari, limoncello and orange juice in a cocktail shaker half-filled with ice and stir well. Pour into a tall glass, top with a dash of soda water and serve.

Makes 1

CRANBERRRY COSMOPOLITAN

DRUNK, PUNCH, LOVE

SWEET. YOU CAN FINALLY THINK ABOUT SOMETHING ELSE, DO OTHER THINGS AND LET OUT THE ODD AIR PUNCH FOR YOUR RECOVERING HEART AS YOU WALK DOWN THE STREET IN THE SUN.

INGREDIENTS
700 g (1 lb 6 oz/6 cups) frozen cranberries
440 g (15½ oz/2 cups) caster
  (superfine) sugar
1 tbsp finely chopped rosemary leaves
1.1 litres (39 fl oz/4½ cups) water
750 ml (26 fl oz/3 cups) vodka
crushed ice

Place the cranberries, sugar, rosemary and water in a large saucepan over medium heat and simmer, stirring occasionally, for 30 minutes until the cranberries start to burst and the liquid is slightly syrupy.

Pour the syrup through a sieve into a bowl, discarding the cranberries. Cover and chill the syrup in the fridge.

Combine the syrup and vodka in a bowl or jug. Serve over the crushed ice.

Serves 8–10 generously sized

BLUE MARTINI ICE POPS

ICE, ICE BABY

IF SOMEONE MENTIONS HIS NAME AGAIN, YOU'LL VOMIT. REST ASSURED NOTHING CAN KEEP A GOOD WOMAN DOWN, OR OFF THE MARKET.

INGREDIENTS
375 ml (13 fl oz/1½ cups) water
55 g (2 oz/¼ cup) caster (superfine) sugar
6 wide strips of lemon zest
60 ml (2 fl oz/¼ cup) gin
40 ml (1¼ fl oz) dry vermouth
20 ml (½ fl oz) blue Curaçao

Simmer the water, sugar and lemon zest in a small saucepan, stirring until the sugar has dissolved. Cool the syrup, then stir in the gin and vermouth. Mix in the Curaçao and discard the zest. Pour into freezer-proof moulds and freeze for 1 hour. Add paddle-pop sticks and freeze for at least another 24 hours.

Makes 4 using a small ice-block mould

CINNAMON CAIPIRINHA

EVENTS AND DIVERSIONS

THIS IS A DRINK ENGINEERED FOR A LIFE LIVED IN FULL — ACUTE INTELLIGENCE AND EXQUISITE GOOD TASTE.

INGREDIENTS
1 lime, cut into 8 wedges
40 ml (1¼ fl oz) cachaça (white rum)
crushed ice
1 cinnamon stick

Cinnamon sugar
3 tsp caster (superfine) sugar
1 tsp ground cinnamon

For the cinnamon sugar, combine the sugar and cinnamon in a small bowl and mix well.

Squeeze the lime wedges over the cinnamon sugar and muddle so the lime wedges are pressed and the juices released in the bottom of your glass. Add the cachaça and stir. Pour over the crushed ice into a double old-fashioned glass. Garnish with the cinnamon stick.

Makes 1

ELDERFLOWER AND GIN SODA

TOM, DICK AND HARRY

THIS IS THE KIND OF DRINK YOU COULD LOSE WHOLE WEEKENDS TO. YOU GO OUT ONE EVENING, CONSUME A FEW OF THESE PRETTY LITTLE GEMS, ONLY TO WAKE UP THREE DAYS LATER IN THAILAND WEARING SOMEONE ELSE'S UNDERWEAR WITH THE WORDS 'CALL ME, BRAD' WRITTEN IN LIPSTICK ON THE PILLOW.

RECOVERY IS IMMINENT.

INGREDIENTS
60 ml (2 fl oz/ ¼ cup) gin
35 ml (1 fl oz) lemon juice
50 ml (1¾ fl oz) elderflower cordial
crushed ice
soda water (club soda)
2 lemon slices

Combine the gin, lemon juice, and elderflower syrup in a cocktail shaker half-filled with crushed ice. Mix well, strain into a tall glass, top with the soda, garnish with the lemon slices and serve.

Makes 1

The make-up

I'd always considered the 'make-up' a slightly suspect, can't-move-on, bit of a dirty and desperate sex-with-your-ex sort of thing. As if a break-up the first time round wasn't traumatic enough then you decide to give all of it — the various incarnations of glorious lover to dirt-bag ex and back again — another go. It's madness.

Then I swallowed the bitter pill of my own making, and decided to give in to the need for an emotional money-shot at the end of a 'will they, won't they' story arc, and had a happy outcome. A blissful one. So I'd like this to be my printed retraction.

People who break up then make up tend to fall prey to what both first-hand experience and voyeuristic research indicate to be three typical scenarios, all of which sadly are clichés and more often than not result in tears ... and copious amounts of make-up sex.

It's not you, it's me. For whatever reason your yin ain't fittin' with their yang and, let's face it, you want the bed to yourself. You want to go to the gym at 8 a.m. on Saturday and spend as damn well long as you please on the phone, at the farmers' markets or shopping online; and enjoying their memory as one that is preferably far and distant. Then the bed feels too big, the gym still sucks, there is no one to help you carry your stuff at the markets, and shopping online has lost its appeal when you can't do a twirl in your new dress and say 'What, this old thing?'

The grass is always greener. Oops, actually it's not. It's brown. And dry. And not comfortable to sit with. Or on. (I mean that both metaphorically and physically.)

A visit to shady town. One of you had a moment. A moment of morphing into a commitment phobe; a selfish, loveless self-absorbed soul with roving eyes who lost their clothes at someone else's house and spent a considerable amount of time and emotional angst trying to get the hell out of Dodge. The challenge, then,

is not only getting over the act but living with the outcome, which is all tangled up in pre-feminist ideas about relationships and propriety. If the act is not the end (wow, hats off to your — or their — generous and forgiving heart), then the break-up is merely the necessary process of working through remorse, recrimination and then retribution before love can, again, blossom.

They say time heals all wounds, and I'm sure it does, but sometimes all you need is a bandage. One that comes in the form of the ex. Just be warned: your friends (and your mother) will hate the idea, advise you against it, then worry about it endlessly. But if you think you have a chance; if you want your BF to again be your BFF, or your GF to no longer be the GFC, then call your little shining glowstick of love and reunite.

Menu 1

Buffalo mozzarella and nectarine stack with Champagne dressing and jamón

–

Pork shoulder with apple, fennel and pomegranate salsa

–

Mixed berry and elderflower baked clafoutis

Menu 2

Drunken scallops with ponzu granita

–

Duck pie with spiced figs

–

Vanilla, raspberry and Frangelico chocolate ice cream sandwiches

XXX

MIXED BERRY
AND ELDERFLOWER
BAKED CLAFOUTIS

XXXXXXXXXXXXXXXXXXXXXXXX STRAWBERRY FIELDS XXXXXXXXXXXXXXXXXXX
ARE FOREVER

A PERFECT DESSERT IS A FLEETING THING. SOMETHING TO BE CAPTURED, HELD LOVINGLY, AND MOMENTARILY ADMIRED BEFORE IT IS GONE FOREVER. THIS LITTLE PUD IS LIKE THE MAKE-UP — A COMBINATION OF OLD FRIENDS WITH NEW BEGINNINGS. THE FAMILIARITY OF CINNAMON AND VANILLA IS CUT THROUGH BY THE SLIGHT BITTERNESS OF THE FRUIT, WHILE THE TANTALISING POTENCY OF ELDERFLOWER ECHOES THE SENSUAL THRILLS OF DELAYED GRATIFICATION.

ALL IN ALL, A PERFECT UNION.

INGREDIENTS
melted butter, for greasing
6 egg yolks
150 ml (5 fl oz) cream
1¹/₂ tbsp icing (confectioners') sugar
1 vanilla bean, split lengthways and
    seeds scraped
50 g (1³/₄ oz/¹/₃ cup) plain (all-purpose)
    flour, sifted
100 g (3¹/₂ oz) strawberries, hulled and sliced
100 g (3¹/₂ oz) blueberries
100 g (3¹/₂ oz) raspberries
2 tbsp elderflower cordial

To serve
vanilla bean or panna cotta ice cream

Preheat the oven to 180°C (350°F/Gas 4). Brush two 250 ml (9 fl oz/1 cup) ramekins with melted butter.

Whisk the egg yolks, cream and sugar in a bowl until slightly frothy. Add the vanilla seeds and flour and whisk well.

Line the base of the prepared ramekins with the berries and pour on the elderflower cordial. Spoon the clafouti batter over the berries, filling the ramekins almost to the top. Bake for 20–25 minutes, or until puffed and golden.

Serve with vanilla or panna cotta ice cream.

Serves 2

DRUNKEN SCALLOPS WITH PONZU GRANITA
LOOKING FORWARD, FALLING BACKWARDS

THIS DISH IS THE FOOD EQUIVALENT OF THE JAPANESE AESTHETIC PRINCIPLE KNOWN AS 'WABI-SABI'. AN OFFSHOOT OF ZEN BUDDHISM, WABI-SABI REFERS TO A PROFOUND APPRECIATION OF THE TRANSIENT, FLEETING BEAUTY THAT PERVADES THE NATURAL WORLD — OR IN THIS CASE, YOUR KITCHEN.

INGREDIENTS

Ponzu granita

60 ml (2 fl oz/¼ cup) mirin

60 ml (2 fl oz/¼ cup) soy sauce

60 ml (2 fl oz/¼ cup) sake

2 tbsp fresh or bottled yuzu juice (substitute with lemon juice at a pinch)

1 tsp sugar

60 ml (2 fl oz/¼ cup) water

Filling

8–10 scallops, in the shell

2 chorizo sausages, finely chopped

sea salt and freshly ground black pepper

a small handful of coriander (cilantro), finely chopped

Butter sauce

50 g (1¾ oz) butter, roughly chopped

60 ml (2 fl oz/¼ cup) sake

1 small garlic clove, very finely chopped

01

For the granita, combine the ingredients in a freezer-proof container and stir until the sugar dissolves. Cover and transfer to the freezer for an hour, or until frozen.

02

For the butter sauce, melt the butter in a small saucepan over medium heat. Add the sake and garlic and sauté for 5 minutes until fragrant.

03

Pour half the butter into a frying pan and place over medium heat. Add the finely chopped chorizo sausage and cook until brown. Add the coriander, toss to combine, then remove from the pan and keep warm.

04

Remove the ponzu granita from the freezer, scrape with a fork to lighten the texture. Return to the freezer until ready to serve. Gently remove the scallops from the shell. Pour the remaining butter into the pan and fry the scallops for 1 minute per side or cooked to your liking.

05

Place a teaspoon of chopped chorizo meat on the scallop shell. Top with the cooked scallop. Repeat with remaining chorizo and scallops. Serve the scallops hot with the granita on the side.

Serves 2

Any left-over duck is
fantastic tossed through pasta

DUCK PIE
WITH SPICED FIGS
MISCHIEF AND MAYHEM

DINNER AND SEX. A PRETTY SIMPLE PATH TO HAPPINESS. AND IF THE WAY TO THE HEART IS THROUGH THE STOMACH, THEN THIS PIE IS THE FRIEND WITH BENEFITS. THE DUCK AND FIG COMBO HAS THE POWER TO PLAY HUMPTY DUMPTY AND HELP PUT IT ALL TOGETHER AGAIN … ALTHOUGH IT MAY MAKE THINGS GO BUMP IN THE NIGHT.

YOU CAN MAKE THE CHUTNEY SAUCE FOR THE DUCK WELL AHEAD OF TIME, AND USE A BARBECUED DUCK IF YOU'D RATHER DWELL ON YOUR REUNION THAN YOUR ROASTING.

INGREDIENTS
Pie
1 x 1 kg (2 lb 4 oz) duck (or barbecued duck, meat picked, bones discarded)
sea salt and freshly ground black pepper
1 tsp ground cinnamon
1 garlic clove, finely chopped
1 small onion, finely chopped
1 sheet of ready-made shortcrust (pie) pastry
1 large starchy potato (such as sebago), thinly sliced

Fig chutney
50 g (1¾ oz) caster (superfine) sugar
½ cinnamon stick
1 star anise
5 large figs, quartered
1 large strip of orange zest
a pinch of ground cumin
125 ml (4 fl oz/½ cup) red wine
1½ tbsp port

To serve
green salad or green bean salad

Preheat the oven to 180°C (350°F/Gas 4).

Season the duck with salt, pepper and cinnamon, place snugly in a roasting tin, breast side down, and add the garlic and onion. Roast for 1 hour, turning the duck a few times during cooking. About halfway through, scoop out some of the fat from the base of the tin, place in a large bowl, add your sliced potatoes and toss to coat.

While the duck is roasting, make your fig chutney. Place the sugar in a saucepan over medium-high heat, and pour in just enough water to dissolve the sugar. Add the cinnamon and star anise and bring to the boil. Simmer for 5 minutes or until the syrup is reduced and golden. Add the figs, orange zest, ground cumin, wine and port. Turn the heat to low. Keeping an eye on the sauce, maintain the heat until the sauce is a thicker consistency, about 25 minutes. Take the pan off the heat, season and allow to cool.

Pull the duck from the oven and transfer to a clean surface, keeping the oven on. Once slightly cooled, pull the meat from the bones and add to the fig chutney. Stir to combine.

Line two 250 ml (9 fl oz/1 cup) ramekins or 8 cm (3 inch) diameter pie tins with the pastry and blind bake, using pastry weights or uncooked rice grains for 10 minutes. Remove from the oven and spoon in the duck mixture. Layer the duck-fat-coated potato slices over the top of the duck mixture, overlapping each slice. Place the pies in the oven and cook for 25 minutes until the potato is golden and crisp, and the duck mixture is warmed through.

Serve with a simple green salad.

Serves 2

VANILLA, RASPBERRY AND FRANGELICO CHOCOLATE ICE CREAM SANDWICHES

L'AMOUR

THESE ICE CREAM SANDWICHES ARE BENEFIT RIDDLED, BRINGING WITH THEM THE SORT OF INVESTMENT THAT NEVER NEED BE DECLARED TO THE TAX OFFICE.

INGREDIENTS

500 g (1 lb 2 oz) vanilla bean ice cream
500 g (1 lb 2 oz) chocolate ice cream
90 ml (3 fl oz) Frangelico

Raspberry compote

235 g (9 oz/2 cups) frozen raspberries
55 g (2 oz/¼ cup) sugar
zest of ½ lemon, removed in a wide strip
   (keep this as a large piece as it will
   be discarded)
2 tsp cornflour (cornstarch)
1 tbsp lemon juice

Sandwich

6 large egg whites, at room temperature
¼ tsp cream of tartare
110 g (3¾ oz/½ cup) caster
   (superfine) sugar
75 g (2¾ oz/½ cup) plain (all-purpose)
   flour, sifted
a tiny pinch of salt, sifted

Preheat the oven to 170°C (325°F/Gas 3). Grease a baking tray and line with baking paper, leaving an overhang on each side. Grease the baking paper.

For the raspberry compote, place the raspberries, sugar and lemon zest in a saucepan and cook over medium–high heat for 2–3 minutes, until the sugar has dissolved.

Combine the cornflour and lemon juice in a small bowl and mix into the raspberry mixture. Bring to the boil and simmer until thickened. Transfer the compote to a bowl, discard the lemon zest and chill in the fridge.

While the compote is chilling, prepare the sandwich. Whisk the egg whites and cream of tartar in a large bowl with electric beaters until soft peaks form. Slowly add the sugar and whisk until thick and glossy. Fold in the flour and salt. Stir carefully: you don't want to deflate the whites, or your enthusiasm.

Spread the batter evenly over the prepared tray. Bake for 20 minutes until golden. Let cool completely, then cut into two even halves.

Remove the ice creams from the freezer to soften slightly.

To make the Frangelico chocolate ice cream, stir the Frangelico into the chocolate ice cream.

Spoon the vanilla ice cream over one sandwich layer, spreading as evenly as possible. Return to the freezer to harden slightly, about 10 minutes. Remove the sandwich from the freezer and spread over compote and return to the freezer. Spoon the Frangelico chocolate ice cream as evenly as possible over the compote and top with the remaining sandwich, pressing down gently. Wrap in plastic wrap and pop back onto the tray and return to the freezer until firm, at least 2 hours.

Transfer the sandwich to a chopping board. Trim the edges, if desired, and cut into eight pieces.

Serves 2 with some very necessary leftovers

There is SOMETHING PRIMITIVE ABOUT EATING AMIDST THE ELEMENTS, *and the impromptu aspect of* EATING WHENEVER **& WHEREVER** YOU ARE IS SOMEWHAT ECCENTRIC **AND** *appealing.*

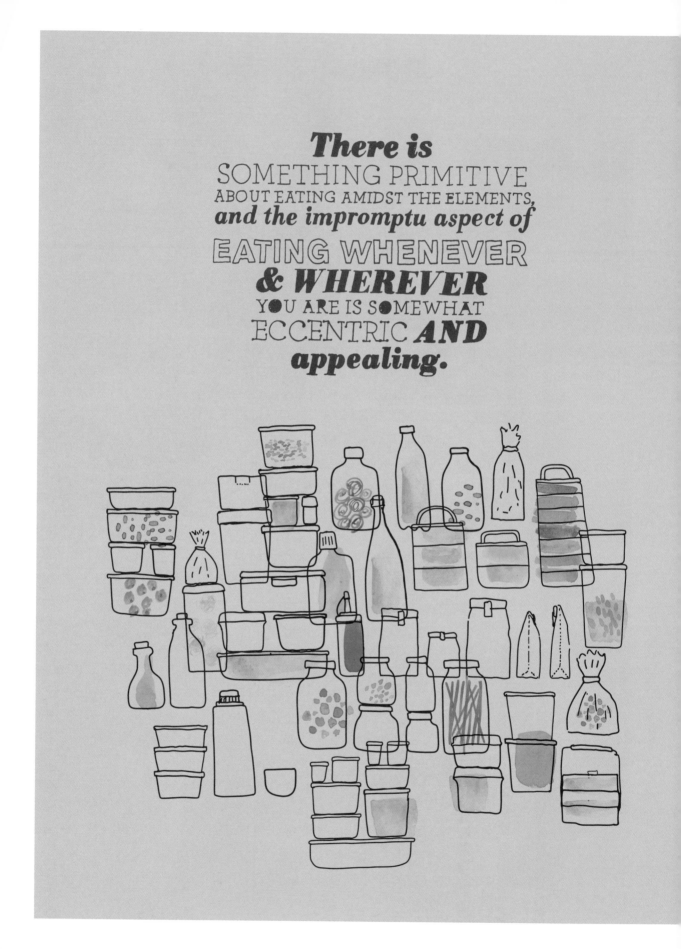

CHAPTER FIVE

MOVEABLE FEASTS

Creating food to move with makes me nervous. I want ready access to condiments and a flushing toilet, and if I have some last-minute epiphany that inspires me to add something to a dish, I want it at my fingertips or, at worst, in the shop down the road.

Add to that the idea of owning a Thermos and planning meals in the minutiae and I feel old. I'm truly scared I'll have some kind of brain fart and wake up in those strange waxy-looking overalls, fly-fishing in Canada — or worse, in some sort of strange ode to MacGyver where I am relying on my hunting skills for survival and find myself trying to run the car on cooking oil.

Even when you put some planning and thought into it — checking the food magazines, tapping friends for recommendations, even reading the world's greatest outdoor foodie cookbooks — it can still all easily go arse-about.

But when there is no (or little) opportunity for planning, when the meal is taken outside the home by either choice or necessity, cooking for movement is also courageous. There is something primitive about eating amidst the elements, and the impromptu aspect of eating whenever and wherever you are is somewhat eccentric and appealing. I've discovered that in these situations it is more about 'how to take' than 'what to take', and more surprisingly, that this can be very tasty.

The food needs to be simple and transportable — something that can be eaten on your lap or on the ground. And the sooner you accept squashed sandwiches, warm fizz and ants in everything, the better for all concerned.

Outdoor cinema

When the outdoor cinema season starts, it means summer has truly arrived: long balmy days, gin on the balcony and Frisbee and cinema in the park. It's all about blankets that stick to the back of your legs in the heat, possums scampering to pick up the scraps, the hum of conversations that only add to the film rather than distract you from it, and food, glorious food.

Little bits and bobs packed in plastic tubs to see you and your friends through the night. I remember *Breakfast at Tiffany's* with Asti spumante and cheese kabanas with pickled onion on toothpicks. And *2001: A Space Odyssey* was accompanied by oversized bowls of Maltesers, warm Guinness and ham off the bone.

Outdoor cinema is different. Better somehow, despite the lack of surround sound and comfy seats. There is no chance to be fiddled with in the back row, and there are no bullies to beat you up outside in the foyer while waiting to see *The Goonies*. It makes the filmgoer as much a part of the experience as the film itself, and the opportunity to match food with your viewing pleasure is simply spectacular.

Menu

Bagels with pork belly, onion
jam and apple cider mustard

–

Corn of the popping kind

–

Homemade Malteser slab

–

Yuzu vanilla cakes with
lime curd

BAGELS WITH PORK BELLY, ONION JAM AND APPLE CIDER MUSTARD

UNDER THE OPEN SKIES

THE BEST THING ABOUT GOING TO SEE A FILM IS THE SUSPENSION OF ANY KIND OF HEALTHY EATING REGIME. IT'S ALL ABOUT CHOC-TOPS, FROZEN COKE AND PICK 'N' MIX, WITH THE MOST DEGENERATE DARING A SNEAKY CHEESIE FROM MACCY D'S OR THIS EPIC BAGEL — THE TASTE AND WEIGHT IN YOUR HANDS IS EQUALLY SATISFYING.

INGREDIENTS

250 g (9 oz/1 cup) dijon mustard
2 garlic cloves, finely chopped
250 ml (9 fl oz/1 cup) apple cider
1 x 800 g (1 lb 12 oz) pork belly
3 tsp grated horseradish (or the bottled at a pinch)
1 tbsp hot English mustard
2 tsp dijon mustard
2 tbsp apple cider
sea salt and freshly ground black pepper
8 plain bagels, halved and lightly toasted
60 g (2¼ oz/2 cups) watercress

Onion jam

2 tbsp olive oil
2 large brown onions, thinly sliced
1 tbsp caster (superfine) sugar
2 apples, peeled, cored and sliced
1 tbsp dijon mustard
2 tbsp apple cider

Preheat the oven to 200°C (400°F/Gas 6). Line a baking tray with baking paper and set aside.

Combine the horseradish, mustards, garlic and apple cider in a bowl. Add the pork belly, meat side down, cover and marinate in the fridge for at least half an hour.

Remove the pork from the marinade and place, skin side up, on the prepared tray. Roast for 1 hour, or until the skin is nice and crisp. Set aside until cool enough to handle. Shred the cooled pork, discarding the skin (except for those who love crackling) and place in a bowl. Cover and set aside.

For the onion jam, heat the oil in a large non-stick frying pan over high heat. Add the onion and sugar and cook, stirring, for 3 minutes, or until soft. Reduce the heat to medium-high, add the apple, dijon mustard, apple cider and cook, stirring, for 3–4 minutes, or until caramelised. Set aside.

Divide the pork between half the bagel halves, spoon on the onion jam, scatter with the watercress and sandwich together with the remaining bagel halves.

Serves 8–10

CORN OF THE POPPING KIND

QUENTIN TARANTINO

AAAHH, A CLASSIC UNDER THE STARS.

INGREDIENTS
4 tbsp vegetable oil
230 g (8 oz/1 cup) popping corn

Spiced goodness
1 tbsp coriander seeds, toasted
2 tsp cumin seeds, toasted
½ tsp fennel seeds, toasted
1 tbsp paprika
a handful of flat-leaf parsley,
   roughly chopped

Burnt butter and sage
200 g (7 oz) butter
a small handful of sage leaves, chopped
sea salt and freshly ground black pepper

Heat the oil in a large heavy-based saucepan over medium–high heat. Add the popping corn, cover and cook, shaking the pan occasionally, for 5 minutes, or until all the corn has popped. Divide the popcorn between two bowls. Add a flavour combination to each bowl and mix thoroughly to evenly coat the popcorn.

Spiced goodness
Combine the spice seeds in a mortar and, using a pestle, grind to a fine powder. Add the paprika and mix well. Evenly coat the popcorn in the spice mixture and stir in the parsley.

Burnt butter and sage
Melt the butter in a saucepan over medium heat and cook until the butter is slightly brown and bubbly. Remove from the heat and add the sage leaves. Pour the butter and sage mixture over the popcorn and stir to combine. Season with the salt and pepper.

Makes approximately 10 cups

HOMEMADE MALTESER SLAB

THE MALTESE FALCON

THIS SLICE IS THE CRYSTAL METH OF THE CINEMA SNACK WORLD — THE KIND OF THING YOUR GRANNY WOULD DO FOR YOU WHEN YOUR PARENTS WERE AWAY AND SHE WAS RULING THE ROOST WITHOUT THE POLICE OF THEIR WATCHFUL EYES.

INGREDIENTS
120 g (1½ oz/1 cup) malted milk powder
120 g (1½ oz/1 cup) instant full cream
   milk powder
250 g (8¾ oz) white chocolate
150 g (5½ oz) milk chocolate

Line a 23 x 33 cm (9 x 13 inch) baking tin with baking paper.

Melt the white chocolate in a heatproof bowl over a saucepan of gently simmering water.

While the chocolate is melting combine the milk powder and malted milk powder in a bowl.

Pour in the melted chocolate and combine until a soft dough forms. This varies given the humidity and heat of the day you make it so if the dough seems a little wet and runny, have some extra malted milk powder on hand to incorporate into the mix.

Press the dough into the base of the pan and place in the fridge for 5 minutes to set.

Melt half the milk chocolate in a heatproof bowl over a saucepan of gently simmering water and stir until smooth.

Pour onto the set Malteser mix and paint over using a pastry brush or flat knife.

Return to the fridge for five minutes to set.

Repeat the process with the other side of the Malteser slab and the remaining milk chocolate.

Makes 10–12 portions

YUZU VANILLA CAKES WITH LIME CURD

THE SEVEN SAMURAI

FRIENDS GATHER IN. THESE ARE A TASTE SENSATION. YOU'LL NEED OUTDOOR SURROUNDS TO MUFFLE THE NOISE OF YOUR FELLOW CINEMA-GOERS' APPRECIATION.

CLAP CLAP CLAP.

SUCH A NOISY BUNCH.

INGREDIENTS
Lime curd
60 g (2¼ oz) butter, softened
40 g (1½ oz) caster (superfine) sugar
2 tbsp lime juice (about 2 limes)
3 egg yolks
zest of 1 lime
½ titanium-strength gelatine leaf, softened in cold water for 5 minutes

Cakes
155 g (5½ oz/1¼ cups) icing (confectioners') sugar
225 g (8 oz/1½ cups) plain (all-purpose) flour
1 tsp baking powder
140 g (5 oz) white chocolate, chopped
125 g (4½ oz) unsalted butter, chopped
60 ml (2 fl oz/¼ cup) soy milk
4 large eggs
1 tbsp vanilla bean paste
60 ml (2 fl oz/¼ cup) yuzu juice
3 tbsp yuzu zest (substitute with lemon zest if unavailable)

To serve
icing (confectioners') sugar, sifted

Preheat the oven to 180°C (350°F/Gas 4). Grease a twelve-hole standard muffin tin and set aside.

For the lime curd, whisk the butter, sugar, lime juice and egg yolks in a heatproof bowl over a saucepan of gently simmering water for 5 minutes or until thick. Stir in the lime zest and remove from the heat. Squeeze the excess water from the gelatine. Add the gelatine to the curd and stir until dissolved. Cover and refrigerate while you make the cakes.

For the cakes, sift the dry ingredients into a bowl. Combine the chocolate, butter and soy milk in a heatproof bowl over a saucepan of simmering water and stir until the chocolate and butter have just melted. Allow to cool. Beat the eggs in a separate bowl until thick and foamy. Gently fold in the chocolate mixture, then fold in the dry ingredients, vanilla, yuzu juice and zest. Pour into the prepared tin and bake for 15–18 minutes until slightly browned on top and a skewer inserted into a cake comes out clean. Allow to cool in the tin then turn out.

Slice the top off each cake and spoon on a dollop of lime curd. Gently place the top back on. Alternatively, you can split the cakes in half, smear the curd over one half and sandwich together. Dust with icing sugar and serve.

Serves 12

Picnics

Picnics are conflicting. Advice differs wildly. Listening to Ratty describing the perfect picnic to an overawed Mole in *The Wind in the Willows*, it seems very innocent and exciting, like a joyous feeding frenzy:

> There's cold chicken inside it ... coldtongue-coldhamcoldbeefpickledgherkinssalad-frenchrollscresssandwichespottedmeatgin-gerbeerlemonadesodawater ...

Then there is the whole *Picnic at Hanging Rock* scenario. Rather sinister, given not one of the white-clad girls with whispering voices is alive to tell the tale. If you follow this tangent, picnics are all Miss McCraw, bloodhounds and rock faces that turn into vortexes, and to that end, not in the least bit appealing.

Maybe it's best to follow the tips on practising safe picnicking from the experts — The Picnic Club of New York:

1. Delay activity until you and your lunch partners are physically and emotionally prepared to swap side dishes.

2. Find a nice grassy spot in the shade. Watch where you sit.

3. Always use a blanket.

4. Regarding relishes, chutneys and dressings: avoid double-dipping unless agreed upon by all.

Menu

Spiced vanilla rice pudding pots with Turkish apricots

–

Smoked salmon and feta salad with mixed greens

–

Quinoa curry salad

–

Gingerbread and violet cream sandwiches

SPICED VANILLA
RICE PUDDING POTS
WITH TURKISH APRICOTS

THE PLEASURE
EXCURSION

A GOOD PICNIC SHOULD BE A TABLEAU OF SORTS, AN ABUNDANCE OF FOODS
LAID OUT FOR VISUAL AND EATING PLEASURE. THIS SLIGHTLY FANCY RICE PUDDING
PROVIDES THE REQUISITE VISUAL SPECTACLE, AND ITS LAYERED CONSTRUCTION IS
MUCH LIKE THE PICNIC ITSELF — WRAPPING UP EVERYTHING, PACKING THE FOOD, AND
THEN UNPACKING AND UNWRAPPING AND PASSING IT
ROUND LIKE GIFTS AT CHRISTMAS.

INGREDIENTS
Rice pudding
750 ml (26 fl oz/3 cups) milk
150 g (5^1/$_2$ oz/^{3}/$_4$ cup) short grain rice
^{1}/$_2$ vanilla bean, seeds scraped
3 egg yolks
75 g (2^3/$_4$ oz/^{1}/$_3$ cup) caster (superfine) sugar
30 g (1 oz) butter, softened

Apricots
350 ml (12 fl oz/1^1/$_2$ cups) water
2 tbsp caster sugar
2 tsp cinnamon
6 cardamom pods, lightly crushed
2 tsp nutmeg
250 g (1^1/$_4$ cups) dried apricots

To serve
Persian fairy floss — vanilla or pistachio

Preheat oven to 180°C (350°F/Gas 4).

For the rice pudding, place the milk and vanilla bean seeds and pod in a saucepan and bring to the boil over medium–high heat. Add the washed rice, stir until it reboils, cover with the saucepan lid and place in the oven for 40 minutes or until tender, stirring occasionally until the milk has been absorbed.

Cream the butter, sugar and egg yolk and mix until smooth. Fold into the rice while still warm and refrigerate until serving.

To make the apricots, combine the water and sugar in a saucepan and heat gently, stirring until sugar has dissolved. Add the cinnamon, cardamom, nutmeg and apricots and increase the heat a touch and let simmer for 15 minutes or until a syrup consistency is achieved. Remove from heat and let the apricots cool in the syrup.

To serve, place rice in portable jars and top with the apricots and syrup. Just before eating, top with fairy floss.

Serves 6–8, depending on the size of your pots

SMOKED SALMON AND FETA SALAD WITH MIXED GREENS

BASKET CASE

IT'S A WEIRD FACT THAT ANYTHING TAKEN ON A PICNIC, NO MATTER HOW YOU PACK IT, EMERGES DISTORTED AND COMPRESSED. I THINK THIS IS NATURE'S VERSION OF SOME ARCANE COOKING ALCHEMY TO LET YOU KNOW YOU'RE IN THE GREAT OUTDOORS. MAYBE IT'S THE STRANGE CHEMICALS EMITTED FROM THE PLASTIC WRAP WHICH, JUST LIKE MSG, MAKES THINGS TASTE BETTER.

INGREDIENTS

155 g (5^1/$_2$ oz/1 cup) freshly shelled peas
185 g (6^1/$_2$ oz/1 cup) podded broad beans
500 g (1 lb 2 oz) baby asparagus spears
110 g (3^3/$_4$ oz/^{3}/$_4$ cup) crumbled
    Persian feta cheese
60 g (2^1/$_4$ oz/2 cups) watercress
500 g (1 lb 2 oz) sliced smoked salmon,
    coarsely torn

Vinaigrette

60 ml (2 fl oz/^{1}/$_4$ cup) white wine
80 ml (2^1/$_2$ fl oz/^{1}/$_3$ cup) olive oil
juice of 1 lemon
sea salt and freshly ground black pepper

Bring a saucepan of water to the boil. Add the peas and broad beans and cook for 2 minutes. Drain and refresh under cold water.

Thinly cut the asparagus at an angle up to the tip, blanch and refresh, then mix with the feta, peas, broad beans and watercress. Add the salmon and toss to combine.

To make the vinaigrette, combine the white wine, olive oil and lemon juice in a bowl and whisk to combine. Season with salt and pepper.

Just before serving drizzle the vinaigrette on the salad. Season to taste.

Serves 6

QUINOA CURRY SALAD
MEAL TICKET

FLY LIKE A BUTTERFLY. STING LIKE A BEE.

INGREDIENTS

----

40 g (1½ oz/¼ cup) whole
    almonds

200 g (7 oz/1 cup) white quinoa

2 cups water

1 tsp honey

1 spring onion (scallion),
    finely chopped

2 tsp curry powder

2 tbsp lemon juice

sea salt and freshly ground
    black pepper

2 tbsp extra virgin olive oil

2 tbsp currants

2 tbsp sultanas (golden raisins)

1 small red apple, cut into
    matchsticks

a small handful of mint leaves,
    roughly chopped, plus extra
    to garnish

01

Preheat the oven to 190°C (375°F/Gas 5).
Line a baking tray with baking paper
and set aside.

02

Spread the almonds on the prepared tray
and toast in the oven for 7 minutes until
fragrant. Let cool, then coarsely chop.

03

Rinse the quinoa thoroughly. Bring a
saucepan of water to the boil, add the
quinoa and reduce heat to low. Simmer
for 15 minutes until the quinoa is tender
but still chewy. Strain, add to a bowl,
then fluff up the quinoa with a fork.
Add the currants, sultanas, apple, mint
and almonds.

04

Whisk together the honey, spring onion,
curry powder and lemon juice in a large
bowl. Season with the salt and pepper.
Add the oil in a slow, steady stream and
continue whisking until the dressing is
combined. Drizzle over the quinoa salad.

05

Toss well and garnish with the
extra mint.

Serves 4

GINGERBREAD AND VIOLET CREAM SANDWICHES
GET IN MY BELLY

THE SUCCESS OF THIS VIOLET AND GINGERBREAD PAIRING IS THE FOOD EQUIVALENT OF THE PERFECT PICNIC SPOT. THE MOUTH ZING OF GINGER AND THE PRETTINESS OF VIOLET CREAM IS THE SENSORY EQUIVALENT OF SHADE AND THE COMFORT OF GRASS.

INGREDIENTS

----

125 g (4½ oz) butter

115 g (4 oz/½ cup) sugar

90 g (3¼ oz/¼ cup) molasses

1 egg

2 tbsp sour cream

175 g (6 oz/1¼ cups) plain (all-purpose) flour

1 tsp baking powder

2 tsp ground ginger

1 tsp freshly grated ginger

½ tsp ground cinnamon

Violet cream

100 ml (3½ fl oz) cream, whipped

20 g (¾ oz) icing (confectioners') sugar

½ vanilla bean, seeds scraped

50 g (1¾ oz) crystallised violets

2 tsp violet liqueur

01

Preheat the oven to 170°C (325°F/Gas 3). Line a 23 x 13 cm (9 x 5 inch) loaf tin with baking paper.

02

Cream the butter and sugar in a large bowl until pale and fluffy. Beat in the molasses, the egg and the sour cream.

In a separate bowl, combine the dry ingredients and freshly grated ginger.

03

Sift the dry ingredients into the creamed mixture and pour into the prepared tin. Bake for 1 hour and 45 minutes, or until a skewer inserted in the centre of the gingerbread comes out clean. Turn out onto a wire rack to cool.

04

Combine the cream, icing sugar, vanilla and violet liqueur in a bowl and whisk until combined and thickened. Gently stir through the crystallised violets.

05

Smear a thick dollop of cream over a piece of gingerbread. Gently top with another piece of gingerbread. Repeat with the remaining gingerbread and violet cream.

Serves 6 (makes 1 large loaf)

Road trip

Road trips were ruined by *Thelma & Louise*: the unfavourable ratio of Brad Pitt to serial killer is a roadside motel discovery most would prefer not to make. Add overzealous parents who planned family trips in wood-panelled wagons and played I Spy With My Little Eye to avert backseat sibling mutiny ... well you can hear the collective sigh of understanding.

But I'd like to advise an amendment.

I met a couple who used to shut their eyes, point to somewhere on a map and just drive there. Never mind that you could reach anywhere in the country within five hours; that was beside the point. It was the unknown adventure that appealed: the throw-reason-and-cost-of-petrol-to-the-wind-and-see-what-happens mentality that reignited a road trip curiosity.

It's a pity I can't read maps. And that I don't own a car. But as a seasoned backseat driver and battler of all things car-sick related I can offer two steadfast rules.

One: avoid where possible a road trip that involves public transport.

Two: when it comes to food, one hand on the wheel, one hand on your meal. (Interpret as you will.)

Menu

Pumpkin and haloumi
risotto cakes

–

Mixed leftovers biscuits

–

Cheesy cornflake bars

PUMPKIN AND HALOUMI RISOTTO CAKES

ARE WE THERE YET?

A ROAD TRIP HELPS OVERCOME ANY NATURE-DEFICIT DISORDER, WITH THE BENEFIT OF CUSHIONED SEATING AND AIR-CONDITIONED COMFORT.

INGREDIENTS

155 g (5½ oz/1 cup) butternut pumpkin (squash), peeled and diced
60 ml (2 fl oz/¼ cup) sweet chilli sauce
80 ml (2½ fl oz/⅓ cup) olive oil
1 red onion, finely chopped
2 garlic cloves, finely chopped
110 g (3¾ oz/½ cup) arborio rice
125 ml (4 fl oz/½ cup) white wine
500 ml (17 fl oz/2 cups) chicken stock
60 g (2¼ oz/½ cup) grated parmesan
100 g (3½ oz) haloumi cheese, finely diced
a small handful of coriander (cilantro), finely chopped
sea salt and freshly ground black pepper
60 g (2¼ oz/1 cup) fresh breadcrumbs
2 eggs

Preheat the oven to 180°C (350°F/Gas 4). Line a baking tray with baking paper and set aside.

Combine the pumpkin, sweet chilli sauce and half the oil in a roasting tin and toss to coat well. Roast in the oven for 40 minutes, or until cooked to your liking.

Heat the remaining oil in a saucepan over medium heat, add the onion and garlic and sauté until the onion is soft. Stir in the rice to coat. Increase the heat slightly, pour in the wine and stir until all the liquid is absorbed. Slowly add the stock, a ladleful at a time, stirring well after each addition; make sure it is absorbed before you pour in the next ladleful. When the rice is tender (between 15-20 minutes, depending on the quality of the grain) and the stock has been fully absorbed, remove the pan from the heat and stir in the parmesan.

Transfer the risotto to a bowl and stir in the pumpkin, haloumi and coriander. Season with the salt and pepper. Roll tablespoons of the risotto mixture into walnut-sized balls. It often helps to lightly oil your hands so the rice doesn't stick.

Place the breadcrumbs in a shallow bowl and lightly beat the eggs in a separate shallow bowl. Roll the risotto balls in the egg and then in the crumbs. Place on the prepared tray and roast in the oven for 20 minutes until crisp on top and firm to touch.

Makes 10

MIXED LEFTOVERS BISCUITS
A ROAD LESS TRAVELLED

THE SAD LITTLE BAG OF SCROGGIN MIX WAS THE ONLY THING THAT GOT ME THROUGH GIRL GUIDES AND SCHOOL EXCURSION LONG-HAUL BUS TRIPS. I USED TO LOVE THE COMBINATION OF SEEDS, CHOCOLATE AND WHAT SEEMED LIKE ANYTHING ELSE THAT COULD BE SCRAPED OFF THE KITCHEN FLOOR INTO A SNAP-LOCK BAG. ITS CONTENTS WERE AS MUCH A TEST OF SURVIVAL AND WIT AS WERE YOUR CAMPING SKILLS. A REAL LIVE GAME OF SURVIVOR: YOUR SCROGGIN.

THIS RECIPE IS MY ADAPTATION OF THE MOMOFUKU MILK BAR COMPOST (AKA SCROGGIN) COOKIES. THE FACT THAT I AM EVEN TALKING ABOUT NEW YORK AND SCROGGIN IN A SINGLE SENTENCE REALLY DOES PROVE YOU NEVER KNOW WHERE LIFE IS GOING TO TAKE YOU.

INGREDIENTS

----

250 g (9 oz) butter, softened

220 g (7¾ oz/1 cup) caster (superfine) sugar

110 g (3¾ oz/½ cup) soft brown sugar, firmly packed

1 tbsp corn syrup

2 large eggs

1 tsp natural vanilla extract

260 g (9¼ oz/1¾ cups) plain (all-purpose) flour

2 tsp baking powder

1 tsp bicarbonate of soda

2 tsp sea salt

3 cups chocolate chips, marshmallows, rolled oats, cocoa pops, tiny teddies, pretzels, raisins, Tim Tams, potato chips (basically anything you like)

01

Cream the butter, sugars and corn syrup in a bowl until pale and fluffy. Add the eggs and vanilla and continue to beat until the mixture has doubled in volume. Add the flour, baking powder, bicarbonate of soda and salt and mix until just incorporated. Stir in the remaining ingredients, cover the bowl with plastic wrap and refrigerate for at least 1 hour. It is important not to bake from room temperature as the biscuits (cookies) don't hold their shape.

02

Preheat the oven to 200°C (400°F/Gas 6). Line a baking tray with baking paper.

03

Place dollops of mixture on the prepared tray — about a dessertspoon per biscuit. Bake for 10–12 minutes, or until just browned on the edges. Allow the biscuits to cool completely on the tray before transferring to a plate or airtight container.

The biscuits will keep, stored in an airtight container, for 5 days, and probably far less in the glovebox.

Serves 8–10

CHEESY CORNFLAKE BARS
TRUCK STOP

A PACKED WEEKENDER, YOUR FAVOURITE TUNES AND A TUB OF CHEESY CORNFLAKE BARS — THIS ROAD MAP IS FULL OF MORE GOOD NEWS.

TIME FOR THE OPEN ROAD.

INGREDIENTS

----

150 g (5½ oz/1½ cups) grated smoked cheddar

1 tbsp worcestershire sauce

170 g (6 oz/1 cup) raisins, chopped

105 g (3¾ oz/3½ cups) cornflakes

01

Melt the cheese in a non-stick saucepan over low heat.

02

Add the worcestershire sauce, raisins and cornflakes, stirring to coat.

03

Drop heaped tablespoons of the mixture into muffin paper cases.

04

Refrigerate for 15 minutes until set.

Makes 6

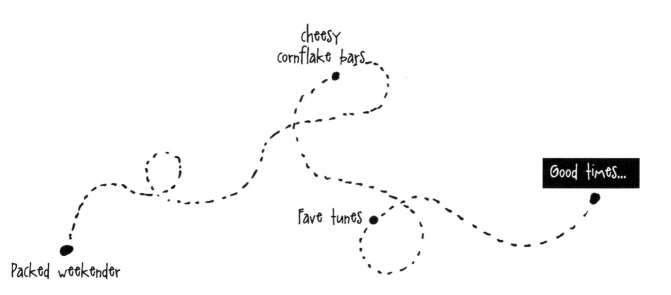

cheesy cornflake bars

Good times...

Fave tunes

Packed weekender

Stealth food

When I'm not allowed to eat I get very hungry.

Lecture theatres, libraries, art galleries, or five minutes into a long-haul flight. Work meetings are the worst. Someone utters the word 'agenda' and my stomach lets out a small grumble. By the time we're talking 'brainstorming' and 'strategy' my stomach is howling like a pack of lonely dogs in the pound.

It's important to plan ahead for these sorts of situations: situations requiring food that stays on your person and is small enough to avoid detection, while providing nourishment. The following bites are discreet, easy to access and above all, small and portable.

Menu 1 — Food for flight

Asian brittle
–
Hot 'n' spicy rocky road

Menu 2 — Gallery gazing

Salt and vinegar parmesan crisps
–
Chocolate Guinness cupcakes

Menu 3 — The work drawer

Chocolate-dipped almond dates
–
Butternut pumpkin, chilli and feta loaf

Menu 4 — Libraries

Black-bottomed coconut and cranberry bars
–
Peppermint crispies

ASIAN BRITTLE
THE EXIT ROW

Sweet, spicy and unexpected. This brittle is leg room and unexpected upgrades.

INGREDIENTS

240 g (8¾ oz/1½ cups) whole almonds
235 g (8½ oz/1½ cups) cashew nuts
55 g (2 oz/½ cup) wasabi peas
40 g (1½ oz/¼ cup) sesame seeds
1 tsp dried chilli flakes
1 tbsp furikake seasoning (optional)
1 tsp ground ginger
220 g (7¾ oz/1 cup) sugar
125 ml (4 fl oz/½ cup) water
60 ml (2 fl oz/¼ cup) soy sauce

Line a tray with baking paper and set aside.

Combine the almonds, cashews, wasabi peas, sesame seeds, chilli flakes, furikake and ground ginger in a bowl.

Place the sugar and water in a saucepan and bring to the boil over high heat, stirring until the sugar has dissolved. Cook, without stirring, for 10 minutes, or until the sugar is bubbling considerably and dark brown in colour. Remove from the heat and, working quickly, carefully add the soy sauce and nut mixture, stirring to coat. Pour onto the prepared tray, flatten the surface with the back of a spoon and allow to cool. Break into bite-sized pieces.

Makes 600 g (1 lb 5 oz)

HOT 'N' SPICY ROCKY ROAD
WILLY WONKA'S CHOCOLATE SMASH

One of those bizarre combinations that seems to work with the added portability to fit in your overnight bag on the plane.

INGREDIENTS

185 g (6½ oz/¾ cup) Starburst babies
50 g (1¾ oz/1 cup) Coco Pops (Cocoa Krispies)
100 g (3½ oz) red hot cinnamon liquorice
100 g (3½ oz/⅔ cup) sour cola sweets (candy)
250 g (9 oz) dark chocolate (70 per cent cocoa solids), roughly chopped

Line a 3 cm (1¼ inch) deep, 23 x 8 cm (9 x 3 inch) loaf tin with baking paper and set aside.

Chop the liquorice and sour cola sweets into chunks. Place the liquorice, Starburst babies and sour cola sweets in a bowl with the Coco Pops.

Melt the chocolate in a heatproof bowl over a saucepan of gently simmering water and stir until smooth.

Pour the chocolate over the sweets and stir gently to combine.

Pour the mixture into the prepared tin. Cover with plastic wrap and refrigerate for half an hour or until set.

Cut into thick slices or squares.

Makes 8–10

SALT AND VINEGAR PARMESAN CRISPS
ARTFUL EXECUTION

POPPING ONE OF THESE BAD BOYS WHILE STARING AT THE GREATS OF AMERICAN IMPRESSIONISM WILL CERTAINLY SORT THE WOMEN FROM THE GIRLS, AND THE WHEAT FROM THE CHAFF.

INGREDIENTS
100 g (3½ oz/1 cup) finely grated grana cheese
   or parmesan, or a mix of the two
salt and vinegar seasoning

Preheat oven to 180°C (350°F/Gas 4).

Use an egg ring (about 10 cm (4 inch) diameter) to make circles on a sheet of silicon paper (use silicon as it prevents the cheese from burning).

Finely grate the cheese and place dessert-spoonfuls onto the lined tray inside the marked circles. Gently sprinkle the salt and vinegar seasoning over the top of the cheese.

Bake in the oven until just golden (about 5 minutes) and transfer onto a cooling rack. Sprinkle over additional salt and vinegar seasoning and store in an airtight container.

Makes 10–12

CHOCOLATE GUINNESS CUPCAKES
PICTURE THIS

THESE LITTLE CUPCAKES HAVE JUST ENOUGH ALCOHOL TO NUMB THE MUTTER OF THOSE OUTSPOKEN ART TYPES AND THE TASTE IS PERFORMANCE ART IN FOOD FORM.

INGREDIENTS
125 ml (4 fl oz/½ cup) Guinness
125 g (4⅓ oz) unsalted butter
40 g (1½ oz/¼ cup) cocoa powder
200 g (7 oz/1⅓ cups) caster (superfine) sugar
1 egg
55 ml (1¾ fl oz) sour cream
55 ml (1¾ fl oz) buttermilk
140 g (5 oz) plain (all-purpose) flour
1 tsp bicarbonate soda
¼ tsp baking powder
100 g (3½ oz) dark chocolate (70 per cent
   cocoa solids), broken into chunks

Icing
50 g (1¾ oz) butter
2 tbsp Guinness
300 g (10½ oz/2 cups) icing sugar
dark chocolate shaved for dusting

Preheat oven to 170°C (325°F/Gas 3). Grease a six-jumbo or 12-small muffin pan.

Place the Guinness and butter in a saucepan and warm over low heat until the butter has melted. Add the sugar and cocoa powder, stir until combined and remove from the heat.

Combine the eggs, cream and buttermilk in a bowl then add to the Guinness mixture.

Add the flour, bicarbonate soda, baking powder and dark chocolate in a bowl. Add the Guinness mixture and whisk until all ingredients are incorporated.

Pour the batter into the muffin pan and bake for 25–30 minutes or until the cupcakes press back to the touch or a skewer inserted comes out clean. Allow to cool for five minutes in the tin before turning out onto a wire rack to cool.

For the icing, mix the butter and Guinness with the icing sugar until fully combined. Top the cupcakes generously with the frosting and grate over the chocolate shavings.

Makes 6 jumbo or 12 small cupcakes

CHOCOLATE-DIPPED ALMOND DATES

KPI FOR THE ROI, FYI

NOT REALLY WORTH A RECIPE GIVEN ITS SIMPLICITY BUT DEFINITELY WORTH THE TIME GIVEN ITS PORTABILITY AND TASTE REVELATION.

INGREDIENTS

10 fresh dates
10 whole almonds
75 g (5½ oz) dark chocolate (70 per cent cocoa solids), roughly chopped

Line a tray with baking paper.

Using a small sharp knife, cut an incision in one end of each date and slip in an almond.

Melt the chocolate in a heatproof bowl over a saucepan of gently simmering water.

Dip half each date into the melted chocolate. Place on the prepared tray and allow to set. Store in an airtight container until ready to eat.

Makes 10

BUTTERNUT PUMPKIN, CHILLI AND FETA LOAF

DESKTIME

LUNCH IN A LOAF. PERFECT

I DON'T ENCOURAGE THE WORKING THROUGH LUNCH THING — I THINK SANITY CALLS FOR A BIT OF TIME OUTSIDE, IT KEEPS THOSE 'I HAVE TO GET THE F*$K OUT' MOMENTS TO A MINIMUM AND GIVES SOME SPACE TO RECOLLECT YOUR THOUGHTS. BUT WHAT WOULD I KNOW? I WORK FROM HOME RIGHT NOW. IT'S 11.45 A.M. AND I'M STILL IN MY PYJAMAS. AFTER AN EXTREMELY LONG NIGHT WORKING IN FRONT OF THE TV, I JUST HAD A VERY IMPORTANT TELECONFERENCE WITH MOLLY.

MOLLY IS MY DOG.

INGREDIENTS

400 g (14 oz) butternut pumpkin (squash), chopped
2 tsp olive oil
3 small red chillies, deseeded and finely sliced
sea salt and freshly ground black pepper
1 onion, roughly chopped
185 ml (6 fl oz/¾ cup) buttermilk
2 eggs, lightly beaten
a small handful of basil leaves, finely chopped
2 tsp sugar
450 g (1 lb/3 cups) self-raising flour
200 g (7 oz) feta cheese

Preheat the oven to 160°C (315°F/Gas 2–3). Butter a 23 x 8 cm (9 x 3 inch) loaf tin.

Place the pumpkin, oil, chilli and salt and pepper in a bowl and toss well. Transfer to a baking tray and roast for 15 minutes, or until the pumpkin is tender. Set aside.

Combine the onion, buttermilk, eggs, basil, salt and sugar in the bowl of a food processor and process until smooth. Transfer to a bowl and stir in the flour. Crumble in the feta and add the pumpkin and stir gently to combine.

Spoon the dough into the prepared tin and bake for 1 hour, or until a skewer inserted in the centre of the loaf comes out clean. Allow to cool for 10 minutes in the tin before turning out onto a wire rack to cool completely.

Makes 10–12 slices

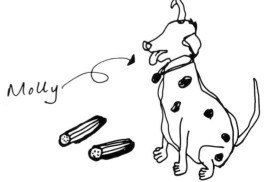

Molly

BLACK-BOTTOMED COCONUT AND CRANBERRY BARS

THE PLEASURE EXCURSION

MOST PEOPLE THESE DAYS ONLY HAVE TIME FOR READING ON THE BUS TO PASS THE TIME AND ON HOLIDAYS TO FEEL RELAXED. A GOOD BOOK AND COCONUT — THIS IS AS CLOSE AS YOU'LL GET TO YOUR VACATION READ AND THAILAND'S BEACHES.

INGREDIENTS

125 g (4½ oz) unsalted butter, melted
110 g (3¾ oz/½ cup) sugar
¼ tsp salt
1 large egg
30 g (1 oz/¼ cup) unsweetened cocoa powder
35 g (1¼ oz/¼ cup) plain (all-purpose) flour

Coconut topping

2 large eggs
165 g (5¾ oz/¾ cup) sugar
1/2 tsp natural vanilla extract
150 g (5½ oz/1 cup) plain
  (all-purpose) flour
190 g (6¾ oz/1 cup) dried cranberries,
  finely chopped
200 g (7 oz) sweetened shredded coconut

Preheat the oven to 190°C (375°F/Gas 5).

Line a 23 cm (9 inch) square baking tin with baking paper, leaving a slight overhang and set aside.

Combine the butter, sugar and salt in a bowl and whisk well.

Add the egg, cocoa and flour to the butter mix and stir until smooth.

Spread the batter into the prepared tin and bake for 15 minutes, or until firm to the touch.

For the coconut topping, whisk the eggs, sugar and vanilla in a bowl.

Gently mix in the flour, cranberries and 165 g (5¾ oz/2½ cups) of the coconut.

Spread the topping over the chocolate base and sprinkle on the remaining coconut.

Bake for 25–30 minutes until slightly golden and bounces back to the touch.

Allow to cool in the tin then gently lift the cake from the tin, peel off the baking paper base and cut into bars.

Keep stored in an airtight container for up to 4 days.

Makes 24

PEPPERMINT CRISPIES

ON BORROWED TERMS

EATING WHILE READING IS A DELICATE PRECIPICE, EQUAL PARTS ILLICIT THRILL AND FEAR OF MARKING SOME LITERARY TOME. THIS WHITE CHOCOLATE-BASED CRISPY WILL AT LEAST KEEP THE PAGES CLEAN, ENOUGH FOR THAT PLAUSIBLE DENIABILITY CLAUSE.

INGREDIENTS

250 g (9 oz) white chocolate, chopped
2 tsp peppermint essence
60 g (1³/₄ oz/1 cup) Coco Pops
  (Cocoa Krispies)

Line a tray with baking paper and set aside.

Melt the chocolate in a heatproof bowl over a saucepan of gently simmering water. Add the peppermint essence and stir to combine. Mix in the Coco Pops and smear the mixture onto the prepared tray.

Refrigerate until set. Break into shards.

Serves 8

Moving
out of home
.... & ....
SETTING UP HOUSE
is a chance to
PLAY
GROWN-UPS.

CHAPTER SIX

PLAYING HOUSE

Moving out of home and setting up house always seems so novel — a chance to play grown-ups, even though you already are one. It's an opportunity to buy fresh flowers every week, stock the fridge with goodies, have our buds over for dinner and spend lazy Sunday afternoons taking drives to the countryside scouring the vintage stores for the perfect little knick-knacks to make the house a home.

The sad reality is that the flowers we couldn't really afford from last month are still in the vase and the scent is more dirty creek-bed than fresh floral. And worse, Mum isn't there to miraculously appear when it all gets too hard to say it's dinner time.

The fridge is bare and the 'India Hicks'-style bedroom is looking more dog's breakfast than inspirational design. So by the time friends or family announce they are dropping by, we tend to get a bit frantic, have a mini panic attack and end up serving the most predictable homemade dishes. But it doesn't have to be that way — just remember that if they wanted to eat restaurant-quality food, they'd go to a restaurant. They visit to see you, to sift through your things, and play a little house. If only they would help with the clean-up afterwards.

These recipes should help when you feel like playing pretend.

Grandma for a cup of tea

Remember when you were little, spending school holidays with your gran, following her from room to room in her pearls, her pied-à-terre feeling like the most wondrous place on earth as you nibbled on the cocotte of wonderful stories she spun, and which now you struggle to recall?

Then there was the food. Toast with butter, real butter, and lamb chops and meringues. Biscuits — Monte Carlos, ginger snaps, the Scotch Fingers for dipping in tea, and orange creams. Life was perfect.

Except for the odd glimpse of old lady's flesh-toned underwear on the clothesline, flapping like a national flag in the breeze.

Menu

Red velvet cake

—

Spiced apple cake

RED VELVET CAKE

AGING GRACEFULLY

THIS IS HAUTE GATEAU; A BUTTER-BORNE MARRIAGE OF INGREDIENTS ONE
SPENDS MONTHS OF AFTERNOONS LOOKING FOR. AND PERFECT FOR AN AFTERNOON
CUP OF TEA WITH YOUR OLDEST FRIEND.

INGREDIENTS

125 g (4^1/$_2$ oz) unsalted butter, softened
330 g (11^1/$_2$ oz/1^1/$_2$ cups) caster (superfine)
  sugar
3 large eggs
3 tsp unsweetened cocoa powder
1^1/$_2$ tbsp red food colouring
300 g (10^1/$_2$ oz/2 cups) self-raising flour
290 ml (10 fl oz) buttermilk
1 tsp baking powder
small pinch salt
1 tsp apple cider vinegar
1 tsp natural vanilla extract

Icing

50 g (1^3/$_4$ oz) butter, softened
500 g (1 lb 2 oz) cream cheese, softened
250 g (9 oz/2 cups) icing
  (confectioners') sugar
1 tsp natural vanilla extract

Preheat the oven to 170°C (325°F/Gas 3). Grease and line two 20 cm (8 inch) diameter cake tins and set aside.

Cream the butter and sugar in a bowl with electric beaters until pale and fluffy. Add the eggs one at a time, beating well after each addition. Combine the cocoa and food colouring and stir into the creamed mixture.

Sift in half the flour and add half the buttermilk stirring until just incorporated. Repeat with the remaining flour and buttermilk. Fold in the baking powder, salt, vinegar and vanilla.

Pour into the prepared tins and bake for 30 minutes, or until a skewer inserted into the middle comes out clean and the cake springs back to the touch. Remove from the oven, turn onto a wire rack and allow to cool before icing.

For the icing, combine the butter and cream cheese in a bowl. Add the icing sugar and mix well, being careful not to overmix: the icing should be smooth not light and fluffy. Stir in the vanilla.

Ice the top of one cake and gently sandwich together with the second cake. Ice over the top and sides with the remaining icing and serve.

Makes 8–10

SPICED APPLE CAKE

A WHOLE LOT
OF LOVE

THIS SPICED APPLE TEA CAKE WILL GIVE GRAN A TASTE OF HOME. THE APPLE KEEPS
THE TEXTURE LUSCIOUS, AND THE MIXED SPICE PERMEATES EVERYTHING, INCLUDING
YOUR KITCHEN, WITH ITS HUSKY HEAT.

INGREDIENTS

2 granny smith apples, peeled, cored
   and diced
220 g (7³/₄ oz/1 cup) caster (superfine) sugar
125 g (4¹/₂ oz) butter, softened
1 large egg
170 g (6 oz/1 cup) sticky raisins
225 g (8 oz/1¹/₂ cups) plain (all-purpose) flour
1 tsp bicarbonate of soda
¹/₂ tsp salt
1 tsp ground cinnamon
1 tsp freshly grated nutmeg
1 tsp mixed spice
60 g (2¹/₄ oz/¹/₂ cup) chopped walnuts

To serve
icing sugar, sifted, for dusting and mascarpone

Preheat the oven to 180°C (350°F/Gas 4). Grease a 22 cm (8¹/₂ inch) ring cake tin, line with baking paper and set aside.

Mix the apple and sugar in a bowl and let stand for 3 minutes.

Combine the butter and egg in a bowl and beat until light and fluffy. Fold in the apple mixture and the raisins and set aside. In another bowl, sift together the dry ingredients and add to the apple mixture, stirring sparingly.

Fold in half the walnuts, pour into the prepared tin and sprinkle on the remaining walnuts. Bake for 50 minutes, or until a skewer inserted in the centre of the cake comes out clean.

Cool for 10 minutes in the tin before turning out onto a wire rack to cool completely.

Serve with a dusting of icing sugar and a dollop of mascarpone.

Makes 8–12 slices, depending on how Gran takes her cake

Friends for breakfast, lunch and tea

There used to be an implicit understanding that the place of cooking, like a woman's nether regions, should remain a secret, hidden from all but the most intimate of acquaintances. It was the epicentre of delicate preparation where everyday fare was transformed, by way of heat, physical exertion and creativity, into delicious tastes to be offered up to a select and appreciative few.

So one cannot be blamed for being shocked by the arrival of the unannounced. One minute you are pottering about in your undies, only to find yourself called to stove duty the next. The house is a mess, and friends who are 'just passing by' drop in for a drink, stay for dinner and somehow expect miracles. You do love them but they violate your inner sanctum and open kitchen plan with ease, pour themselves a drink, lean against the sink for a chat, then expect dinner on the fine china with about as much decorum as, well ... asking to see your nether regions.

There is nothing like a series of MasterChef and the growing culture of foodie wank to cause mild-mannered home-cook types to try to transform themselves into leotard-wearing superhero chef types. It is a recipe for disaster. And completely unnecessary. Never forget you are cooking for friends — the people that have seen you at your absolute worst and still want to come over for tea.

Menu 1 — Breakfast

Vegemite croque monsieur

–

Rosewater yoghurt with Middle Eastern spiced granola

Menu 2 — Brunch

Banana and coconut French toast with caramelised banana

–

Bacon and egg piroshki

–

Squid ink couscous with smoked salmon and poached egg

Menu 3 — Lunch

Trashy tortilla española

–

Wagyu beef skewers with maple and tamarind glaze

–

Spanish corn

–

Limoncello tiramisu

Menu 4 — Dinner

Beef toasts with smoked paprika mayonnaise

–

Roast leg of lamb with plum and soy marinade

–

Wasabi butter beans

–

Chocolate and Galliano milkshake ice cream with balsamic strawberries

VEGEMITE
CROQUE MONSIEUR

FRANCE IN YOUR
PANTS

ANY FRIEND THAT IS AROUND FOR BREAKFAST IS A GOOD FRIEND INDEED SO THERE IS NO NEED TO FUSS. THE IMPORTANT THING IS TO PUT ON A FILLING SPREAD, LIKE THIS VEGEMITE CROQUE MONSIEUR, SO THEY WALK AROUND ALL DAY WITH THEIR STOMACH PUSHING UNCOMFORTABLY AGAINST THEIR PANTS AS A CONSTANT REMINDER OF THE STELLAR SPREAD YOU PROVIDED.

INGREDIENTS

8 croissants, halved lengthways
2 tbsp Vegemite
8 slices of smoked cheddar
100 ml (3¹/₂ fl oz) cream
100 g (3¹/₂ oz/1 cup) coarsely grated cheese
   (cheddar, parmesan, gruyere or whatever
   you have on hand will do)
3 eggs

Preheat the oven to 200°C (400°F/Gas 6).

Layer half the croissant pieces into a 21 x 30 cm (8¼ x 12 inch) ovenproof dish. Smear the Vegemite over the croissant base and layer the smoked cheddar on top. Cover with the remaining croissant pieces.

Whisk together the cream, cheese and eggs and pour over the croissants. If you have time, refrigerate for half an hour to let the cream mixture be absorbed. Bake for 25 minutes, or until golden and crisp.

Serves 8

MIDDLE EASTERN Spiced GRANOLA

ROSEWATER YOGHURT WITH MIDDLE EASTERN SPICED GRANOLA

AGAINST THE GRAIN

YOU COULD DO A LOT WORSE THAN MAKE THIS SENSATIONAL GRANOLA FOR A BUNCH OF PEOPLE YOU REALLY LOVE — THEY'LL LOVE YOU EVEN MORE AFTERWARDS, AND EVEN BETTER, THE LEFT-OVER GRANOLA KEEPS FOR WEEKS IN AN AIRTIGHT CONTAINER, WHILE THE YOGHURT IS GOOD ENOUGH TO EAT FROM BREAKFAST THROUGH TO DESSERT.

INGREDIENTS

Spiced granola

450 g (1 lb/4^1/$_2$ cups) rolled (porridge) oats
175 g (6 oz) apple puree
2 tsp ground cardamom
1 tsp ground ginger
1 tsp ground cumin
2 tsp ground cinnamon
120 g (4^1/$_4$ oz) golden syrup (light treacle)
115 g (4 oz/^{1}/$_3$ cup) honey
100 g (3^1/$_2$ oz) soft brown sugar
150 g (5^1/$_2$ oz) unsalted pistachio nuts,
   lightly crushed
100 g (3^1/$_2$ oz) hazelnuts, roughly chopped
100 g (3^1/$_2$ oz) dried figs, roughly chopped
100 g (3^1/$_2$ oz) dried strawberries,
   roughly chopped
100 g (3^1/$_2$ oz) coconut chips

Yoghurt

a pinch of saffron threads
2 tbsp rosewater
800 g (1 lb 12 oz) Greek yoghurt
1 tsp ground cinnamon
1 tsp ground cumin
1 vanilla bean, split lengthways and
   seeds scraped

Preheat the oven to 170°C (325°F/Gas 3). Line two baking trays with baking paper and set aside.

For the granola, combine the rolled oats, apple puree, ground spices, golden syrup, honey, sugar and nuts in a large bowl and mix with your hands to ensure everything is evenly coated. Spread the mixture onto the prepared trays and toast for 20–25 minutes. Remove from the oven, stir and return to the oven for a further 20–25 minutes until fragrant and an even golden colour. Allow to cool. Stir in the dried fruits and coconut chips.

Combine the saffron threads and rosewater in a bowl and set aside for 5 minutes to infuse. Mix the yoghurt with the cinnamon, cumin and vanilla and stir through the infused rosewater. Refrigerate until required.

Serve the granola and a healthy dollop of rosewater-infused yoghurt.

Serves 8

BANANA AND COCONUT FRENCH TOAST WITH CARAMELISED BANANA

NANANNANANA

THE VERY PREMISE OF BRUNCH IS ABOUT SLEEP-INS, CHAMPAGNE BEFORE MIDDAY, AND I-HAVE-ALL-THE-TIME-IN-THE-WORLD SORT OF SENTIMENTS. IT'S DEFINITELY THE BEST MEAL OF THE DAY.

TRY TO MAKE THE BANANA BREAD AHEAD OF TIME, SO ALL YOU HAVE TO DO ON THE SPOT IS MAKE THE FRENCH TOAST AND CARAMELISE THE BANANA.

INGREDIENTS

Banana bread
150 g (5^1/$_2$ oz/1 cup) plain (all-purpose) flour
1 tsp baking powder
25 g (1 oz/^{1}/$_4$ cup) desiccated coconut
a small pinch of salt
60 g (2^1/$_4$ oz) unsalted butter, softened
110 g (3^3/$_4$ oz/^{1}/$_2$ cup) caster (superfine) sugar
1 egg, lightly beaten
2 overripe bananas, mashed
125 g (4^1/$_2$ oz/^{1}/$_2$ cup) sour cream

Caramelised banana
60 g (2^1/$_4$ oz) butter, chopped
3 bananas, halved lengthways
110 g (3^3/$_4$ oz/^{1}/$_2$ cup) soft
   brown sugar, firmly packed

French toast
8 large eggs
55 g (2 oz/^{1}/$_4$ cup) sugar
3 tsp ground cinnamon
45 g (1^3/$_4$ oz) unsalted butter

To serve
250 g (9 oz) crème fraîche

Preheat the oven to 180°C (350°F/Gas 4). Line a 23 x 8 cm (9 x 3 inch) loaf tin with baking paper and set aside.

For the banana bread, sift the flour, baking powder, coconut and salt into a bowl. Cream the butter and sugar in a separate bowl until pale and fluffy. Add the egg and beat until combined. Stir in the banana, then alternately add the dry ingredients and the sour cream, mixing well after each addition. Pour into the prepared tin and bake for 50 minutes, or until a skewer inserted in the centre of the bread comes out clean. Leave to cool in the tin for 10 minutes before turning out onto a wire rack to cool completely.

For the caramelised banana, melt the butter in a large frying pan over medium–high heat. Add the bananas and cook, turning once, for 3 minutes. Add the sugar and continue to cook until the bananas are golden brown and caramelised. Transfer to a plate.

For the French toast, using a fork, beat the eggs in a large shallow dish. Dip the slices of banana bread in the egg and stand, turning the slices once, for 5 minutes, or until the egg is absorbed. Stir the sugar and cinnamon together on a large plate and set aside. Melt the butter in a large frying pan over medium heat. Add the eggy banana bread slices and cook for 2 minutes per side until golden and crunchy and heated through. Immediately drench in the cinnamon sugar, turning to coat completely.

Divide the French toast among serving plates, top with a caramelised banana and a dollop of crème fraîche and serve.

Serves 6

BACON AND EGG
PIROSHKI

EVERYTHING TASTES
BETTER WITH BACON

THIS IS AN INCREDIBLY 'AUSSIFIED' VERSION OF THE RUSSIAN PIROSHKI — A
SPECTACULAR PASTRY TRADITIONALLY STUFFED WITH CABBAGE OR MINCE. HERE I'VE
USED BACON AND EGG. TO MAKE IT REALLY PUNCH ABOVE ITS WEIGHT, SERVE WITH
A CHUNKY TOMATO RELISH OR GOOD QUALITY SMOKY BARBECUE SAUCE.

INGREDIENTS
180 ml (6 fl oz/³/₄ cup) milk
62.5 g (2¹/₄ oz) butter
1 tsp salt
1 tbsp caster (superfine) sugar
1 tsp dried yeast
225 g (8 oz/1¹/₂ cups) plain (all-purpose)
    flour, sifted
1 egg yolk, lightly beaten
beaten egg to glaze

Filling
8 rashers bacon
8 eggs
8 tsp good quality tomato relish

Preheat the oven to 200°C (400°F/Gas 6). Line a baking tray with baking paper and set aside. Heat the milk, butter, salt and sugar in a saucepan over low heat until just lukewarm.

Sift the flour into a large bowl. Add the yeast and salt and stir to combine. Make a well in the centre and pour in the milk mixture and lightly beaten egg yolk. Gently incorporate then turn out onto a clean and floured surface and knead the dough until smooth, shiny and elastic. Sprinkle over a little flour and set aside, covered, until doubled in size — usually about 30 minutes.

Fry the bacon in a frying pan over medium heat until cooked through. Remove from heat and cut away fat.

Bring a large pot of water to the boil, add the eggs and cook for one minute. You only want to just cook the eggs enough to remove the shell, not cook the egg through. Remove and carefully crack and remove the shell, keeping the egg whole.

Roll out discs of the pastry to about 10 cm (4 inch) diameter. Place a rasher of bacon in the centre, top with a teaspoon of tomato relish and one egg. Gently encase the pastry over the top of the mixture and press together with your fingertips to seal. Brush with the egg wash. Repeat with remaining pastry, bacon, relish, eggs, and egg wash to seal.

Brush over the egg wash and bake in the oven for 10 minutes. Serve hot with tomato relish or barbecue sauce.

Makes 10

SQUID INK COUSCOUS WITH SMOKED SALMON AND POACHED EGG
THE BREAKFAST CLUB

THE COLOURS OF THIS DISH ARE SO LUSH AND IT IS DEAD, DEAD EASY.

OH, AND DID I MENTION IT IS ALSO A COMPLETE TASTE REVELATION.

INGREDIENTS

----

500 g (1 lb 2 oz) Israeli couscous

2–3 tsp squid ink

1 tsp olive oil

sea salt and freshly ground black pepper

6 eggs

60 ml (2 fl oz/¼ cup) white wine vinegar

450 g (1 lb) smoked salmon

45 g (1½ oz/1 cup) baby rocket (arugula)

To serve

3 lemons, halved

01

Cook the couscous in boiling water according to the packet instructions. Drain and return to the pan. Add the squid ink and olive oil, then stir well until the ink has evenly coated the grains. Season with salt and pepper.

02

While the couscous is cooking, poach the eggs by filling a large frying pan with water and bringing to the boil over medium heat. Reduce the heat to low and stir in the vinegar. Crack one egg into a coffee cup and then gently pour the egg into the simmering water. Repeat with remaining eggs. Cook the eggs for 3 minutes, or until the whites are set but the yolks are still runny. Using a slotted spoon, carefully remove the eggs and set aside. Repeat with the remaining eggs.

03

Place a large spoonful of couscous on a plate, top with a few rocket leaves and then layer over the salmon. Top with a poached egg. Season with salt and pepper and serve immediately with fresh lemon.

Serves 6

The colours of this dish are so lush

and it is dead, dead easy.

TRASHY
TORTILLA ESPAÑOLA

PABLO ESCOBAR

THIS IS MEXICAN STREET FOOD MEETS MACCAS. A LITTLE BIT CHEAP, A LITTLE BIT TRASHY, AND AN EASY THROW-TOGETHER TO WASH DOWN WITH BEER, WHILE SHOOTING THE BREEZE WITH SOME MATES IN THE SUN.

THROW IN ANY LEFTOVERS YOU WANT. FOLLOW YOUR INSTINCTS AND USE THIS AS A GUIDE ONLY.

INGREDIENTS

2 large serves of McDonald's fries
8 eggs
125 ml (4½ fl oz/½ cup) milk
2 small handfuls flat-leaf parsley,
    roughly chopped
cheese (whatever is in the fridge), shredded,
    grated or crumbled
sea salt and freshly ground black pepper
Tabasco sauce
8 rashes of bacon or 4 chorizo sausage,
    sliced

Preheat the oven to 180°C (350°F/Gas 4).

Grease a casserole dish or a cast-iron saucepan, whatever you have on hand. You can even use individual 250 ml (9 fl oz/1 cup) ramekins for individual serves.

Dump the fries in the dish, pan or divided among the ramekins if using, and place in the oven to keep warm.

Beat the eggs and milk in a large bowl. Submerge the parsley in the eggs and fold in some cheese. Season with salt and pepper.

Add a glug of Tabasco and if you have some bacon or chorizo, fry, drain and crumble it in.

Peer into your fridge for any leftovers that smell okay and pop those in too — semi-dried tomatoes, a bit of onion, a few peas — all work well.

Pour the egg mixture over the fries, pushing down on the fries to make sure they are covered. Bake for 5–10 minutes until the casserole poofs up and turns brown and the egg mix is just cooked through.

Serves 6–8

WAGYU BEEF SKEWERS WITH MAPLE AND TAMARIND GLAZE

RETURN OF THE NATIVE

THESE TASTE BEST WHEN SLIGHTLY CHARRED FROM THE BARBECUE. THERE IS SOMETHING ABOUT MEAT SEARED AT FISSION-INDUCING TEMPERATURES WITH THE MARINADE CRUSTED AT THE EDGES THAT WILL GLADDEN YOUR HEART AND SHOCK YOUR GP.

INGREDIENTS

6 x 150 g (5^1/$_2$ oz) wagyu steaks
1 tbsp coriander seeds
^{1}/$_2$ tbsp black peppercorns
125 ml (4 fl oz/^{1}/$_2$ cup) pure maple syrup
125 ml (4 fl oz/^{1}/$_2$ cup) beef stock
2 tbsp finely chopped ginger
2 tbsp tamarind pulp
2 tbsp grapeseed oil
1 tbsp unsalted butter
1 tbsp coriander leaves, finely chopped

Heat a small frying pan over medium heat and toast coriander until fragrant, or a shade darker, for about 3 minutes. Transfer to a bowl to cool. Toast peppercorns in the same manner.

Grind toasted spices to a powder in a grinder or with a mortar and pestle. Stir together the maple syrup, beef stock, ginger, and tamarind pulp in a small saucepan and simmer until reduced to a coating consistency, for about 10 minutes. Add salt and toasted spices to taste, then cover and keep warm.

Pat beef dry and cut into cubes and push down onto metal skewers (if using wooden skewers make sure they are wet with water before cooking or they will burn). Heat the oil on a barbecue hot plate or in a frying pan until it shimmers, then cook the skewers, turning regularly until cooked to your liking.

To serve skewers, drizzle over glaze and top with the coriander leaves.

Serves 6–8

SPANISH CORN
IT'S NOT JUST FOR CORNFLAKES

THE LASHINGS OF AÏOLI, LIME AND COTIJA CHEESE ENSURE THAT EVERY HAVE-A-GO-HERO TRYING HIS OR HER HAND AT TAMING THE BLAZING COALS WILL CONSIDER THIS SPANISH CORN A RAGING SUCCESS. THEY DON'T LOOK THAT PRETTY, BUT TRULY GOOD FOOD RARELY DOES.

INGREDIENTS
12 corn cobs, with husks
juice of 3 limes
350 g (12 oz) store-bought aïoli
120 g (4¼ oz/1 cup) grated cotija cheese
3 limes, halved

Preheat the barbecue to medium.

Peel back the husks of the corn without removing them. Remove the silks and recover the corn with the husks. Soak in a large bowl of cold water for 30 minutes.

Combine the lime juice and aïoli in a bowl and set aside.

Remove the corn from the water and shake off the excess. Place on the barbecue, close the cover and cook for 15–20 minutes. Alternatively you can cook these in a frying pan covered with a lid. Unwrap the corn from the husk and serve with a healthy dollop of aïoli, a sprinkle of cotijia cheese and a squeeze of lime.

Serves 8–12

ROAST LEG OF LAMB WITH PLUM AND SOY MARINADE
PLUM LAMB

THIS LAMB IS IDIOT-PROOF AND CAPABLE OF MAKING EVEN HARDENED FOODIES WEAK AT THE KNEES. CATERING FOR A CROWD TENDS TO BE AN ONSLAUGHT RATHER THAN AN EBB AND FLOW, AND THE FOOD ALL HAS TO BE READY AT THE SAME TIME, SO THIS IS PERFECT FOR SHOVING IN THE OVEN AND FORGETTING ABOUT UNTIL THE TIMER BEEPS.

INGREDIENTS
250 ml (9 fl oz/1 cup) soy sauce
1 tbsp worcestershire sauce
1 tbsp English mustard
320 g (11¼ oz/1 cup) plum jam
sea salt and freshly ground black pepper
2 x 1.4 kg (3 lb 2 oz) legs of lamb
6 garlic cloves, thinly sliced
4 tbsp sesame seeds

Preheat the oven to 180°C (350°F/Gas 4).

Combine the soy sauce, worcestershire sauce, mustard and plum jam in a bowl and stir until the jam breaks down and a thick sauce-like texture is achieved. Season with salt and pepper.

Make small slits in the lamb and insert a slice of garlic in each incision. Spread the soy sauce mixture over the lamb and sprinkle on the sesame seeds. Place each lamb leg in a tight-fitting ovenproof dish (to prevent the jam from burning) and roast for 1½ hours, basting with the soy sauce mixture at least once. Rest for 5 minutes and serve with wasabi butter beans.

Serves 8–10

WASABI BUTTER BEANS
BEAN TOWN

INGREDIENTS
500 g (1 lb 2 oz) green beans
15 g (½ oz) butter
1 tbsp wasabi, or more to taste

Place a large saucepan of water over high heat and bring to the boil, add the beans and cook for 1-2 minutes. Drain and refresh under cold water.

Melt the butter and wasabi in a saucepan over low heat, stirring well until butter has just melted and is beginning to foam.

Drizzle the wasabi butter over the beans, toss to combine and serve.

Serves 8–10 as a side dish

CHOCOLATE AND GALLIANO MILKSHAKE ICE CREAM WITH BALSAMIC STRAWBERRIES
SWEET RELEASE

THIS DELIGHTFUL SWEET, CREAMY AND SLIGHTLY NUTTY MILKSHAKE-INSPIRED ICE CREAM IS ONE TO BE SAVOURED SPOON BY SPOON AND IS THE PERFECT ENDING TO A MEAL. THIS IS CHILDHOOD GOODNESS WITH ADULT INTENTIONS. I LIKE TO THINK BREAST MILK TASTED LIKE GALLIANO AND MALT-SPICED ICE CREAM.

YOU'LL NEED TO **BEGIN THIS RECIPE A DAY AHEAD.**

INGREDIENTS

Ice cream

3 large eggs, at room temperature

75 g (2¾ oz/⅓ cup) soft brown sugar, firmly packed

2 tsp ground cinnamon

80 ml (2½ fl oz/⅓ cup) Galliano liqueur

300 g (10½ oz) good quality chocolate

170 ml (5½ fl oz/⅔ cup) sour cream

½ tsp natural vanilla extract

40 g (1½ oz/⅓ cup) malted milk powder

Balsamic strawberries

250 g (9 oz) strawberries, hulled

3 tbsp caster (superfine) sugar

1 tbsp balsamic vinegar

01

For the ice cream, beat the eggs and sugar in a heatproof bowl over a saucepan of simmering water for 6–8 minutes, or until the mixture coats the back of a wooden spoon. Remove the bowl from the heat, stir in the cinnamon and Galliano and chill the mixture for 10 minutes until cool.

02

Melt the chocolate in a heatproof bowl over a saucepan of simmering water. Add the chocolate to the egg mix and set aside.

03

In a separate bowl, whip the sour cream, vanilla and malted milk powder until soft peaks form. Stir one-third of the cream mix into the egg mixture to lighten it, then gently fold in the remaining cream mix.

04

Pour into individual ramekins or a 1 litre (35 fl oz/4 cups) capacity loaf tin lined with plastic wrap and place in the freezer for 4 hours, or until frozen.

05

For the strawberries, combine all the ingredients in a bowl and stand for an hour.

Remove ice cream from the freezer to soften 10 minutes prior to serving and top with the balsamic strawberries.

Serves 4–6

A month of Sundays

There comes a time, not for all, but for many, when the thought of being out and about pales in comparison to a day and/or night in.

I've always hated nightclubs — I never got off with anyone, and when I did have enough cash for drinks (which was rare by the third night out in a row) I spent it on hideous, disturbingly colourful (both going down and coming up) concoctions such as Cock-Sucking Cowboys or Midori Illusions, only to finish the night trawling the streets with a girlfriend or two trying to find a cab home.

At home you can choose your company, no one is likely to squeeze your arse unless you'd actually like them to, and your money can be spent on far more carefully selected entertainment.

Such as food.

When you work, weekends become sacrosanct. They must be filled with good times, spectacular food and enough escape to prepare you for the week that always follows.

Maybe it's because I love to cook that I embrace the idea of a Sunday involving no real plans, flaffing about the house in my jim-jams, cooking a roast or maybe a spot of pasta, or even deciding to cook a feast for a few friends for a late lunch. The following recipes are the type that sit quietly in the kitchen until you need them — they're deeply practical or slightly sparkling so they earn a spot at a more dressed table if needed.

Perfect for a Sunday on a whim.

Menu 1

Fish tacos with papaya, lemongrss and chilli

–

Sashimi salad

–

Red miso chicken pies with lemongrass and coriander mushy peas

–

Blood plum and sparkling pinot sorbet with sour cherry, star anise and chocolate biscotti

Menu 2

Hickory croquettes with beery garlic and lemon ricotta dip

–

Lamb shoulder and quinoa salad

–

Lindt chocolate puddings

FISH TACOS WITH PAPAYA, LEMONGRASS AND CHILLI

THE DAY BEFORE THE WEEK AHEAD

THERE WAS ONCE A TIME, A FAR EASIER TIME, WHEN HARD-PRESSING DECISIONS WERE MADE WITH A GAME OF 'YOU'RE IT' OR ROCK, PAPER, SCISSORS. THESE TACOS PUT A STOP, EVEN IF ONLY FOR A MOMENT, TO ALL THOSE OTHER EVERYDAY ADULT MAD THINGS — GOING TO WORK, PAYING BILLS AND DONNING CONSERVATIVE WARDROBES — TAKING YOU BACK TO SIMPLER TIMES LIKE EATING WITH COMPLETE IGNORANCE OF CUTLERY, WHILE BEING DELICIOUS ENOUGH FOR GROWN-UP DINNERTIME SITUATIONS.

INGREDIENTS

2 x 150 g (5½ oz) snapper fillets or other
   firm white fish
2–4 flour tortillas

Marinade

1 tbsp olive oil
60 ml (2 fl oz/ ¼ cup) lime juice
1 tbsp chopped coriander (cilantro)
2 tbsp finely chopped lemongrass,
   white part only
1 small red chilli, deseeded and finely chopped
1 garlic clove, smashed

Salsa

½ red onion, finely chopped
1 small red chilli, deseeded and finely
   chopped
275 g (9¾ oz/1½ cups) papaya, cut into cubes
a small handful of coriander (cilantro) leaves,
   stems and roots, rinsed and finely chopped
a small handful of Thai basil, coarsely torn
a small handful of Vietnamese mint,
   coarsely torn
juice of 1 lime

Sauce

3 dried long red chillies, deseeded
3 garlic cloves, peeled
3 red Asian shallots, peeled
2 tbsp vegetable oil
4 tbsp grated palm sugar
80 ml (2½ fl oz/⅓ cup) tamarind water
2 tbsp fish sauce
100 ml (3½ fl oz) water
a pinch of salt
80 ml (2½ fl oz/⅓ cup) light sour cream

Place the fish fillets in a large, shallow dish and add the marinade ingredients. Toss to coat. Cover with plastic wrap and allow to infuse for 30 minutes but preferably up to 2 hours in the fridge.

For the salsa, combine all the ingredients in a bowl, cover and refrigerate until serving.

For the sauce, soak the dried chillies in hot water for 3 minutes until softened. Discard the stems and roughly chop the chillies. Blitz the chillies, garlic and shallots to a paste in a food processor.

Heat a frying pan over high heat, add the oil and the chilli paste and cook until fragrant. Add the sugar, tamarind water, fish sauce, water and salt. Reduce the heat to low and simmer for 3 minutes, or until the sauce has thickened. Set aside to cool. Stir in the sour cream.

Preheat a chargrill pan or barbecue to medium-low and brush with oil. Cook the fish for 2–3 minutes per side, or until cooked through. Transfer the fish to a platter and, using a fork, gently shred the meat.

Heat the tortillas on the barbecue or in the chargrill pan for about 30 seconds on each side.

Serve the fish and tortillas hot with the salsa and sauce.

Serves 2

SASHIMI SALAD
GO FISH

SOMETIMES A FISH OUT OF WATER IS A TRULY GOOD THING. DON'T GET ME WRONG I DO CARE ABOUT OUR SEAFARING FRIENDS. I'M RIGHT THERE WITH GREENPEACE, PULLING UP ALONGSIDE THOSE FISHING BOATS TO SHAKE MY FIST FROM THE ALL-INTIMIDATING RUBBER DINGHY OF MY MIND. HELL, WHEN ARIEL DECIDED TO GIVE UP HER LIFE IN THE SEA FOR THE LOVE OF A PRINCE, I LOST SLEEP FOR WEEKS …

BUT PUT A PIECE OF PERFECTLY FRESH FISH AND A TOUCH OF WASABI IN FRONT OF ME AND IT'S ALL MONSTERS AND LIVE-ACTION ADVENTURE IN EPIC *20,000 LEAGUES UNDER THE SEA* PROPORTIONS. I SIMPLY CANNOT RESIST.

THIS WARM, CRUNCHY, FISH SALAD WITH A TOUCH OF GINGER AND WASABI IS THE ONE TO EAT IF YOU FEEL THE NEED FOR AN UNDERWATER, OTHER-WORLD KIND OF MOMENT.

INGREDIENTS
210 g (7½ oz/1 cup) sushi rice
125 ml (4 fl oz/½ cup) sushi rice vinegar
120 g (4¼ oz/2 cups) edamame bean pods
200 g (7 oz) sashimi-grade salmon
a handful of coriander (cilantro),
    roughly chopped
40 g (1½ oz/¼ cup) sesame seeds
45 g (1¾ oz/¼ cup) pickled ginger

Soy-mirin dressing
125 ml (4 fl oz/½ cup) mirin
125 ml (4 fl oz/½ cup) soy sauce
60 ml (2 fl oz/¼ cup) rice wine vinegar
½ tsp miso paste

Cook the sushi rice according to the packet instructions. Drain the rice and pour on the vinegar, gently stirring to coat the rice. Place in the fridge until required.

Bring a saucepan of water to the boil over high heat, add the edamame and cook for 2 minutes. Drain and pod the beans into a large bowl. Add the sashimi, coriander, sesame seeds and pickled ginger, and toss gently.

Heat the sushi rice in a microwave on medium heat for 2 minutes, or until piping hot. Mix the rice through the salad.

For the dressing, combine the ingredients in a bowl.

Pour the dressing over the salad, toss gently and serve.

Serves 4

RED MISO CHICKEN PIES WITH LEMONGRASS AND CORIANDER MUSHY PEAS
THE BAKED ESCAPE

IT REALLY IS A BEAUTIFUL THING TO DO NOTHING, EAT A PIE, AND THEN REST AFTERWARDS.

YOU SHOULD ALWAYS USE THIGH FILLETS OR CHICKEN MARYLANDS FOR THE ULTIMATE CHICKEN PIE. BREAST MEAT IS TOO LEAN AND OFTEN ENDS UP DRY AND DISAPPOINTING. AND THAT IS SOMETHING YOU NEVER WANT IN YOUR PIE.

INGREDIENTS
Pies
500 g (1 lb 2 oz) skinless chicken thighs
2 tsp olive oil
sea salt and freshly ground black pepper
150 g (5½ oz/½ cup) red miso paste
125 ml (4 fl oz/½ cup) soy sauce
2 tsp lime juice
1 tbsp soft brown sugar
250 ml (9 fl oz/1 cup) cream
1 x 375 g (13 oz) sheet of shortcrust (pie) pastry
375 g (13 oz) puff pastry
1 egg yolk, for egg wash
half bunch spring onions (scallions), finely chopped
2 tsp sesame seeds

Lemongrass peas
500 g (1 lb 2 oz) frozen peas
1 tbsp lemongrass, white part only, very finely diced (approximately 1–2 stems depending on their size)
a handful of coriander (cilantro), roughly chopped
75 g (2¾ oz) crème fraîche
a few Thai basil leaves

Preheat the oven to 180°C (350°F/Gas 4). Line a baking tray with baking paper.

Place the chicken on the prepared tray, drizzle on the oil and season with the salt and pepper. Roast for 20 minutes. Set aside until cool enough to handle, and shred the meat.

Combine the miso paste, soy sauce, lime juice, sugar and cream in a saucepan over low heat and cook for 10 minutes, stirring regularly, until the sauce thickens slightly. Add the shredded chicken and stir well.

Roll out the shortcrust pastry on a lightly floured surface until 5 mm (¼ inch) thick. Cut out six circles to line the bases and sides of six 9. 5 cm (3¾ inch) pie tins. If you are fussy about your pastry, you can blind bake the pastry in the oven for 15 minutes by placing a piece of baking paper over the pastry and lining it with pastry weights (dried chickpeas work equally well). Or you can just skip this step and spoon the filling into the pastry cases and brush the edges with the egg yolk.

Roll out the puff pastry until 5 mm (¼ inch) thick and cut out six circles slightly larger than the pie tins. Place the puff pastry tops on the pies and press around the edges with a fork to seal. Brush the pastry with the egg yolk and make three piercings with a sharp knife in the top of each pie. Sprinkle over the sesame seeds then bake in the oven for 35 minutes, or until golden.

For the lemongrass peas, about 10 minutes before the pies are ready to be pulled from the oven, cook the peas in boiling water until tender. Drain and tip into a blender with the lemongrass, coriander and crème fraîche and blitz until pureed to your liking. Season to taste.

Serve the pies with a side of mushy lemongrass peas, topped with a few Thai basil leaves.

Makes 6–8 pies

BLOOD PLUM AND SPARKLING PINOT SORBET WITH SOUR CHERRY, STAR ANISE AND CHOCOLATE BISCOTTI
THE SWEETEST THING

YOU CAN MAKE THE BISCOTTI WHENEVER YOU LIKE. THEY LAST ABOUT 3 WEEKS STORED IN AN AIRTIGHT CONTAINER.

INGREDIENTS
Sorbet
800 g (1 lb 12 oz) ripe blood plums
165 g (5¾ oz/¾ cup) sugar
500 ml (17 fl oz/2 cups) sparkling pinot noir
2 tbsp light corn syrup
1 tbsp lemon juice

Biscotti
80 g (2¾ oz) caster (superfine) sugar
1 egg
100 g (3½ oz/⅔ cup) plain (all-purpose)
  flour, sifted
½ tsp baking powder
50 g (1¾ oz) unsweetened cocoa powder
40 g (1½ oz) sour cherries, finely chopped
40 g (1½ oz) dark chocolate (70 per cent
  cocoa solids), chopped into chunks

For the sorbet, place the plums in a large saucepan. Add the sugar and 375 ml (13 fl oz/1½ cups) of the sparkling pinot and simmer over medium heat for 14 minutes until the plums are soft. Strain through a fine sieve into a bowl, reserving the poaching liquid. Allow the plums to cool so you can handle them. Remove the skin from the plums and cut the flesh into chunks; discarding the skin and stones. Puree the plums in a food processor with the reserved poaching liquid. Stir in the remaining sparkling pinot, the corn syrup and lemon juice.

Pour the mixture into a shallow container and freeze until frozen at the edges. Remove from the freezer and beat with electric beaters. Pour back into the container and refreeze. Repeat two or three times. Alternatively, use an ice-cream machine following the manufacturer's instructions.

Preheat the oven to 180°C (350°F/Gas 4). Line a large baking tray with baking paper and set aside.

For the biscotti, beat the sugar and egg in a large bowl until pale and thick. Fold in the flour, baking powder, cocoa, cherries and chocolate. Use your hands to lightly knead the dough on a floured work surface until smooth. Divide the dough in half and shape into two long logs about 5 cm (2 inches) wide. Place on the prepared tray, leaving space between each log. Bake for 20–25 minutes until firm to touch and slightly golden. Set aside to cool completely (about an hour).

Reduce the oven temperature to 140°C (275°F/Gas 1).

Using a serrated knife, cut each log on the diagonal into thin slices. Lay the slices flat on the tray and return to the oven for 15–20 minutes, turning once, until crisp. Allow to cool completely.

When the sorbet is firm, place scoops in serving cups or dishes and serve with the biscotti.

Makes 6–8

HICKORY CROQUETTES WITH BEERY GARLIC AND LEMON RICOTTA DIP
SOUL FOOD

THERE IS NEVER EVER ANYTHING WRONG WITH CROQUETTES. LITTLE BITE-SIZED, BARELY THERE CYLINDERS OF CREAMY GOODNESS ENCASED IN CRISPY BREADCRUMBS. DEMONIC FOOD FOR HEAVENLY PEOPLE.

INGREDIENTS
Croquettes
3 starchy potatoes (such as sebago), peeled
2 garlic cloves, finely chopped
25 g (1 oz/¼ cup) shaved parmesan
60 ml (2 fl oz/¼ cup) hickory sauce
½ tsp dried chilli flakes
sea salt and freshly ground black pepper
1 egg
1 tbsp cold water
100 g (3½ oz) fresh breadcrumbs or
   panko crumbs
olive oil, for shallow frying

Ricotta dipping sauce
250 g (9 oz) ricotta
zest of 1 lemon
1 garlic clove, finely chopped
100 g (3½ oz) natural yoghurt
125 ml (4 fl oz/½ cup) beer

To serve
lime halves

Cook the potatoes in boiling water until tender, then push through a mouli or large strainer into a bowl. Add the garlic, parmesan, hickory sauce and chilli flakes. Season with salt and pepper and mix well. Cool, then roll tablespoons of the mixture into oval-shaped croquettes.

Beat the egg and water in a shallow bowl. Spread the breadcrumbs or panko crumbs on a plate. Dip the potato croquettes in the egg wash, then in the breadcrumbs. Place on a tray, cover with plastic wrap and refrigerate for 30 minutes.

For the dipping sauce, combine the ricotta, lemon zest, garlic, yoghurt and beer in a bowl and set aside.

Heat the oil to 180°C (350°F) in a large saucepan or deep-fryer or until the oil is hot enough to turn a cube of bread immediately golden. Add the croquettes, in batches, and fry for 3–5 minutes, or until golden. Drain on paper towel.

Serve warm with lime halves and the ricotta dipping sauce.

Makes 24

LAMB SHOULDER AND QUINOA SALAD
ONE QUIET NIGHT

I'M HAPPY TO SAY THAT THE ONLY WAY YOU CAN STUFF UP THE COOKING OF A LAMB SHOULDER IS IF YOUR OVEN EXPLODES. YEP, THIS IS SUNDAY-NIGHT ROAST EATING AT ITS FINEST. THE LAMB COOKS FOR HOURS, TRANSFORMING YOUR HOUSE INTO GUSTATORY HEAVEN, SO WHEN THE NEIGHBOURS WALK THEIR DOGS PAST YOU CAN HEAR THEM EFFUSING, 'OH MY GOD, THAT DINNER SMELLS AMAZING'.

ON A DAY SPENT IN, IT'S THE LITTLE THINGS THAT COUNT.

INGREDIENTS

1 tbsp rosemary leaves, bruised
3 tbsp roughly chopped lemon thyme
½ tbsp sage leaves, bruised
4 garlic cloves, finely chopped
1 tbsp olive oil
2 kg (4 lb 8 oz) boned shoulder of lamb, trimmed of excess fat and at room temperature
3 red onions, thinly sliced
250 ml (9 fl oz/1 cup) white wine
2 preserved lemon quarters, rinsed, flesh removed, peel thinly sliced
130 g (4¾ oz/¾ cup) dried black olives, thinly sliced

Salad

200 g (7 oz/1 cup) quinoa
1 bunch spring onions (scallions)
10 French shallots, peeled
1 large handful watercress or beetroot or mustard leaves
a large handful of mint leaves, torn
80 ml (2½ fl oz/⅓ cup) olive oil
60 ml (2 fl oz/¼ cup) sherry vinegar
sea salt and freshly ground black pepper

Preheat the oven to 100°C (200°F/Gas ½).

Combine the herbs and garlic in a bowl, add the oil, then massage into the lamb.

Heat a large non-stick frying pan over high heat and sear the lamb on all sides until browned. Set aside. Return the pan to the heat, turn down to low, add the oil and sweat the onion until translucent.

Transfer the onion to a large roasting tin and place the lamb on top. Slow cook the lamb in the oven for 3 hours, basting on occasion. Remove the lamb from the heat, turn, scatter on the preserved lemon and dried olives, pour over the white wine and return to the oven for a further 3 hours. Cover with foil and set aside to rest.

For the salad, place the quinoa in a large saucepan with 500 ml (17 fl oz/2 cups) of water. Bring to the boil. Reduce the heat to medium and simmer for 8 minutes, or until the quinoa is cooked (the grain should have a natural crunch). Drain, fluff the grains with a fork and leave to cool.

Place the spring onions in a chargrill pan on low heat, turning quickly so the outside chars and the inside caramelises. Discard the blackened outside skin and transfer to a bowl to cool. Just before serving combine the quinoa, spring onions, shallots, watercress and mint in a large bowl.

Whisk the oil and vinegar in a small bowl, season with the salt and pepper and toss through the salad.

Shred the lamb into large pieces and serve with the quinoa and grilled onion salad.

Serves 4 with a few leftovers for lunch

LINDT CHOCOLATE PUDDINGS
THE SWEET SPOT

YES, I DID JUST SAY LINDT. LOTS OF IT.
AND, YES, THIS PUDDIN' IS ABSOLUTELY
FREAKIN' AWESOME.

INGREDIENTS
8 Lindt white chocolate balls
200 g (7 oz) dark chocolate (70 per cent
  cocoa solids), chopped
100 g (3½ oz) butter, chopped
3 eggs
115 g (4 oz/½ cup) caster (superfine) sugar
2 tbsp plain (all-purpose) flour

Topping
100 g (3½ oz) milk chocolate, chopped
25 g (1 oz) butter

To serve
vanilla bean ice cream or gelato

Place the white chocolate balls in the freezer for at least an hour.

Preheat the oven to 200°C (400°F/Gas 6).

Place the dark chocolate and butter in a heatproof bowl over a saucepan of gently simmering water and stir until just melted. Set aside to cool.

Place the eggs, sugar and flour in a bowl and mix until just combined. Gradually stir in the melted chocolate mixture. Pour the mixture into four 250 ml (9 fl oz/1 cup) ramekins and place on a baking tray. Gently push two white chocolate balls into the centre of the mixture until just submerged. Bake for 15 minutes until the edges are set.

While the puddings are baking, make the topping. Melt the chocolate and butter in a heatproof bowl over a saucepan of gently simmering water and stir until smooth.

Pour the milk chocolate topping over the puddings and serve with ice cream or gelato.

Serves 4

LINDT
choc puddings

Reacquainting with acquaintances

Friends come and go. Not the true friends, but the transient ones who fall off the radar after misunderstandings over money, successes, failures and troubled relationships, to become an acquaintance and friend from lives past.

Then there are the other ones. You know when you were once inseparable and swore you came from the same mother until they, or at the very least something in the dynamic, changed, leaving you despondently clutching your melting Mars Bars and BFF bracelet in a cloud of dust.

A lot of spicy spatchcock, plums and pinot passes under the bridge, memories fade, and then by way of personal crisis, loneliness, sheer random run-in, or a cruel bout of Facebook stalking, the friendship is awkwardly reignited.

Someone once said to me the only friends you should surround yourself with are those who'd go 'Rhonda' on anyone who did or said anything to hurt you. Remember Rhonda — Muriel's fabulous friend and saviour in *Muriel's Wedding*? I always loved the take-down at Chook and Tania's hibiscus wedding:

> 'Stick your drink up your arse, Tania. I'd rather swallow razor blades than drink with you. Oh, and by the way, I'm not alone. I'm with Muriel.'

You might be unsure about the friendship, but rest assured the cooking manages the 'caring' component of reacquainting with an acquaintance. The rest is up to you.

Menu

Quince and blue cheese pastry

—

Chocolate ricotta kisses

—

Butterscotch and white chocolate muffins

QUINCE AND BLUE CHEESE PASTRY

GONE WITH THE WIND

THIS PASTRY IS LIKE A RESURRECTED FRIENDSHIP; THE SWEETNESS OF THE QUINCE IS LIKE A WARM HUG FROM THE PAST — COMFORTING AND ALL-KNOWING. THE TANG OF CHEESE ADDS THE SLIGHTLY BITTERSWEET TASTE OF RESENTMENT.

INGREDIENTS
2 tsp water
170 g (6 oz) blue cheese, softened
1 tbsp sugar
¼ tsp natural vanilla extract
170 g (6 oz/⅔ cup) quince paste
1 tbsp lemon juice
1 sheet puff pastry
1 large egg, whisked for egg wash

Preheat the oven to 220°C (425°F/Gas 7). Line a baking tray with baking paper and set aside.

Place the blue cheese, sugar and vanilla in a bowl and stir until well combined. Combine the quince paste and lemon juice in a bowl and stir until smooth.

Roll out the pastry to a 27 x 22 cm (11 x 9 inch) rectangle on a lightly floured surface, then cut rectangle in half. Place the other piece on the prepared tray and spread the blue cheese mixture down the middle, leaving a border of about 3 cm (1¼ inches) on all sides. Dollop the quince mixture along the centre of the cheese mixture.

Fold the remaining pastry in half lengthways, putting the folded edge closest to you. Leaving a 3 cm (1¼ inch) border on the sides and top, cut slits through the folded edge to create a criss-cross effect. Brush on the egg wash, then gently unfold the cut pastry and lay over the filling. Press down on the edges to seal. Bake for 20 minutes until golden.

This is best served warm.

Serves 4–6

CHOCOLATE RICOTTA KISSES

FRENEMIES

I'VE LEFT THE QUANTITY FAIRLY LARGE, AS IT'S HARD TO KEEP THESE BUNDLES OF MAGIC ON A PLATE.

INGREDIENTS
230 g (8 oz/1 cup) ricotta
2 eggs
75 g (2¾ oz/½ cup) strong 00 flour (bakers' flour)
30 g (1 oz/¼ cup) unsweetened cocoa powder
1½ tsp baking powder
½ tsp ground cinnamon
a pinch of salt
1 tbsp caster (superfine) sugar
½ tsp natural vanilla extract
vegetable oil, for frying
2 tsp icing (confectioners') sugar

Combine the ricotta and eggs in a bowl and mix until smooth. Sift in the flour, cocoa, baking powder, cinnamon, salt and caster sugar. Add the vanilla and mix to form a smooth batter.

Fill a deep frying pan with vegetable oil to a depth of 2 cm (¾ inch). Heat over medium heat until a dollop of batter sizzles when dropped in the oil. Drop dessertspoons of batter, about four at a time, into the pan. When the batter puffs and a golden-brown crust appears on the underside (about 90 seconds), flip the kisses and allow to brown again for another minute. Transfer to paper towel to drain. Continue until you have used all the batter.

Plate the kisses and sift over the icing sugar. Serve immediately.

Makes 30

BUTTERSCOTCH AND WHITE CHOCOLATE MUFFINS
GET THEE BEHIND ME NOSTALGIA

SEX AND THE CITY PUT A LOT OF UNNECESSARY PRESSURE ON FEMALE FRIENDSHIPS. CARRIE AND HER POSSE OF SHOE-LOVING PROSTITUTES WERE ALL ABOUT HUGGING, LEARNING AND GROWING AS PEOPLE UNDER THE RISQUÉ GUISE OF SEXUAL COMPLICATION AND HIGH-END FASHION BUT, IN THE REAL WORLD, THE MORE SUPERFICIAL FRIENDSHIPS ARE DRIVEN MAINLY BY SELF-SERVING INSTINCTS. TOXIC FRIENDSHIPS ARE RARELY RECOGNISED, AND NOTHING IS DONE TO EVICT SUCH FRIENDS FROM OUR OTHERWISE HAPPY LIVES. DISTANCE IS ATTEMPTED, THEN A PHONE CALL, A CHANCE RUN-IN AND THE NOSTALGIA FOR WHAT WE ONCE HAD SEEMS TO FAR OUTWEIGH BREAKING UP WITH SO-CALLED 'FRIENDS'. BEFORE YOU KNOW IT, YOU'VE LOVINGLY WELCOMED THEM BACK INTO THE FOLD. AND PROBABLY WITH A HUG AND A BUTTERSCOTCH AND WHITE CHOCOLATE MUFFIN.

INGREDIENTS

300 g (10½ oz/2 cups) plain (all-purpose) flour
1 tsp baking powder
pinch salt
100 g (3½ oz) white chocolate chips, plus extra to sprinkle
100 g (3½ oz) butterscotch morsels
110 g (3¾ oz/½ cup) caster (superfine) sugar
2 eggs, lightly beaten
250 ml (9 fl oz/1 cup) milk
60 ml (2 fl oz/¼ cup) melted butter

Butterscotch sauce

170 ml (5½ fl oz/⅔ cup) cream
165 g (5¾ oz/¾ cup) soft brown sugar, firmly packed
50 g (1¾ oz) butter, cubed
2 tsp natural vanilla extract

Preheat the oven to 190°C (375°F/Gas 5). Line a muffin tin with paper cases and set aside.

For the butterscotch sauce, place the cream, sugar, butter and vanilla in a heavy-based saucepan and stir over medium heat for 5 minutes. Bring to the boil, then reduce the heat to low and simmer, stirring often, for 5 minutes, or until the sauce thickens. Set aside until cooled.

Mix the flour, baking powder, salt, chocolate chips, sugar and butterscotch morsels in a bowl. Add the eggs, milk and butter, stirring only enough to dampen the flour; the batter should not be smooth. Add three-quarters of the butterscotch sauce, and stir once or twice, being careful not to overwork the mixture.

Spoon into the prepared muffin tin and gently pour the remaining butterscotch sauce over the top. Sprinkle on the remaining chocolate chips and bake for 20–25 minutes or until a skewer inserted comes out clean.

Makes 6 jumbo or 12 regular muffins

CHAPTER SEVEN

A TIME FOR FUSS

It is such a generous and thoughtful thing to invite people into your home. It's the time when you clean the house, buy flowers, dust off the fine china and wheel out your own personal 'best of' collection. The key, with all the window dressing on such occasions, both literal and figurative, is to never let it spill over into the food.

Sadly, having people over for an occasion is a dying tradition. I'm not sure why but the idea has become unmentionable and seems to invoke a stressful sense of duty and stiffness. People are afraid to have others over, but it's brave and real. And a completely different experience. You can spend five hours at a table, roll onto the couch, then have fights on anything from politics to holiday destinations while feeding the dog your scraps. You and your guests can get properly hammered and let your hair down in a way that might not work quite so well in a public setting.

It's time for a full-on comeback.

Cooking for the potential in-laws

The concept of in-laws is truly bizarre. How, in this day and age when arranged marriage is largely a thing of the past, did something as important as adding to our 'family' leave us with absolutely no opportunity for selection whatsoever. It's frightening. And cruel. And further complicated by the fact that it is incredibly difficult to know what to cook for an entirely new category of people who in an indeterminable period of time you will be calling your own.

I once cooked for some potentials, and it was a Hiroshima-like disaster. The smoke from the barbecue and our fake conversation was odourless, colourless and deadly. I had visions of its toxicity spreading to my neighbours and the surrounding suburbs. Static radios hissing and crackling with community health announcements urging people to retreat indoors; with children being plucked from parks and sandpits for fear of radioactive jump-ropes, dirty dirt pies and toxic swing sets, while my 'potentials' sat stony faced, placing the kiss of certain and excruciating death on my relationship with their offspring.

Menu 1

Harissa tomato soup with smoky Welsh rarebit toasties

–

Caramelised chipotle chicken with chipotle glaze and parsnip fries

–

Fig, raspberry, pistachio and burnt-butter cake with mascarpone

Menu 2

Mustard miso beef with Japanese salad

–

Pork belly and crab salad

–

Sticky date syrup pudding

HARISSA TOMATO SOUP WITH SMOKY WELSH RAREBIT TOASTIES

THE HAND THAT ROCKS THE LADLE

LIKE SO MANY OTHER BIG LIFE OCCASIONS, YOU'LL MAKE IT TO THE OTHER SIDE RELATIVELY UNSCATHED. THE CONVERSATION WILL BE MILDLY ANNOYING AT BEST, YOUR IN-LAWS CRUEL OBNOXIOUS FOOLS AT WORST. THINK OF IT LIKE A MILESTONE. A RELATIONSHIP, LIKE FOOD, NEEDS CURIOSITY; THE MOMENT IT BECOMES FAMILIAR, IT'S NO LONGER A CHALLENGE. ULTIMATELY IT IS AN IDEAL OPPORTUNITY TO DISCOVER WHAT YOU ARE IN FOR.

SOUP SEEMS A BIT HUMDRUM TO SERVE WHEN TRYING TO IMPRESS — BUT ROASTED TOMATO SOUP IS DEAD EASY AND THE TASTE IS, QUITE POSSIBLY, PURE CULINARY MAGIC.

INGREDIENTS

2 thick slices of day-old sourdough bread
    (about 80 g/2¾ oz), torn into chunks
800 g (1 lb 12 oz) vine-ripened tomatoes,
    blanched, peeled and cut into rough chunks
1 garlic clove, finely chopped
2 tsp harissa paste
a squeeze of lemon juice
30 ml (1 fl oz) nip of tequila
2 tbsp tomato paste
sea salt and freshly ground black pepper
1½ tbsp olive oil
2 tbsp sherry vinegar
a pinch of caster (superfine) sugar
1 tsp paprika
a handful of coriander (cilantro) leaves,
    roughly chopped

Spiced rarebit toastie

50 g (1¾ oz) butter
1 tbsp plain (all-purpose) flour
80 ml (2½ fl oz/⅓ cup) beer
1 tsp smoked paprika
1 tsp ground coriander
110 g (3¾ oz) haloumi, grated
110 g (3¾ oz) strong smoked
    cheddar, grated
1 egg yolk
4 slices of sourdough bread

Blitz the bread in a food processor until you have coarse breadcrumbs. Add the tomato, garlic, harissa, lemon juice, tequila and tomato paste and blend until smooth. Season and, while the motor is running, slowly add the oil. Transfer to a large saucepan and place over low heat. Stir in the vinegar and sugar and continue to stir for 5 minutes until the sugar has dissolved and the soup is warmed through. If the soup is too thick, add a dash of water.

Combine the paprika and coriander in a small bowl and set aside.

For the toastie, melt the butter in a saucepan over low heat, stir in the flour and cook, stirring constantly, for 1 minute. Add the beer, spices and cheeses, and stir until creamy, but don't allow to boil. Remove from the heat and mix in the egg yolk until well combined.

Toast the bread slices, then evenly spread with the spiced rarebit mixture, and place under a hot grill (broiler) until bubbling.

Pour the soup into four large glasses or soup bowls, top with a pinch of the reserved coriander and paprika and serve with a rarebit toastie.

Serves 4

CARAMELISED CHIPOTLE CHICKEN WITH CHIPOTLE GLAZE AND PARSNIP FRIES

BAKED GLUTTONY

THE EPIC TASTE OF THIS SMOKY, DARK AND INTENSE CHICKEN WILL PROVE TO THE MOTHER-IN-LAW THAT YOU COULD TURN SOWS' EARS INTO SILK PURSES.

THIS DISH ISN'T SHY WITH THE GARLIC, WHICH IF SUPERSTITION IS TO BE BELIEVED HELPS WARD OFF EVIL SPIRITS — THAT CERTAINLY CAN'T HURT THE SITUATION AT HAND.

PREPARE THE GLAZE IN ADVANCE — IT WILL KEEP FOR UP TO A WEEK SEALED IN THE FRIDGE. I'VE LEFT THE QUANTITY FAIRLY LARGE HERE — IT'S TOO GOOD NOT TO HAVE LEFTOVERS. AND IT'S PERFECT ON ANYTHING FROM COLD MEAT SANDWICHES TO SCRAMBLED EGGS.

INGREDIENTS

Glaze

2 tbsp olive oil

1 onion, finely chopped

5 garlic cloves, finely chopped

800 g (1 lb 12 oz) roma (plum) tomatoes

300 ml (10½ fl oz) orange juice

300 ml (10½ fl oz) chicken stock

85 g (3 oz) tinned chipotle chillis

75 g (2¾ oz/⅓ cup) soft brown sugar, firmly packed

a large handful of coriander (cilantro) leaves, roughly chopped, plus extra to serve

Chicken

1½ tbsp olive oil

4 garlic cloves, smashed

1 onion, finely chopped

60 g (2¼ oz/¼ cup) tomato paste

60 g (2¼ oz/¼ cup) smoky barbecue sauce

3 dried chipotle chillis, softened in warm water and finely chopped

1 tbsp worcestershire sauce

2 tsp kecap manis

sea salt and freshly ground black pepper

1 x 1.6 kg (3 lb 8 oz) chicken jointed into 8 pieces

Parsnip fries

1 tbsp olive oil

8–10 parsnips, peeled and cut into thin sticks

35 g (1¼ oz/¼ cup) sea salt

Garlic salt

a good pinch of celery salt

a good pinch of sea salt

a good pinch of dried garlic

01

Preheat the oven to 220°C (425°F/Gas 7).

02

For the glaze, heat the oil in a large frying pan over medium heat, add the onion and garlic and sauté for 7-10 minutes, or until caramelised. Add the remaining ingredients and reduce the heat to low. Cover and cook, stirring occasionally, for 30 minutes until the sauce thickens. Remove from the heat and blitz in a food processor until thick and smooth. Set aside.

03

For the chicken sauce, heat the oil in a frying pan over medium heat and cook the onion and garlic until softened. Add the tomato paste, barbecue sauce, chipotles, worcestershire sauce and kecap manis. Turn the heat to low and simmer for 25 minutes. Season with salt and pepper.

04

Seal the chicken in a large frying pan over medium heat until just browned all over. Remove and place snugly in a 6 cm (2½ inches) deep, 8 cup capacity ovenproof dish.

05

Pour the sauce over the chicken, turning to evenly coat the pieces. Roast in the oven for 25 minutes, turn the chicken pieces and cook for an additional 20 minutes.

06

For the fries, add the oil and parsnip to a roasting tin, season with salt and toss to coat. Roast for 30 minutes, or until the parsnip is golden.

07

For the garlic salt, combine the salts and garlic in a small bowl and set aside.

08

Remove the chicken from the oven and set aside covered. Pour the glaze from the roasting dish into a saucepan and cook over a low heat until reduced by a third.

09

Plate the chicken, drizzle over the glaze and serve with the hot parsnip fries and garlic salt on the side. Scatter over the extra coriander if using.

This is also great with a simple green side salad of shredded cucumber, coriander and mint.

Serves 4

FIG, RASPBERRY, PISTACHIO AND BURNT-BUTTER CAKE WITH MASCARPONE

FIG IT

MY FIRST IN-LAW BAKING ATTEMPT WAS A LEMON SYRUP CAKE. QUELLE DISASTER. IT WAS MEANT TO BE A THANK YOU FOR RUSHING ME TO THE HOSPITAL WHEN I COULDN'T SWALLOW AND ALLOWING ME TO LIVE UNDER THEIR ROOF WHILE I WAS JOBLESS AND SINKING IN DEBT FOLLOWING A DRUNKEN, EXTENDED JAUNT OVERSEAS. IN BETWEEN CREATING AN IMPRESSION THAT I WAS WARMING UP FOR LIFE AS A LADY OF LEISURE AND THE POTENTIAL ONSET OF SOME KIND OF STRANGE THROAT-INDUCED PALSY, MY CAKE LEFT THEM VERY FRIGHTENED FOR THE FUTURE.

WHO AM I DEAR IN-LAWS? WHY, I AM THE MALFUNCTIONING CAKE KILLER. I'M LUCKY I LACK THE PHYSICAL PROPORTIONS TO APPEAR THREATENING OR THEY WOULD HAVE TAKEN THEIR SON AND RUN.

BAKING IS A KITCHEN ALCHEMY REQUIRING PRECISION, FOCUS AND CONCENTRATION. LUCKILY, THIS CAKE IS FORGIVING AND THERE IS ENOUGH FRUIT TO HOLD THE CAKE TOGETHER LONG ENOUGH FOR YOU TO STICK YOUR MIDDLE FINGER UP THE IDEA OF ANY IN-LAWS AT ALL.

INGREDIENTS

6 figs, thinly sliced
100 g (3½ oz) raspberries
60 g (2 oz) pistachio nuts, roughly chopped
120 g (4¼ oz) unsalted butter, roughly
  chopped and chilled
165 g (5¾ oz /¾ cup) caster (superfine) sugar
3 large eggs, separated
300 g (10½ oz /2 cups) self-raising
  flour, sifted

Caramel

50 g (1¾ oz) unsalted butter
1 vanilla bean, split lengthways and
  seeds scraped
70 g (2½ oz /⅓ cup) demerara sugar
2 tbsp golden syrup (light treacle)

To serve

150 g (5½ oz) raspberries
80 g (2¾ oz/¼ cup) pistachio nuts,
  roughly chopped
125 g (4⅓ oz/½ cup) mascarpone

Preheat the oven to 170°C (325°F/Gas 3). Line a 25 cm (10 inch) round cake tin with baking paper and set aside.

For the caramel, combine the butter and vanilla bean and seeds in a saucepan over medium–high heat and cook for 4–5 minutes until the mixture turns a nutty, dark brown colour. Cool slightly and remove the vanilla bean. Add the sugar and golden syrup and stir until the sugar has dissolved.

Combine the figs, raspberries and ground pistachios in a bowl and set aside.

Cream the butter and sugar until pale and fluffy. Beat in the egg yolks and gently fold in flour. Whisk the egg whites in a separate bowl until stiff peaks form and fold into the egg yolk mixture. Pour into the prepared tin and gently sprinkle on the fig and pistachio mixture. Bake for 35 minutes. Remove the cake from the oven and, working quickly, pour on the caramel. Return to the oven for 15 minutes, or until the fruit is looking dark and golden and a skewer inserted into the middle of the cake comes out clean.

To serve, place the cake on a serving platter. Scatter the extra raspberries and pistachios on top. Slice and top with a healthy dollop of mascarpone..

Serves 4–6

MUSTARD MISO BEEF WITH JAPANESE SALAD
JAPANESE FUNHOUSE

BEGIN WITH LOVING COUPLE (HIS PARENTS) AND FORNICATION (DON'T LAUGH, IT HAPPENED). ENTER CHILDREN. TWO, MAYBE THREE. MOTHER BASKS IN MATERNAL GLORY. CHILDREN LOVE THEIR MUM, RAGE TOP 50, 7 ELEVEN SLURPEES, REDSKINS AND BUILDING FORTS. THEN EACH CHILD IS GIVEN WINGS. CHILDREN FLY FAR FROM THE NEST (WITH THE ODD MOVE IN AND OUT BY WAY OF VARIOUS CRISES). TRAGEDY STRIKES WHEN GROWN MAN-CHILD FINDS LOVE IN THE ARMS OF ANOTHER. MOTHER DEFLATES AND PARENTAL UNIT BECOMES DEFENSIVE. EMOTIONALLY DIABOLICAL SITUATION ENSUES …

AND THEN YOU INVITE THEM FOR DINNER.

AND RIGHT THERE, NO MATTER HOW YOU PLAY IT, IS THE PROBLEM. THERE ARE SOME MOTHERS-IN-LAW WHO ABSOLUTELY DESPISE YOU FOR THE REASONS THAT MOTHERS-IN-LAW GENERALLY DESPISE ANYONE WHO IS MARRYING THEIR OFFSPRING. SO NOW YOU KNOW IT ISN'T YOU, TRY AND ENJOY YOUR TEA.

YOU'LL NEED TO **BEGIN THIS RECIPE A DAY AHEAD.**

INGREDIENTS

125 ml (4 fl oz /½ cup) mirin
125 ml (4 fl oz /½ cup) sake
60 ml (2 fl oz /¼ cup) soy sauce
2 tbsp soft brown sugar
1 tbsp white miso paste
2 tsp Japanese mustard powder
   (if you can't find Japanese mustard powder, replace with wasabi)
350 g (12 oz) wagyu beef
1 garlic clove, finely chopped
1 tbsp olive oil
750 ml (26 fl oz /3 cups) water
150 g (5½ oz) packet of udon noodles
1 red radish, thinly sliced
1 tbsp sesame seeds, toasted
30 g (1 oz /1 cup) watercress
1 small red onion, finely chopped
a large handful of coriander (cilantro) leaves, chopped
40 g (1½ oz /½ cup) dried sweetened coconut chips

Combine the mirin, sake, soy sauce, sugar and miso paste in a saucepan over medium heat and cook, stirring occasionally, until slightly thickened. Remove from the heat and stir in the mustard powder. Pour into a non-reactive bowl, add the beef and garlic, cover with plastic wrap and refrigerate overnight (or for at least 2 hours).

Preheat the oven to 200°C (400°F/Gas 6).

Heat a flameproof roasting tin over high heat and add the oil. Remove the beef from the marinade, reserving the juices, add to the tin and cook until sealed on all sides and the meat looks just browned all over. Transfer the tin to the oven and roast for 10 minutes for medium-rare (if a thick cut of steak), or until cooked to your liking. Cover with foil and rest in a warm place for 5 minutes.

While the beef is in the oven, bring the water to the boil in a saucepan. Add the udon noodles and cook according to the packet instructions. Drain and tip into a large bowl. Add the radish, sesame seeds, watercress, onion and coriander.

Pour the reserved meat juices into a saucepan and cook over high heat for 1 minute, or until warmed through and reduced by a third. Toss through the noodle mixture.

Thinly slice the beef. Plate the noodles and top with the slices of beef. Sprinkle over the coconut chips and serve.

Serves 4

PORK BELLY
AND CRAB SALAD

EASTERN PROMISES

ENTERTAINING THE IN-LAWS IS NOT THE TIME FOR SHORT SHORTS THAT SHOW WHAT YOU ATE FOR LUNCH, BREASTS THAT SWING LOW (SWEET CHARIOT) … NOR THE REEF 'N' BEEF COMBO. NO OTHER DUO IN HISTORY, APART FROM WINNIE BLUES AND VB CANS, COULD SCREAM BOGAN MORE LOUDLY. NORMALLY I AM ALLERGIC TO MEAT AND FISH AFFECTATIONS, BUT THIS MORE HIGHBROW VERSION IS TRULY SENSATIONAL, TASTES LIKE YOU SLAVED AWAY FOR HOURS, AND WILL HAVE THE IN-LAWS UNDER YOUR THUMB BEFORE YOU CAN ASK 'OWS IT GARN?'.

INGREDIENTS

1 x 600 g (1 lb 5 oz) pork belly
400 g (14 oz) picked fresh crabmeat
1 small red chilli, thinly sliced
1 green papaya, finely shredded using a
    mandolin or grater
3 kaffir lime leaves,
    finely chopped
50 g (1¾ oz) fresh coconut, shaved
a small handful of coriander (cilantro) leaves
a small handful of Vietnamese
    mint leaves
a small handful of Thai basil leaves
65 g (2½ oz/½ cup)
    crushed peanuts
1 tsp peanut oil

Dressing

1 tbsp grated palm sugar
1 tbsp fish sauce
2 tsp lemon juice
1 tbsp water

Place the pork in a saucepan, cover with cold water and bring to the boil over high heat. Reduce the heat to low and simmer for 2 hours. Drain the pork, transfer to a bowl, cover and refrigerate.

For the dressing, place the sugar, fish sauce, lemon juice and water in a bowl and stir until the sugar dissolves.

Combine the crabmeat, chilli, papaya, kaffir lime leaves, coconut, herbs and peanuts in a large bowl and gently toss.

Cut the pork into small cubes. Heat a non-stick frying pan over high heat, add the oil and pork and sauté for 3 minutes until the pork is crisp. Drain on paper towel. Add to the salad, pour over the dressing, and serve immediately.

Serves 4

STICKY DATE
SYRUP PUDDING

PUDDING AND PEAKS

INDULGING IN A WELL-BAKED STICKY PUDDING — THE TYPE THAT MAKES YOU DIG IN AND BURN THE ROOF OF YOUR MOUTH WITH THE SPOON ONLY TO COOL IT SECONDS LATER WITH ICE CREAM OR CUSTARD — IS THE EARTH'S WAY OF SHOWING US EVERYTHING IS OKAY. THIS IS IMPORTANT AT A TIME WHEN THE CONVERSATION IS HEAVY WITH EXPECTATION. A LIGHT DATE-LACED SPONGE SLATHERED IN A BUTTERY TOFFEE SAUCE HAS ENJOYED A CULT FOLLOWING FOR DECADES — A MORE-THAN-FAIR INDICATION THAT THIS DISH CAN ONLY IMPRESS.

INGREDIENTS

200 g (7 oz) pitted dates
375 ml (13 fl oz/1½ cups)
   boiling water
1 tsp bicarbonate of soda
150 g (5½ oz/1 cup) self-raising flour, sifted
1 tsp ground ginger
110 g (3¾ oz/½ cup) soft brown sugar,
   firmly packed
70 g (2½ oz) unsalted butter, melted
1 egg, lightly beaten
60 ml (2 fl oz/¼ cup) milk
1 tbsp golden syrup (light treacle)
1 tsp natural vanilla extract

Syrup

100 g (3½ oz/½ cup) soft brown sugar, lightly
   packed
2 tbsp golden syrup (light treacle)
150 ml (5 fl oz) hot water

To serve

vanilla bean ice cream

Preheat the oven to 190°C (375°F/Gas 5). Lightly grease four 250 ml (9 fl oz/1 cup) ramekins and set aside.

Cover the dates with the boiling water, add the bicarbonate of soda and set aside to soften for 20 minutes. Drain and finely chop the dates.

Combine the flour, ground ginger and sugar in a bowl. Add the butter, egg, milk, golden syrup and vanilla and stir until everything is combined. Stir in the chopped dates and spoon the batter evenly into the prepared ramekins.

For the syrup, mix the sugar, golden syrup and hot water together until the sugar has dissolved and a thin syrup has formed.

Carefully pour 2 tablespoons of the syrup evenly over the batter in the ramekins.

Bake for 20 minutes, or until just firm. Serve with the ice cream.

Serves 4

Vegetarian friends

A vegetarian friend of mine went to a wedding where she was served a slightly warm square of tofu on a plate, no salad, no dressing, no seasoning — and to add insult to injury, a glass of Fanta (obviously, if you don't eat meat, you don't drink wine). How rude, inconsiderate and backward. Our vegetarian friends continue to be marginalised, ostracised and left with scant dining choices.

It's a wonder they're allowed to vote.

Thoughtless menus and sometimes-thoughtless friends see the big Vs outed at restaurants, and left with the side dishes to act as a main meal. It's probably why they are generally thinner and why they are usually so nice about being invited over for dinner because they are grateful to have somewhere to go. So they deserve a bit of fuss, a bit of looking after at our dinner table, and some choices that move beyond the tofu option.

And the Fanta.

Maybe the lack of vegetarian menu options is the result of jealousy on our meat-eating part. Vegetarians get to be a bit sanctimonious about meat-eaters living a life of denial about all those slaughtered animals and saturated fats clogging our arteries — not to mention what our meat-eating ways are doing to the planet. And what makes it even worse, while they bask in their ecologically correct glory, is that all our meat-eating presumptions about vegetarians are simply not true. They are not all pale and wan and listless. They are generally vibrant, dynamic and lovely people. And credit where credit is due — their cupboards are stocked with puy lentils, split peas and all those types of ingredients that take longer than your natural life to cook. That shows dedication.

And probably regular bowel movements worthy of a TV show.

Menu

Burnt butter, sage and
pumpkin pancakes
with apple, celery and
walnut salad

–

Zucchini flower, caramelised
red onion and goat's
curd tart

–

Vodka-spiked tomato, three
cheese and olive bread
pudding

–

Sticky roasted pumpkin and
chickpea dumplings with
smoked aïoli and cumin salt

–

Edamame 'n' beans with
ginger, miso and walnuts

–

Mushroom and
celeriac lasagne

BURNT BUTTER, SAGE
AND PUMPKIN PANCAKES WITH APPLE,
CELERY AND WALNUT SALAD

FOOD FOR
THOUGHT

VEGETARIAN RESTAURANTS ARE, ON AVERAGE, DISGUSTING. VEGETABLES, HOWEVER, ARE NOT. THEY ARE AMAZING — ONE OF THE BEST FOODS ON THE PLANET, RIGHT UP THERE WITH MEAT AND FISH. AND THERE IS CERTAINLY UNBELIEVABLE FOOD THAT IS VEGETARIAN LIKE THESE BURNT BUTTER, SAGE AND PUMPKIN PANCAKES.

INGREDIENTS
Salad
30 g (1 oz/¼ cup) halved walnuts
2 celery stalks, finely chopped
2 red delicious apples, cored and thinly sliced
    into matchsticks
35 g (1¼ oz/½ cup)
    shaved gruyere
60 ml (2 fl oz) apple cider vinegar
30 ml (1 fl oz) olive oil
juice of 1 lemon juice

Pancakes
150 ml (5 fl oz) buttermilk
165 g (5¾ oz) pureed butternut pumpkin
    (squash)
1 egg
85 g (2¾ oz) butter
a small handful of sage leaves
190 g (6¾ oz) plain (all-purpose) flour
1 tsp bicarbonate soda
1 tsp allspice
1 tsp ground cinnamon
1 tsp ground ginger
pinch salt

For the salad, combine the walnuts, celery, apple and cheese in a bowl. Whisk the vinegar, oil and lemon juice in a small bowl, pour over the salad and toss to combine.

For the pancakes, mix together the buttermilk, pumpkin and egg in a bowl. In a separate bowl, sift in the flour, bicarbonate of soda, allspice, cinnamon, ginger and salt, then stir into the pumpkin mixture just enough to combine.

Brown the butter in a frying pan over medium heat until a warm nutty brown colour. Add the sage and quickly fry until crisp and the leaves are dark and start to turn in at the edges. Remove from the heat and gently place the sage leaves on some paper towel.

Heat a lightly oiled frying pan over medium–high heat. For each pancake, pour 60 ml (2 fl oz/¼ cup) of the batter into the pan. Once bubbles begin to appear, scatter over a few sage leaves until they are just submerged in the mixture, then gently flip the pancakes and cook the other side until brown on both sides.

Keep warm.

Stack the pancakes on each plate, top with the salad, and serve hot.

Serves 4

ZUCCHINI FLOWER, CARAMELISED RED ONION AND GOAT'S CURD TART

WHERE'S THE BEEF?

WE ARE THE ONLY ANIMAL WHO CAN CHOOSE WHAT WE EAT, SO WE CAN CHOOSE TO DO WHAT'S HUMANE AND ALSO MUCH HEALTHIER. I RESPECT THIS VEGETARIAN ADAGE, BUT I AM WEAK … THE PULL OF MEAT TOO GREAT — THAT IS, UNTIL GOAT'S CHEESE COMES TO THE TABLE. THIS IS DELICIOUS AND COMPLETELY SATISFYING TO BOTH VEGETARIANS AND THEIR MEAT-EATING FRIENDS.

INGREDIENTS

2 tbsp olive oil
3 leeks, white part only,
    thinly sliced
1 garlic clove, finely chopped
1 tbsp finely grated lemon zest
60 ml (2 fl oz/¼ cup) white wine
sea salt and freshly ground
    black pepper
3 eggs, lightly beaten
120 g (4¼ oz) goat's curd
80 g (2¾ oz/⅔ cup) coarsely grated
    parmesan
2 x 375 g (13 oz) sheets of ready-made
    puff pastry
6 zucchini (courgette) flowers,
    stamens removed
1 tbsp thyme leaves

Caramelised onion jam

2 red onions, thinly sliced
2 tbsp olive oil
2 tbsp balsamic vinegar
1 tbsp soft brown sugar

Preheat the oven to 200°C (400°F/Gas 6). Line a baking tray with baking paper and set aside.

For the onion jam, toss the onion rings in the oil, then cook in a frying pan over medium heat for 10 minutes, or until soft and starting to brown. Add the vinegar and sugar and stir well. Turn the heat to low and cook for a further 10 minutes, or until caramelised.

For the tart, heat the oil in a saucepan over low heat, add the leek, garlic and lemon zest and cook for 2–3 minutes until the leek is soft. Add the wine and simmer for 3 minutes, or until all the liquid is absorbed. Season to taste and set aside to cool.

Combine the leek mixture, eggs, goat's curd and parmesan in a bowl.

Roll out each sheet of pastry on a lightly floured surface to 5 mm (¼ inch) thick and cut into four rectangles about 9 x 20 cm (3½ x 8 inches). Carefully transfer the pastry rectangles to the prepared tray and cut a 1 cm (½ inch) border around the edge, being careful not to cut all the way through. Divide the leek mixture among the pastry rectangles, keeping the filling inside the border.

Carefully stuff each zucchini flower with the onion jam and top the tarts with the filled flowers and scatter the thyme leaves over the top. Bake for 20 minutes, or until puffed and golden.

Serves 4

VODKA–SPIKED TOMATO, THREE CHEESE AND OLIVE BREAD PUDDING

VEGGIE MIGHT

THIS IS A NEVER-FAIL HOMELY WINNER. BAKED IN THE OVEN UNTIL SLIGHTLY PUFFY, THIS EGGY, DENSER BAKED VERSION OF A CAPONATA SALAD IS BRILLIANT SERVED WITH SOME SIMPLE GREENS.

INGREDIENTS

1.3 kg (3 lb) roma (plum) tomatoes, halved
125 ml (4¹/₄ fl oz/¹/₂ cup) vodka
2 tbsp balsamic vinegar
2 tbsp brown sugar
125 ml (4¹/₄ fl oz/¹/₂ cup) olive oil
1 tsp grated lemon zest
10 thick slices olive sourdough
   cut into cubes
375 ml (13 fl oz/1¹/₂ cups) milk
250 ml (9 fl oz/1 cup) cream
8 eggs
1 cup fontina cheese, grated
120 g (4¹/₄ oz/1 cup) parmesan, grated
2 large buffalo mozzarella balls, torn
a small handful of basil leaves, coarsely torn
salt and freshly ground pepper to season

Preheat oven to 180°C (350°F/Gas 4). Grease a large 20 x 30 cm (13 x 9 inch) baking dish and set aside.

Stir together vodka, vinegar, sugar, half the olive oil and zest until sugar has dissolved. Pour over tomatoes and gently toss to coat. Pour into a shallow baking dish and roast in the oven cut side up and roast for 40 minutes.

Toss the bread cubes in the remaining oil and roast in the oven until brown and crisp for 5–10 minutes. Remove and allow to cool.

Whisk together milk, cream, eggs, cheeses and basil leaves. Season with salt and pepper. Transfer bread to the baking dish, pour over the egg mixture and gently press the tomatoes in between the bread cubes.

Bake for 30 minutes, or until golden brown on top and firm to touch.

Serves 8

STICKY ROASTED PUMPKIN AND CHICKPEA DUMPLINGS WITH SMOKED AÏOLI AND CUMIN SALT

IN GOOD TASTE

THE TAKE-NO-PRISONERS PUNCH OF THE SMOKED
AÏOLI AND CUMIN SALT MAKES THESE DUMPLINGS SERIOUSLY MORE-ISH WHEN
ACCOMPANYING A BEER OR TWO.

INGREDIENTS
1 kg (2 lb 4 oz) butternut pumpkin (squash),
  peeled and seeds removed
1 tbsp olive oil
½ red onion, finely chopped
70 g (2½ oz/⅓ cup) tinned chickpeas, drained
2 tsp ground cumin
150 ml (5 fl oz) vegetable stock
a small handful of coriander (cilantro) leaves,
  chopped
sea salt and freshly ground
  black pepper
30 wonton wrappers

Aïoli dipping sauce
1 garlic clove, crushed
235 g (8½ oz/1 cup) whole-egg mayonnaise

Cumin salt
2 tsp ground cumin
½ tsp smoked paprika
1 tbsp sea salt

Preheat the oven to 200°C (400°F/Gas 6).

Chop the pumpkin into large chunks, place on a baking tray, drizzle with some of the oil and toss to coat. Roast for 45 minutes, or until beginning to caramelise at the edges.

Combine the pumpkin, onion, chickpeas, cumin, stock and coriander in a food processor, season with the salt and pepper, then blitz until a thick paste forms.

Place a teaspoonful of the pumpkin mixture in the centre of each wanton wrapper. Brush the edges with water, fold to enclose and pinch the edges to seal.

Place a frying pan over high heat and cover the base in a thin coating of oil. Cook the dumplings, in batches, for 2 minutes or until golden and crispy. You can also cook the dumplings, in batches, in a large saucepan of boiling water if you want the healthier option, but be careful — if the seals on your dumplings aren't watertight you might end up with pumpkin water and not much else. The frying option is failsafe. You can pop the dumplings in the oven as you make them — these are best served piping hot.

For the aïoli, combine the garlic and mayonnaise in a small bowl and stir thoroughly.

For the cumin salt, mix the spices with the salt in a small bowl.

Serve the dumplings with the aïoli dipping sauce and the cumin salt.

Serves 4

EDAMAME 'N' BEANS WITH GINGER, MISO AND WALNUTS

MEATLESS INDULGENCE

The combo of edamame, lip-tweaking ginger and a hit of nuts will see you making this time and time again. You can make more of a dish out of it by adding glass noodles and some lightly fried tofu and peanuts.

Edamame is available frozen from most Asian grocers. It's frozen but seems no worse off for it.

INGREDIENTS

120 g (4¼ oz/2 cups) edamame beans
150 g (5½ oz) sugar snap peas
1 tsp grated fresh ginger
150 g (5½ oz/½ cup) white miso paste
65 g (2¼ oz/½ cup) walnuts
2 tbsp light soy sauce
a small handful of mint leaves, coarsely torn
a small handful of coriander leaves, coarsely torn
3 tbsp sesame seeds, toasted

In a blender, combine the ginger, miso, walnuts and soy sauce to make a loose paste. Season and set aside.

Bring a pot of water to the boil over high heat. Blanch and refresh the sugar snap peas and cut on the diagonal. Add the peas to a bowl with the mint, coriander and sesame seeds.

Add the edamame beans (still in their weird hairy pods) to the boiling water for 5 minutes. Drain and when cool enough to handle, push out the pods into the salad bowl.

Pour over the loose paste and toss to combine.
Serve slightly warm.

Serves 4

MUSHROOM AND CELERIAC LASAGNE

WHEN STEAK IS SHUNNED

THIS LASAGNE WILL HAVE YOU DIPPING YOUR TOES IN VEGETARIAN WATERS BEFORE YOU CAN SHOUT HAIRY ARMPITS, MUNG BEANS AND REEF VELCRO SANDALS.

INGREDIENTS

15 g (½ oz/¾ cup) dried porcini mushrooms
375 ml (13 fl oz/1½ cups)
   boiling water
a handful of basil leaves,
   roughly torn
zest of 1 lemon
1 tbsp olive oil
10 g (¼ oz) butter
2 garlic cloves, finely chopped
500 g (1 lb 2 oz) portobello mushrooms,
   thinly sliced
sea salt and freshly ground black pepper
1 celeriac, peeled and thinly sliced
40 g (1½ oz/⅓ cup) grated parmesan, plus
   extra for garnish
190 g (6¾ oz/1½ cups) grated mozzarella
500 g (1 lb 2 oz) ricotta
2 x 30 cm (12 inch) fresh lasagne sheets

Preheat the oven to 200°C (400°F/Gas 6).

Soak the porcini in the water for 15 minutes. Drain, reserving the liquid in a small bowl. Chop the porcini and set aside. Combine the basil, lemon zest and oil in a bowl and set aside.

Place a frying pan over high heat, add the butter and once it starts to bubble, stir in the garlic and portobello mushrooms. Reduce the heat to low and cook, stirring occasionally, for 5 minutes until softened. Add the porcini mushrooms and 2 tablespoons of the reserved porcini liquid. Stir until the liquid has evaporated, season with the salt and pepper and remove from the heat.

Place the celeriac slices on a plate, cover with plastic wrap and microwave on high for 3 minutes. Remove and set aside.

Combine the cheeses and 2 tablespoons of the reserved porcini liquid in a bowl and mix well.

Line a 20 x 30 cm (13 x 9 inch) rectangular ovenproof dish with baking paper and add a sheet of lasagne. Evenly spread half the cheese mixture over the lasagne sheet, top with half the mushroom mixture, smoothing it out to cover the cheese, then add a layer of slightly overlapping slices of celeriac. Repeat the layers, finishing with a sprinkle of the extra parmesan. Cover with another piece of baking paper and bake for 50 minutes, removing the top piece of baking paper for the last 10 minutes of cooking.

Serve the lasagne topped with the reserved basil and lemon mixture.

Serves 4

Dinner parties

People have dinner parties for many different reasons — to spend time with friends, to meet new friends, or to have a buffer when newly formed friendships may need, well, a buffer. Each has benefits for the host and guest.

Dinner parties don't mean candelabras, waitstaff and dishes full of fancy foams and reductions. No one wants to spend a Saturday fluffing egg whites and fine-tuning seating arrangements for mates who bring cheap red wine then dirty your plates and pretty hand towels. But you might like to pick up last Saturday night's shoes from the living room floor and push the lean cuisines to the back of the freezer. It's all about a happy medium — impressing with big flavours and limited fuss.

The full-on shebang (12+) is more challenging to organise, but gives you the opportunity to invite people you would like to get to know better — a gathering of friends of friends. The danger, given its sheer size, is that you could get very panicky and suddenly want everybody out, immediately.

The medium-sized dinner (8+) is a mix of friends and new faces — you can decide if you like someone through the handy filter and judgment of well-known friends.

But to me, the best sort of dinner party is an intimate do — one that inspires expectation, devotion and Nigella Lawson fan-dom as you cook for those you hold nearest and dearest. You don't think twice about the money you spend on ingredients, and it is the perfect Saturday night entertainment option for those who don't really like parties. At parties you meet strangers. It's probably hideously antisocial but the older I get, I really, really want to just meet with my dearest friends.

The following dishes will help you cater for your dinner parties with ease and dexterity — garnering a reputation that might see you holding these soirées a little more often than you'd like.

Menu 1

Roasted quail with golden syrup glaze and goat's curd mash

–

Moroccan lamb tartlet with feta and pomegranates

–

Cardamom and rosewater semifreddo with mango shards

Menu 2

Waldorf sandwiches

–

Spice-crusted veal with masala potatoes and split peas

–

Liquorice bullet deluxe

ROASTED QUAIL WITH GOLDEN SYRUP GLAZE AND GOAT'S CURD MASH
MEAL TICKET

SOME OF US JUST AREN'T CUT OUT FOR COOKING FOR PEOPLE OUTSIDE OF THOSE WE LIVE WITH. YOUR FAMILY ALWAYS EAT THE BURNT BITS, GRUMBLE WHEN IT'S TOO SPICY, TOO BLAND, BLAH BLAH BLAH; YET THERE IS NEVER ANY DOUBT THEY'LL BE THERE AT THE TABLE OR IN THE KITCHEN PICKING AT THE PAN WHEN YOU TURN YOUR BACK THE VERY NEXT DAY. THAT'S JUST WHAT FAMILIES DO. THEN GUESTS ARRIVE, AND AMIDST THE FLURRY OF GETTING OUT THE NICE PLATES WE UNINTENTIONALLY PUT ON AIRS AND GRACES. THE TRUTH IS, THEY TOO WILL LOVE THE BURNT BITS — AND DIPLOMACY ENSURES THEY'LL NEVER TELL YOU THAT IT'S TOO SPICY OR BLAND. EVEN WHEN IT IS.

INGREDIENTS
a handful of thyme sprigs
3 garlic cloves, finely chopped
185 ml (6 fl oz/¾ cup) olive oil
125 ml (4 fl oz/½ cup) brandy
8 quail
sea salt and freshly ground black pepper

Mash
1 kg (2 lb 4 oz) starchy potatoes (such as sebago), peeled and chopped
50 g (1¾ oz) butter
1 garlic clove, finely chopped
120 g (4¼ oz/1 cup) goat's curd
60 ml (2 fl oz/¼ cup) milk

Golden syrup glaze
310 ml (10¾ fl oz/1¼ cups) chicken stock
175 g (6 oz/½ cup) golden syrup (light treacle)

Peas with jamon
60 ml (2 fl oz/¼ cup) olive oil
½ red onion, finely chopped
50 g (1¾ oz) sliced jamon iberico, coarsely torn
310 g (11 oz/2 cups) shelled fresh peas
small handful mint leaves, coarsely torn

Place the thyme, garlic, oil, brandy and quail in a large bowl and toss to coat. Season well with the salt and pepper. Cover and marinate in the fridge for 3 hours.

Preheat the oven to 190°C (375°F/Gas 5). Line a baking tray with baking paper and set aside.

For the mash, place the potato in a saucepan of cold, salted water, bring to the boil and cook for 15 minutes, or until tender. Drain, return to the pan and mash. Stir in the butter, garlic, goat's curd and milk and season well. Keep warm.

Place the quail on the prepared tray, and roast for 8–10 minutes, or until cooked through and golden.

For the glaze, place the stock and golden syrup in a non-stick frying pan over high heat. Bring to the boil and cook for 3–4 minutes, or until slightly thickened.

For the peas with jamon, heat the oil in a saucepan over low heat, add the onion and sauté for 4–5 minutes until soft. Stir in the jamon and cook for 1 minute, then set aside. Bring a saucepan of salted water to the boil, add the peas and cook for 5 minutes until just tender. Drain and add to the onion mixture, season to taste and stir in the mint.

To serve, spoon the mash onto serving plates, top with the quail and spoon on the glaze. Serve with a side of peas and jamon.

Serves 8

MOROCCAN LAMB TARTLET WITH FETA AND POMEGRANATES
PARTY POLITICS

YOU KNOW HOW SOMETIMES WHEN YOU CHUCK A SOIRÉE YOU CAN GET ALL PARANOID THAT YOUR FRIENDS WON'T SHOW UP, THAT THEY MIGHT NOT HAVE FUN, OR THEY MIGHT NOT LIKE THE FOOD? THIS DISH IS YOUR INSURANCE POLICY — IT'S LIKE THE ULTIMATE PARTY ALBUM ON A PLATE AND I DARE SAY GUARANTEES GOOD TIMES ALL ROUND … THERE MIGHT EVEN BE THE ODD FOOT TAP UNDER THE TABLE.

INGREDIENTS
3 tsp ground fennel
3 tsp ground cumin
3 tsp ground coriander
45 ml (1½ fl oz) pomegranate molasses
450 g (1 lb) lamb backstraps
sea salt and freshly ground black pepper
3 garlic cloves, finely chopped
165 g (5¾ oz/¾ cup) ready-made smoky
   baba ghanoush
6 x 10 cm (4 inch) savoury pastry cases
100 ml (3½ fl oz) olive oil
6 tsp ground sumac
65 g (2½ oz/1½ cups) baby rocket (arugula)
195 g (7 oz/1½ cups) crumbled
   Persian feta
5 tbsp pomegranate seeds (about
   2 small pomegranates)

Preheat the oven to 180°C (350°F/Gas 4).

Combine the ground fennel, ground cumin, ground coriander and pomegranate molasses in a small bowl.

Smear the mixture all over the lamb. Season the lamb with the salt, pepper and garlic.

Sear the lamb in a frying pan over high heat for 5–7 minutes, or until cooked to your liking. Remove from the heat, cover with foil and rest.

Spoon the baba ghanoush into the pastry cases. Place the cases on a baking tray and warm in the oven for 15 minutes.

While the pastry cases are warming, combine the olive oil and sumac in a large bowl. Add the rocket leaves and feta and loosely mix to ensure the rocket is evenly coated.

Thinly slice the lamb and add to the salad mixture. Fill each pastry case with a small handful of the lamb and salad mixture.

Sprinkle with the pomegranate seeds and serve immediately.

Serves 6

CARDAMOM AND ROSEWATER SEMIFREDDO WITH MANGO SHARDS

SWEET FINALE

THIS DESSERT **NEEDS TO BE STARTED ONE DAY AHEAD**, BUT THE UPSIDE OF SUCH PLANNING IS THAT YOUR FRIENDS/PARENTS/WORKMATES/ RANDOM INVITEES WILL KNOW YOU TO BE AN AWESOME INDIVIDUAL OF IMPECCABLE TASTE AND FINESSE.

INGREDIENTS

½ tsp saffron threads

2 tbsp rosewater

4 eggs

100 g (3½ oz) icing (confectioners') sugar

780 g (1 lb 11½ oz/3 cups) Greek yoghurt

2 tbsp honey

1½ tsp cardamom pods

40 g (1½ oz/¼ cup) whole almonds, roughly chopped

70 g (2½ oz) unsalted pistachio nuts, roughly chopped

4 mangoes, sliced

Line a 1 litre (35 fl oz/4 cup) freezer-proof container with plastic wrap, making sure the plastic wrap hangs over the sides and is long enough to fold back over the semifreddo.

Combine the saffron and rosewater in a small bowl and set aside to infuse for 5 minutes.

Beat the eggs and sugar in a bowl with electric beaters until doubled in volume. Stir in the yoghurt and honey. Lightly crush the cardamom pods using a mortar and pestle, discard the husks, then grind the seeds into a coarse powder. Combine the ground cardamom with the nuts and stir three-quarters of the nut mixture into the yoghurt mixture. Add the saffron and rosewater infusion and stir through. Pour into the prepared container and smooth the surface with the back of a spoon. Tap the container on the benchtop to remove any air bubbles. Freeze overnight, or for at least 5 hours.

Soften the semifreddo in the fridge for 30 minutes before serving. Unmould and serve scoops in small bowls, topped with the mango and extra nut mixture or as a log to slice at the table.

Serves 8–12

WALDORF SANDWICHES

APRON ANXIETY

THIS IS A CONFIDENT NOD TO YESTERYEAR, WITH ITS UNCOMPLICATED CONSTRUCTION, AND YET IT DEMONSTRATES AN UNDERSTATED CONFIDENCE IN THE KITCHEN.

INGREDIENTS

1 egg, at room temperature
2 tbsp lemon juice
1 garlic clove, finely chopped
80 ml (2½ fl oz/⅓ cup) olive oil, plus
    extra for brushing
25 g (1 oz) finely grated parmesan
sea salt and freshly ground black pepper
600 g (1 lb 5 oz) picked fresh crabmeat
2 red radishes, cut into matchsticks
1 granny smith apple, cut into matchsticks
2 tbsp finely chopped chervil
70 g (2½ oz/2⅓ cups) picked watercress
16 x 3 mm (⅛ inch) thick slices of
    sourdough bread

Cook the egg in boiling water for 4 minutes. Place in cold water until cool enough to handle, then peel and cut in half. Remove the yolk (which should still be quite soft) and place in a bowl. Set the egg white aside.

Process the egg yolk, lemon juice and garlic in a food processor until combined. With the motor running, slowly pour in the oil in a thin steady stream until the mixture thickens. Add the egg white and parmesan and blitz until combined and the mixture takes on a mayonnaise consistency. Season with salt and pepper, add the crabmeat and stir to combine.

Place the radish, apple, chervil and watercress in a bowl and set aside.

Lightly brush the sourdough pieces with the extra oil and grill (broil) for 40 seconds on each side until golden.

Top half the toasted sourdough pieces with the crab mixture and the salad. Sandwich together with the remaining pieces of toast and serve.

Serves 8

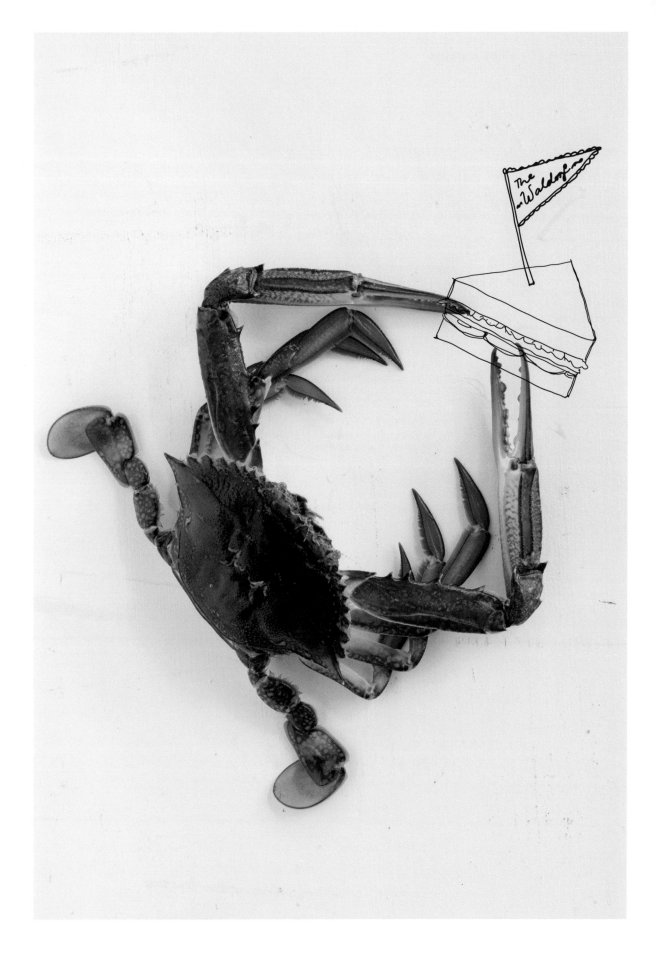

SPICE-CRUSTED VEAL WITH MASALA POTATOES AND SPLIT PEAS
LOOK WHO'S COMING TO DINNER

I DIDN'T FULLY APPRECIATE SOME VERY SAGE ADVICE MY DEARLY DEPARTED GRANDMOTHER ONCE GAVE TO ME. I GUESS THAT'S IT, ISN'T IT? YOU NEVER QUITE APPRECIATE ADVICE AT THE TIME IT IS GIVEN — ALWAYS MUCH LATER, WHEN IT'S FAR TOO LATE TO SAY THANK YOU OR SUCCESSFULLY APPLY IT TO THE SITUATION AT HAND.

MY GRANDMOTHER LOVED — NO, I SHOULD SAY SHE LIVED — TO ENTERTAIN HER FRIENDS AND FAMILY, AND PERHAPS HER ATTITUDE TOWARDS IT IS WHY SHE WAS SO DAMN GOOD AT IT. SO HERE IT IS, SOME FREE ADVICE PASSED ON FROM ME TO YOU. IT CAME FROM A VERY REPUTABLE SOURCE, TRUST ME.

'NEVER, EVER CONCERN YOURSELF WITH AESTHETICS, DARLING. YOU'LL ONLY GIVE YOURSELF A HEADACHE.'

THAT'S THE SORT OF ADVICE THAT APPLIES TO THIS VEAL DISH AND TO A LOT MORE IN LIFE THAN JUST A DINNER PARTY, DON'T YOU THINK?

INGREDIENTS

16 veal medallions (depending on the thickness of the medallions, you may want slightly more or less; the aim is for 180 g (6¼ oz) of meat per person)
2 tsp ground cumin
2 tsp ground coriander
½ tsp chilli powder
50 g (1¾ oz) butter

Masala potatoes

200 g (7 oz/1 cup) yellow split peas, soaked
3 desiree potatoes, peeled and cut into 2 cm (¾ inch) cubes
4 tsp ras el hanout
½ tsp chilli powder
1 tsp ground tumeric
1 tsp cinnamon
125 ml (4 fl oz/½ cup) olive oil
2 onions, thinly sliced
1 tbsp grated fresh ginger
2 cloves garlic, crushed
300 g (10 oz) tomatoes, quartered
6 curry leaves
80 g (2¾ oz) baby spinach leaves

01

Drain the split peas and place in a large saucepan. Cover with water and add a pinch of salt. Cook over medium heat for 1 hour until peas are tender. (If you buy peas that don't require soaking, you can skip this step.) Drain and place in a bowl.

02

Cook potatoes in a saucepan of boiling water until just tender, drain and combine in a large bowl with the split peas.

03

Preheat oven to 200°C (400°F/Gas 6).

04

Combine the masala spices in a small bowl. Heat 2 tablespoons of olive oil in a large saucepan over low heat. Add onions and cook for 10 minutes or until soft. Add the spice mix and cook for 3 minutes. Add the ginger and garlic and cook until fragrant. Add the tomatoes and curry leaves. Reduce heat to low and cook, covered for 10 minutes or until the mix is pulpy and slightly reduced.

05

Stir in the potatoes and split peas, season with salt and pepper. Stir through the spinach and keep warm.

06

For the spice-crusted veal, combine the spice mix in a bowl and gently toss the veal medallions until coated in the spice.

07

Heat the remaining oil in an ovenproof frying pan over high heat, brown the medallions for 1-2 minutes, turning on all sides then transfer to an oven and roast for 5 minutes. Remove and allow to rest, covered, for 5 minutes.

08

To serve, spoon a generous amount of masala potato onto each plate. Top with veal medallions (usually 2-3 per person) and serve hot.

Serves 8

LIQUORICE BULLET DELUXE

IN GOOD COMPANY

THIS IS A VERY GROWN-UP VERSION OF A LIQUORICE BULLET. IT'S THE KIND OF DISH THAT WILL HAVE EVERYONE SILENT AT THE TABLE WITH THAT 'CAN'T TALK, EATING' REACTION WE ALL DREAM OF INSPIRING. THE TASTE IS WONDROUS AND OPULENT — TINGLING ANISEED, WITH THE CLOAKING MOUTH-FEEL OF CARAMEL, AND A COLLECTIVE RICHNESS, THICK AND HEAVY AS AN OIL SPILL. THIS IS REAL DESSERT.

YOU CAN PREPARE THE BASE AND ICE CREAM THE DAY BEFORE, SO YOUR TIME IN THE KITCHEN WILL BE MINIMAL ON THE DAY.

INGREDIENTS

Sandwich

150 g (5½ oz/1 cup) plain (all-purpose) flour
½ tsp baking powder
¼ tsp bicarbonate of soda
¼ tsp salt
2 tbsp unsweetened cocoa powder
125 g (4½ oz) butter, softened
150 g (5¾ oz/¾ cup) soft brown sugar, firmly packed
1 large egg
½ tsp natural vanilla extract
40 g (1½ oz/⅓ cup) dark chocolate (at least 70 per cent cocoa solids), chopped and melted
1 x 450 g (1 lb) jar dulce de leche (caramel)

Parfait

600 ml (21 fl oz) cream
100 g (3½ oz) caster (superfine) sugar
150 g (5½ oz) liquorice, chopped into pieces
a few drops of black food colouring
4 egg yolks

Preheat the oven to 180°C (350°F/Gas 4). Grease and line two 23 x 33 cm (9 x 13 inch) baking tins.

For the sandwich, sift together the flour, baking powder, bicarbonate of soda, salt and cocoa in a small bowl. Cream the butter and sugar in another bowl with electric beaters until pale and fluffy. Beat in the egg and vanilla. Add the flour mixture in two batches, beating until just combined. Fold in the melted chocolate until mixed through. Divide the batter between the prepared tins and spread into a thin even layer. Bake for 10–12 minutes until just cooked or a skewer inserted comes out clean. Cool completely in the tins.

Spread the dulce de leche over the base of one of the sandwich halves and set aside.

For the parfait, place the cream, sugar and liquorice in a saucepan and stir over low heat until the liquorice has dissolved and the cream coats the back of a wooden spoon. Transfer to a blender and blitz to breakdown any remaining pieces of liquorice. Strain over a bowl to remove any residual liquorice chunks. The liquorice mixture tends to take on a dark green hue so add a few drops of the food colouring to achieve a dark-grey 'liquorice' colour. Beat the egg yolks in a large bowl until pale and thick. Gently combine the cream mixture with the egg yolks, then return to the clean pan and stir over low heat for 5 minutes until thickened. Remove from the heat, pour into a freezer-proof container, cover with plastic wrap and place in the freezer for 20 minutes, or until slightly firm.

Working quickly, pour the softened parfait mixture over the caramel base and gently press the remaining sandwich layer on top. Cover completely with plastic wrap and place in the freezer for at least 3 hours, preferably overnight.

To serve, turn out from the sandwich tin and slice using a hot, wet knife.

Serves 8–10

Wedding feast

The moment I was engaged I started planning the food for the big day. Not because I am organised, but because I'm a fatty and I like to get intimate with my calories — and thinking back to the weddings I've attended, the food, by and large, was invariably a bit hit 'n' miss: cold when it was meant to be hot, lukewarm when it was meant to be hot, reheated so it was hot but then completely devoid of flavour. Or in some cases — the worst ones — completely absent.

Don't get me wrong, some of the food has been spectacular, to the point that I wish I'd kept the menus as reminders — but when there are restrictions by way of budget, location and the need to balance quality versus quantity then there are bound to be issues.

So I think the ideal wedding would be small. A houseful of people that I really care about, and a table groaning with food. I'd rather this type of wedding, with the dogs sniffing round the table hoping for a bite and the smell of cooking wafting from the kitchen, than some soulless function centre.

I love intimate gatherings. Throwing them and going to them. Actually, I adore everything about them and would do anything to prepare a wedding feast for my nearest and dearest — the gentle formality and comfort of old friends and family with great food. It doesn't get much better than that.

When you strip away all the materialistic aspects of a wedding — dress, flowers, invitations and gifts — you're left with the most important parts: love and food. Two things, which taken simultaneously, spell out instant comfort and a pleasure bath for the senses, that mildly illicit coming together of entertainment and nourishment.

Was that a shotgun blast in the distance?

Menu 1

Parmesan financiers with olives and rosemary

–

Saffron-infused prawns wrapped in kataifi pastry with haloumi and watermelon salad

–

Braised wagyu shin with tomato jam and parsley and fennel salad

–

Chocolate mousse with baked doughnuts and granita

Menu 2

Wasabi-crusted trout with udon noodles

–

Lemongrass sarsaparilla and sake beef cheeks

–

Macaroon and meringue white chocolate wedding cake

PARMESAN FINANCIERS WITH OLIVES AND ROSEMARY

HITCHED WITHOUT A HITCH

THESE LITTLE TASTY MORSELS ARE THE ULTIMATE 'TO DO' BEFORE THE 'I DO'.

INGREDIENTS
150 g (5½ oz/1½ cups) ground almonds
90 g (3¼ oz) plain (all-purpose) flour
100 g (3½ oz) parmesan, grated
100 g (3½ oz) gruyere cheese, grated
1 tsp baking powder
280 ml (10 fl oz) egg white (about 7 large eggs)
250 g (9 oz) butter, melted
salt and freshly ground black pepper
  to season
6 kalamata olives, deseeded and halved
2 tsp rosemary leaves, roughly chopped

Preheat the oven to 190°C (375°F/Gas 5). Lightly grease a standard 12-hole muffin tin with butter.

Combine the ground almonds, flour, cheeses and baking powder in a large mixing bowl. Add the egg whites, mixing after each addition. Pour in the butter and whisk until just combined. Spoon the mixture into the muffin tin until they are almost full. Gently place an olive half in the top of each financier and sprinkle over the rosemary leaves. Bake in the oven for 30 minutes, or until they are golden and a skewer inserted in the centre comes out clean.

Turn onto a wire rack to cool and serve.

Makes 12

SAFFRON-INFUSED PRAWNS WRAPPED IN KATAIFI PASTRY WITH HALOUMI AND WATERMELON SALAD
SNAP DECISIONS

POSSIBLY THE MOST SUPERB START TO MARRIED LIFE.

INGREDIENTS
250 ml (8 fl oz/1 cup) grapeseed oil
2 tsp saffron threads
24 large green prawns, peeled and cleaned
200 g (7 oz) kataifi pastry

Salad
50 g (1¾ oz) haloumi, thinly sliced
juice of ½ a lemon
400 g (14 oz) seedless watermelon,
   thinly sliced
½ small red onion, thinly sliced
a large handful mint, coarsely torn
a large handful flat-leaf parsley,
   coarsely torn
seeds of ½ pomegranate
salt and freshly ground pepper to season

Dressing
juice of ½ a lemon
1 tbsp grapeseed oil
2 tsp sumac

To serve
lemon cheeks

Combine the lemon juice, oil and sumac for the dressing in a bowl and set aside.

Pour in enough grapeseed oil to cover the base of a small non-stick frying pan, then place over low heat. Add the saffron threads and stir until dissolved. Remove from heat and allow to cool. Toss prawns in a bowl with 125 ml (4 fl oz/½ cup) of the saffron oil then refrigerate for at least 2 hours.

Separate the kataifi pastry into long strips 6 cm (2½ inches) wide and the length of the prawns. Place a prawn widthwise at the end of each strip and roll up to encase in pastry. Squeeze lightly in your hand to ensure the pastry sticks together. Repeat with remaining prawns and pastry.

Pour enough grapeseed oil to cover the base of a frying pan to 2 cm (¾ inch) high and place over medium heat. Add the wrapped prawns, in batches, and shallow-fry for 2 minutes or until golden and cooked through. Drain on paper towel.

Wipe out the pan and return to the heat, add 1 tablespoon of grapeseed oil, and the haloumi, and cook, turning once, until golden (1–2 minutes each side). Remove from heat, squeeze over a little lemon juice then add to a bowl with the prawns, watermelon, onion, mint, flat-leaf parsley and pomegranate seeds. Season to taste and drizzle over the dressing. Toss gently to combine.

Serve immediately.

Serves 8

BRAISED WAGYU SHIN WITH TOMATO JAM AND PARSLEY AND FENNEL SALAD
THE REAL DEAL

THIS WAGYU SHIN IS THE WEDDING WITH THE WORKS. FOOD FOR A MAGICAL WEDDING THAT EVEN ROYALTY, BORN INTO PARTY-PLANNING FAMILIES AND UNLIMITED BUDGETS, WOULD BE INSPIRED BY.

IF YOU ARE COOKING FOR 12 YOU MAY NEED TO USE TWO CASSEROLE DISHES TO ENSURE YOU HAVE ROOM FOR ALL THE WINE!

INGREDIENTS
Tomato jam
200 ml (7 fl oz) olive oil
1 brown onion, finely chopped
3 garlic cloves, finely chopped
sea salt and freshly ground black pepper
3.2 kg (7 lb/3½ oz) tinned diced tomatoes
250 g (9 oz) sugar
200 ml (7 fl oz) red wine vinegar
2 bay leaves

Braised wagyu
125 ml (4 fl oz/½ cup) olive oil
4 kg (9 lb) wagyu beef shin
2 carrots, finely chopped
2 small onions, finely chopped
2 celery stalks, finely chopped
3 garlic cloves, finely chopped
500 g (1 lb 2 oz) mild pancetta, diced
4 cinnamon sticks
2 vanilla beans, split lengthways and
   seeds scraped
4 x 750 ml (104 fl oz/12 cups) bottles
   of dry red wine

Parsley and fennel salad
1 cup fennel fronds to garnish
1 large fennel bulb
4 very large handfuls of flat-leaf
   parsley leaves
80 g (2¾ oz/½ cup) pine nuts, toasted
1 avocado, thinly sliced
125 ml (4 fl oz/½ cup) buttermilk
2 tsp dijon mustard
1 tbsp white wine vinegar
sea salt and freshly ground black pepper

For the tomato jam, heat the oil in a large saucepan over medium-low heat. Add the onion and garlic, season well and cook until the onion is softened.

Add the tomatoes, sugar, vinegar and bay leaf and bring to the boil. Reduce heat and simmer, stirring occasionally, for 10 minutes or until the mixture thickens. Set aside to cool.

For the braised wagyu, heat the oil in a large saucepan over medium heat and cook the beef, in batches, until browned all over. Transfer the beef to a large bowl and set aside. Add the carrot, onion, celery, garlic, pancetta, cinnamon and vanilla to the pan and cook for 10 minutes, or until soft.

Transfer the beef and carrot mixture to a large casserole dish, pour in the wine and bring to a simmer. Reduce the heat to low,

cover and cook for 2½ hours, or until the beef is very tender. Remove the beef from the pan. Strain the cooking liquid into a clean saucepan and simmer over high heat until syrupy and reduced by a third.

For the salad, tear the fennel fronds into small sprigs. Trim the fennel stalks flush with the bulb. Discard the stalks. Quarter the fennel bulb lengthways and very thinly slice. Toss the sliced fennel with the fennel fronds, parsley, pine nuts and avocado in a large bowl. Place the buttermilk, mustard and vinegar in a bowl, season and whisk lightly to combine. Drizzle the salad with the dressing just prior to serving.

Serve the braised wagyu with the parsley and fennel salad and spoonfuls of the tomato jam.

Serves 10–12

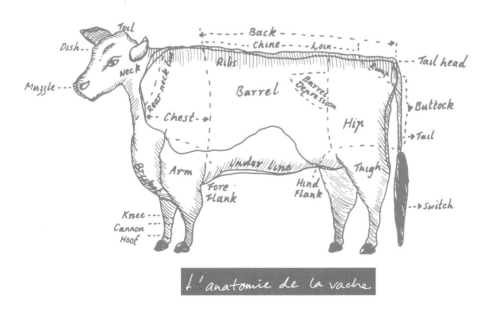

L'anatomie de la vache

CHOCOLATE MOUSSE WITH BAKED DOUGHNUTS AND GRANITA

SAY I DO

THE SUGAR, BUTTER AND CREAM COMMITMENT OF THIS HEADY DESSERT IS THE FOOD EQUIVALENT OF BOLDLY STEPPING INTO THE TULLE-LOVING, FLOWER-HOARDING, TEAR-INDUCING, GUSHY-VOW WEDDING SEASON.

INGREDIENTS

Granita

200 ml (7 fl oz) water
440 g (15½ oz/2 cups) caster
   (superfine) sugar
200 ml (7 fl oz) pomegranate juice
2 tbsp pomegranate molasses
1 tbsp rosewater

Mousse

1 kg (2 lb 4 oz) dark chocolate (70 per cent
   cocoa solids), chopped
280 g (10 oz) butter
1.4 litres (49 fl oz) double (heavy) cream
8 eggs
175 g (6 oz/½ cup) honey

Doughnuts

200 ml (7 fl oz) milk
150 g (5½ oz) unsalted butter, chopped
2 tsp natural vanilla extract
a pinch of salt
200 g (7 oz/1⅓ cups) plain
   (all-purpose) flour
4 eggs, at room temperature
125 ml (4 fl oz/½ cup) vegetable oil
220 g (7¾ oz/1 cup) caster
   (superfine) sugar
1 tbsp ground cinnamon
1 tbsp freshly grated nutmeg

For the granita, bring the water and sugar to the boil in a saucepan until sugar has dissolved and syrup has slightly thickened. Remove from the heat and allow to cool. Add the pomegranate juice, pomegranate molasses and rosewater. Pour into a deep 10 x 20 cm (4 x 8 inch) freezer-proof tray and place in the freezer for at least 4 hours.

For the mousse, melt the chocolate and butter in a heatproof bowl over a saucepan of gently simmering water and stir until smooth. In a large bowl, whip the cream until firm peaks form. In another large bowl, whisk the eggs and honey until pale and thick. Gently fold the chocolate mixture and the cream into the egg mixture. Pour into serving dishes and chill for at least 2 hours.

For the doughnut dough, place the milk, butter, vanilla and salt in a saucepan and bring to the boil over low-medium heat. Add the flour in one batch and stir vigorously until smooth and the mixture comes away from the side of the pan. Continue to stir for another minute to dry out the mixture. Transfer to a large bowl and beat in the eggs, one at a time, until the dough is smooth and glossy. Cover tightly with plastic wrap and refrigerate for 2 hours.

Preheat the oven to 200°C (400°F/Gas 6). Line a baking tray with baking paper.

With oiled hands, shape the doughnut dough into 10 cm (4 inch) flat discs (the number of discs can vary depending on the heat and humidity of your kitchen but usually makes between 10 and 12). Place the vegetable oil in a small bowl and combine the sugar, cinnamon and nutmeg in another bowl. Dip each disc in the oil, then coat in the cinnamon sugar and place on the prepared tray. Bake for 25 minutes, or until golden and cooked through.

Scrape the frozen granita with a fork to create fine ice shards. Place a dollop of granita on top of each mousse and serve with a hot doughnut.

Serves 10–12

WASABI-CRUSTED TROUT WITH SOBA NOODLES

ALL'S FAIR IN LOVE AND WAR

THIS TROUT DISH MAKES ALL THE INSOMNIA, SPOTS AND TRAUMA OF WEDDING PLANNING WORTHWHILE. EASY AND SIMPLE IN WEDDING WORLD WHERE EVERYTHING ELSE IS NOT.

INGREDIENTS

8 x 150 g (5½ oz) ocean trout fillets,
  pin-boned
2 tsp grapeseed oil
sea salt and freshly ground black pepper
4 x 270 g (9½ oz) packets soba noodles
175 ml (6 fl oz/¾ cup) soy sauce
75 ml (3 fl oz/⅓ cup) mirin
2 tbsp sesame oil
4 spring onions (scallions),
  finely sliced
8 tbsp wakame, finely shredded

Wasabi crust

12 tsp wasabi paste (you can use less
  for a milder taste)
120 g (4½ oz/2 cups) panko crumbs
4 tbsp Japanese mayonnaise

Cut out a piece of silicon paper to cover the base of a large frying pan. Grease the silicon paper and pan, to prevent burning, with the grapeseed oil.

For the wasabi crust, combine the wasabi, panko crumbs and mayonnaise in a bowl and stir well. This needs to be a slightly wet breadcrumb consistency . Add more panko crumbs if required.

Gently press the crust mixture onto one side of each trout fillet and cover that side with a piece of silicon paper.

Heat the olive oil in a large non-stick frying pan over medium heat, season the trout and cook, paper side down, for 3 minutes, or until the crust is starting to crisp. Gently turn and cook for 2 minutes, or until cooked to your liking.

Cook the soba noodles according to the packet instructions. Drain, rinse under cold running water and drain again.

Combine the soy sauce, mirin and sesame oil in a large bowl. Add the noodles, spring onion and wakame and toss to combine.

Just prior to serving, cut the trout fillets into thick slices. Serve the noodles topped with slices of wasabi-crusted ocean trout.

Serves 8

LEMONGRASS SARSAPARILLA AND SAKE BEEF CHEEKS
THE VOW FACTOR

YOU FELL IN LOVE. YOU DECIDED THERE WAS A FUTURE. NOW YOU HAVE TO PAY THE PRICE. OF A WEDDING.

WHILE SOME PEOPLE MAY ASPIRE TO BIG, OSTENTATIOUS CELEBRATIONS, THIS DISH IS FOR WHEN YOU WANT TO PULL OFF SOMETHING SIMPLE — THE NO-BIG-DEAL, NO-CEREMONY CEREMONY. IT'S DEAD EASY BUT LOOKS AND TASTES SERIOUSLY IMPRESSIVE. TA DAA!

THIS DISH CAN BE MADE IN ADVANCE, REHEATING THE BEEF CHEEKS PRIOR TO SERVING.

INGREDIENTS
185 ml (6 fl oz/¾ cup) vegetable oil
9 spring onions (scallions), thinly sliced
18 garlic cloves, peeled and halved
3 lemongrass stems, white part only
3 thumb-sized knobs of fresh ginger, finely grated
2.5 litres (88 fl oz/10 cups) sarsaparilla
500 ml (17 fl oz/2 cups) Coca Cola
1 litre (35 fl oz/4 cups) sake
90 g (3¼ oz/¼ cup) dark treacle
3 tsp tamarind paste
2 very large handful of coriander (cilantro) leaves and stems, chopped
1.5 litres (52 fl oz/6 cups) beef stock
300 ml (10½ fl oz) soy sauce
9 small red chillies, finely chopped
6 cinnamon sticks
8 star anise
12 large beef cheeks
sea salt

Coconut rice
1.25 kg (2 lb 12 oz/6 cups) jasmine rice, rinsed
750 ml (26 fl oz/3 cups) coconut milk
500 ml (17 fl oz/2 cups) water
6 lemongrass stems, white part only, lightly bruised and cut into 10 cm (4 inch) pieces
8 kaffir lime leaves

Salad
2 cucumbers, peeled and cut into long thin strips, using a mandoline
1 white radish (daikon), thinly sliced
½ wombok (Chinese cabbage), thinly sliced
12 red radishes, thinly sliced
2 small handfuls of picked watercress
a handful of coriander (cilantro) leaves
a handful of mint leaves
a handful of Vietnamese mint leaves

Dressing
juice of 1 lemon
2 tsp sugar

P.T.O

Preheat the oven to 160°C (315°F/Gas 2–3).

Season the beef cheeks with some salt and sear, in batches, until browned all over in a large casserole dish over high heat. Add the spring onion, garlic, lemongrass, ginger, sarsaparilla, Coke, sake, treacle, tamarind paste, coriander, stock, soy sauce, chilli, cinnamon and star anise and bring to the boil. Reduce the heat to low, cover and braise in the oven for 5 hours.

Heat a large frying pan over medium–high heat, add the remaining oil. Allow the cheeks to cool in the liquid before removing from the dish.

Strain the liquid into a saucepan, bring to the boil and simmer until reduced by half and a syrupy consistency is achieved. Return the beef cheeks to the sauce and gently reheat.

For the coconut rice, combine all the ingredients in a large saucepan. Bring to the boil, stirring continuously, so the rice doesn't stick to the base of the pan. As soon as mixture comes to the boil, reduce the heat to low, cover and simmer for 10–15 minutes or until rice is cooked and coconut milk has been absorbed.

To make the salad, place all the ingredients in a bowl and toss to combine. Add the lemon juice and sugar to a bowl and stir until sugar is dissolved. Pour dressing over salad and gently toss to combine. Serve the rice topped with a beef cheek and some of the salad.

Serves 12

MACAROON AND MERINGUE WHITE CHOCOLATE WEDDING CAKE

WHO. WHAT. WED.

THIS DESSERT IS SENSUALITY PERSONIFIED. THE GENTLE FLAVOURS AND PRETTY COLOURS INSPIRE MOODS OF LANGUID DAYS AND A LIFETIME OF LOVE. YEP, L'AMOUR IS HERE TO STAY, SWEETER THAN EVER THANKS TO YOUR EFFORTS IN THE KITCHEN.

IT'S ENOUGH TO MAKE YOU (LOVE) SICK.

FOR THIS DISH YOU CAN USE ANY MACAROONS THAT TAKE YOUR FANCY (OR ARE AVAILABLE AT YOUR PATISSERIE), BUT TRY TO USE SOME WITH A FRUIT-INSPIRED FLAVOUR SUCH AS STRAWBERRY OR RASPBERRY AND WHICH ARE PALE IN COLOUR — IT MAKES THIS DESSERT A PASTEL WONDERLAND THAT LOOKS OH SO PRETTY … JUST LIKE A WEDDING FEAST SHOULD.

TO SPARE YOURSELF ANY 'I NEED A VALIUM AND LIE DOWN' MOMENTS, **START THIS RECIPE THE DAY BEFORE.** YOU CAN MAKE THE CAKES AND STORE, ONCE COOLED, IN AN AIRTIGHT CONTAINER.

Ingredients

edible rose petals (pale colours work best and you need about 3 roses)
1 egg white, lightly beaten
caster (superfine) sugar, for dusting
15 ready-made macaroons, separated and ganache cream scraped from macaroon shells

Cake

450 g (1 lb/3 cups) plain (all-purpose) flour, sifted
1½ tsp baking powder
a pinch of salt
175 g (6 oz) butter
330 g (11½ oz/1½ cups) caster (superfine) sugar
4 eggs
375 ml (13 fl oz/1½ cups) thickened cream
150 g (5½ oz) white chocolate, melted

White chocolate raspberry cream

250 ml (9 fl oz/1 cup) cream
150 g (5½ oz) white chocolate, melted
100 g (3½ oz) raspberries, lightly crushed

Italian meringue

185 g (6½ oz) caster (superfine) sugar
60 ml (2 fl oz/¼ cup) water
3 egg whites
a pinch of cream of tartar
2 tsp rosewater

More to come . . .

Lightly brush each rose petal with the egg white, then dust generously with the sugar. Place on a wire rack to dry at room temperature for 4 hours or overnight.

Preheat the oven to 180°C (350°F/Gas 4). Grease three 20 cm (8 inch) round cake tins and set aside.

For the cake, sift the flour, baking powder and salt into a bowl. Cream the butter and sugar in a separate bowl using electric beaters until pale and fluffy. Add the eggs, one at a time, beating well after each addition. Beat in half the flour mixture and half the cream, then add the remaining flour and cream. Fold in the chocolate and evenly divide the batter between the prepared tins.

Bake for 30 minutes, or until a skewer inserted in the centre of a cake comes out clean and it is starting to brown on top. If you cook all three cakes at once, you may need to account for a longer cooking time. Leave to cool for 10 minutes in the tins, then turn out onto wire racks to cool completely.

For the white chocolate raspberry cream, whisk the cream and chocolate in a bowl with electric beaters until soft peaks form (about 3 minutes). Be careful not to overmix or the cream will split. Fold in the raspberries and refrigerate for 10 minutes until firm.

Brush one cake with half the white chocolate raspberry cream. Gently place another cake on top and repeat the process with the remaining white chocolate raspberry cream and place the final sponge on top. Cover and refrigerate.

For the Italian meringue, combine the sugar and water in a small saucepan over medium-high heat and stir, brushing down the side of the pan with a wet pastry brush to remove any sugar crystals, until the sugar dissolves. Bring to the boil and simmer, without stirring, for 15 minutes until the syrup reaches softball stage — 115°C (230°F) on a sugar (candy) thermometer.

While the syrup is cooking, whisk the egg whites and cream of tartar in a heatproof bowl using electric beaters until soft peaks form.

Once the syrup reaches 121°C (249°F), slowly and carefully pour the syrup into the egg whites, mixing continuously until thick and glossy and the mixture reaches room temperature. Stir in the rosewater.

Spread the Italian meringue over the top and sides of the assembled cake. Gently press the macaroons into the side of the cake and decorate the top with the sugared rose petals.

Serves 6

* *

CHAPTER EIGHT

WHAT THE F*$K SHOULD WE COOK FOR DINNER?

* *

Enthusiasm is an elusive beast. Ever-present at Friday night drinks, rebellious in the supermarket aisle and completely AWOL come dinner. In the kitchen, as in life, delayed gratification is yesterday's news. Let's face it: you like your pedicures quick dry, your post express overnight and your sauce from a jar.

But in these times of food glitterati, the simple act of preparing food to nourish us through another day sometimes takes on ungodly proportions. There is a time and a place for fuss in the kitchen, and times when shortcuts and conveniences are the only things holding you back from the drive-through.

The following meals are quick and easy. And better yet, they're a bulwark against the epicurean bullying and shame that comes with using oats that are instant, or macaroni 'n' cheese from a tin. This is the ultimate selection to make sure dinner's in the bag.

(Not the KFC bag.)

The following recipes require minimal ingredients, minimal time and minimal thinking and absolutely no forward planning. There is no specific order or menu provided; this is a flick and pick selection with varying levels of effort required.

Can't talk, feed me

You could not be fecked with dinner.

Mother Hubbard ransacked your cupboard, pillaged your enthusiasm, and the takeaway menu is within reach. You know fast food can be bad for you, and you still do it. Me too: Maccas, Chinese, pizza. But making it your dinner option when you otherwise eat pretty well is a bit like using Visa debit instead of credit for an unaffordable shopping spree, or making a late night bootie call to talk about your feelings. It's missing the point.

Sometimes it's enjoyable — the almost forgotten memory of that strange, waxy cheesie-toast from Sizzlers, the deep crust at Pizza Hut, the tingle of salt on the gherkin from your Maccas cheesy, and the potato and gravy dipping pot for your hot chips at KFC. I know, I know ...

But what you eat doesn't need to taste like horse's arse, make you feel like rubbish the next day, or be so full of MSG, stabilisers and whatever else is usually found on that really long list of funky chemicals that go into food that isn't too good for you. As preachy as it sounds, it isn't that hard to chuck a few things on a plate and call it dinner. So put the takeaway menu down and step away. The following recipes are so quick 'n' easy they could hardly be called recipes — giving you a chance to get your house in order, so to speak.

Or use that Visa debit for a little online shopping after tea.

Menu

Spicy lamb chops

–

Steamed asparagus wrapped in prosciutto

–

Posh cheese on toast

–

Chocolate chips

–

Grilled peaches

–

Spaghetti with herbed mascarpone

–

Taco salad with yoghurt

–

Duck and lychee salad

–

Butter-chicken lasagne

–

Lamb and hummus pasties

–

Chilli jam prawns

SPICY LAMB CHOPS

Sprinkle rib lamb chops with a good coarse curry powder or any spice mix you like. Grill quickly, until crisp but not well done. Serve hot, with yoghurt mixed with the same spice rub.

STEAMED ASPARAGUS WRAPPED IN PROSCIUTTO

That's it. Right there. Maybe dip them in some garlic aïoli if this dish is a little too lean for you.

POSH CHEESE ON TOAST

Spread a generous amount of quince paste over some bread — a crunchy sourdough works well. Top with blue cheese and pop under the grill until melted and slightly bubbly.

CHOCOLATE CHIPS

Nuke some milk chocolate in a microwave on medium heat until melted. Dip lightly salted potato chips into the chocolate, then place on a baking tray lined with baking paper and allow to set in the fridge for 10 minutes.

Stop judging. They taste fantastic.

GRILLED PEACHES

Chargrill the fleshy side of halved white peaches, then dress them with dessert wine or moscato and a dash of rosewater. Serve warm, with mascarpone or vanilla gelato.

SPAGHETTI WITH HERBED MASCARPONE

Boil enough spaghetti for two people. Meanwhile chop a fistful of rocket with a small bunch of chives, and another small bunch of mint or basil (or if you prefer, oregano). Combine the herbs with a small tub of mascarpone. Add the juice of half a lemon and 2 tablespoons olive oil. Season with salt and pepper. Drain the cooked pasta — making only a half-arsed effort so the pasta is still slightly wet. Fold the mascarpone mixture through and serve immediately.

TACO SALAD WITH YOGHURT

Preheat the oven to 180°C (350°F/Gas 4). Place 5 taco shells on a baking tray and brown in the oven for 5 minutes. Meanwhile, fry 300 g (10½ oz) beef mince in a frying pan with 1 roughly chopped white onion and the taco seasoning from a taco packet. Roughly chop 1 avocado and 2 roma tomatoes. Add to a large bowl with 100 g (3½ oz/½ cup) black beans, 2 small jalapeños, seeds removed and chopped, and 100 g (3½ oz/2 cups) baby rocket leaves. Add the mince and roughly broken cooked taco shells. Toss to combine, then add 100 g (3½ oz/½ cup) shredded cheddar and serve with a dollop of natural yoghurt.

DUCK AND LYCHEE SALAD

In a bowl combine 2 peeled and halved fresh lychees, 1 grilled chorizo sausage, thinly sliced and a small handful coarsely torn coriander and mint leaves (any Asian herbs will do). Toss 2 duck breasts in a good-quality store-bought chilli jam, then barbecue until cooked to your liking. Thinly slice across the grain and add to the salad.

Prawn/watermelon alternative:
As above, using watermelon instead of lychees, and fresh prawns instead of duck. Skip the chilli jam and add some feta. Combine 3 tablespoons Angostura bitters and 60 ml (2 fl oz/¼ cup) of lemonade, drizzle over the salad and serve immediately.

BUTTER-CHICKEN LASAGNE

Brown 350 g (12 oz) diced chicken, 1 garlic clove and 1 roughly chopped onion in a frying pan over high heat. Pour in a good-quality butter chicken sauce, simmer and reduce by half. Line the base of a baking tray with a naan bread, top with the chicken mixture and repeat with 3 or 4 naan breads. Roast in a 180°C (350°F/Gas 4) oven for 20 minutes. Serve with fresh yoghurt and coriander.

LAMB AND HUMMUS PASTIES

Brown 250 g (9 oz) lamb mince with 1 garlic clove and a pinch each of ground coriander and cumin. Add 110 g (3¾ oz/¾ cup) cranberries. Roll out 1 sheet puff pastry and cut out eight 15 cm (6 inch) circles. Place a small dollop of hummus in the centre of each circle and top with the lamb mixture. Fold the pasties over to enclose the filling, then brush tops with beaten egg. Bake in a 200°C (400°F/Gas 6) oven for 15 minutes.

CHILLI JAM PRAWNS

Chilli jam, fresh prawns and a dash of oil. Stir-fry them in a hot wok until cooked to your liking, add a squirt of fish sauce and lime juice, a handful of coriander or mint leaves, and serve with noodles or steamed rice.

I could stir something

Dinner. Not. Going. To. Happen.

A long day at work, evil carbs, trans fats, mad cow and listeria for your hysteria — eating has become so difficult I don't blame you for waiving it all together; pity about the hunger.

Feeding — it's such a fickle friend.

I'm always fascinated by what people eat when they are tired or they think no one is looking.

Generally it is often one and the same, and because the majority of us only cook when someone else needs feeding.

These are the perfect recipes for when you want it short and sweet. With the odd stir or chop for a taste sensation.

> Peanut butter from the jar over the sink, both halves of an avocado with a teaspoon, or taramasalata on toast in the bath

Menu

Mackerel with bok choy
and oyster sauce
–
Chicken with mustard and
crème fraîche
–
Fontina and meatball
sandwiches
–
Peanut pork
san choy bow
–
Pancetta and cheesy honey
mustard muffins
–
Coriander-crusted chicken
with miso butter
–
Steak Diane salad
–
Pumpkin and burnt-butter
sage ravioli bake
–
Individual fish in a bag
–
Wasabi macaroni and
cheese
–
Black Forest dessert

MACKEREL WITH BOK CHOY AND OYSTER SAUCE
HOLY MACKEREL

THIS RECIPE IS ADAPTED FROM THE 'PRAWN SHACK' OFFERING ON STRADBROKE ISLAND. IT'S A LITTLE LOW-KEY ISLAND ESCAPE AND IS AS EFFORTLESS IN PREPARATION AS THE ISLAND IT CAME FROM.

INGREDIENTS
½ small red onion,
  finely sliced
a small handful of coriander (cilantro),
  roughly chopped
270 ml (9½ fl oz) coconut cream
1 tbsp curry powder
juice of ½ lemon
2 x 150 g (5½ oz) mackerel fillet
80 ml (2½ fl oz/⅓ cup) chicken stock
1 tbsp oyster sauce
2 bok choy (pak choy)

Preheat the oven to 180°C (350°F/Gas 4).

Combine the onion, coriander, coconut cream, curry powder and lemon juice in a shallow bowl, add the mackerel and turn to coat. Leave to marinate for 5 minutes (or up to 30 in the fridge should you be so inclined).

Heat an ovenproof frying pan over medium heat, strain the fish from the marinade, add to the pan and cook for 2 minutes on each side. Pour over the reserved marinade, transfer to the oven and roast for 5 minutes.

While the fish is roasting, combine the chicken stock and oyster sauce in a small dish. Blanch the bok choy in a saucepan of boiling water for 30 seconds. Drain well.

Divide the bok choy between two plates, spoon over the sauce and top with the fish. Serve immediately.

For something a little more substantial, this is great with some steamed rice.

Serves 2

CHICKEN WITH MUSTARD AND CRÈME FRAÎCHE
UPSIDE TO THE DOWNTURN

A ONE-POT WONDER FOR THE MIDWEEK DINNER CRISIS.

INGREDIENTS
4–6 boneless chicken thighs, skin on
250 g (9 oz) crème fraîche
2–3 heaped tbsp wholegrain mustard
2 garlic cloves, finely chopped
sea salt and freshly ground black pepper
3–4 small thyme sprigs
125 ml (4 fl oz/½ cup) white wine
150 g (5½ oz) flat mild pancetta or bacon
  in one piece, cut into thick strips

Preheat the oven to 200°C (400°F/Gas 6).

Place the chicken in an ovenproof dish.

Combine the crème fraîche, mustard, garlic and a little salt and pepper in a bowl. Pull the thyme leaves from their stalks and add them to the crème fraîche. Pour in the wine.

Fry the pancetta or bacon in a non-stick frying pan over medium heat until the fat is golden. Mix in with the sauce, then spoon over the chicken. Bake for 35 minutes until the sauce is bubbling and the chicken skin is nicely coloured.

Serves 2

FONTINA AND MEATBALL SANDWICHES
THE BIG RED

DON'T OPT FOR ANY GOURMET BREAD VARIETY — IT SHOULD BE SO WHITE IT'S ALMOST GLOWING. FOR SOME REASON IT MAKES BETTER MEATBALLS.

INGREDIENTS

4–6 long white, crust rolls or ciabatta rolls, halved lengthways

200 g (7 oz) fontina cheese, thinly sliced

45 g (1½ oz/2 cups) tomato-flavoured potato crisps — 'Big Red' work best

Meatballs

100 g (3½ oz) soft white bread

125 g (4½ oz) minced veal

125 g (4½ oz) minced pork

2 handfuls mint, finely chopped

½ brown onion, finely chopped

1 clove garlic, finely chopped

1 egg

30 ml (1 fl oz) olive oil

salt and freshly ground black pepper

Tomato sauce

3 garlic cloves, peeled and crushed

3 tbsp olive oil

1 x 450 g (1 lb) tin cherry tomatoes

pinch of dried chilli

½ tsp dried mint

½ tsp dried basil

pinch brown sugar

For meatballs, soak bread in 100 ml (3½ fl oz) cold water until just soft. Squeeze out water and tear bread into a large bowl. Add remaining ingredients and mix to combine. Season with salt and pepper. Roll into walnut-sized meatballs and place on a baking tray lined with baking paper. Cover and refrigerate until firm.

For tomato sauce, cook garlic in oil in a frying pan over medium heat for 3 minutes or until golden. Add remaining ingredients and simmer over low heat for an hour.

Fry the meatballs in batches in a large frying pan over medium heat.

Place bases of rolls on an oven tray, divide meatballs among rolls, top with tomato sauce and fontina and grill until cheese melts (2 minutes).

05

Remove from oven, top with tomato crisps and serve.

Serves 4

PEANUT PORK
SAN CHOY BOW

*   THE ORIENT EXPRESS   *

THIS PORK NUMBER IS CHEAP, QUICK AND SUPER TASTY — THE GREAT TRIFECTA
OF DINNER ON THE RUN.

INGREDIENTS

60 ml (2 fl oz/¼ cup) chicken stock
70 g (2½ oz/¼ cup) smooth peanut butter
300 g (10½ oz) minced (ground) pork
2 cloves garlic, crushed
1 egg, lightly beaten
65 g (2½ oz/½ cup) peanuts
   (salted or unsalted), roughly chopped
270 g (9½ oz) soba noodles
1 iceberg lettuce, leaves carefully removed

To serve
2 tbsp ready-made fried shallots (optional)

Preheat the oven to 180°C (350°F/Gas 4). Line a baking tray with baking paper and set aside.

Combine the stock and peanut butter in a large bowl and set aside.

Mix the pork, garlic, egg and peanuts in a bowl and stir to combine.

Roll the pork mixture into small walnut-sized balls and place on the prepared tray. Roast for 20 minutes, or until golden.

While the pork balls are roasting, cook the soba noodles according to the packet instructions. Drain and refresh under cold water.

Tip the noodles into the peanut butter and stock mixture. Add the meatballs and gently toss.

Top each lettuce leaf with some of the meatball and noodle mixture and finish with the fried shallots. Serve immediately.

Serves 4

PANCETTA AND CHEESY HONEY MUSTARD MUFFINS

THE GIFT THAT KEEPS ON GIVING

SURPRISE PIE IN MUFFIN FORM. I'VE USED PANCETTA HERE, BUT YOU COULD USE LEFT-OVER HAM, SAUSAGES, BACON, BASICALLY ANY MEAT YOU HAVE — THEY ALL SEEM TO WORK WELL.

INGREDIENTS

375 g (13 oz) mild pancetta, roughly chopped
375 g (13 oz/2$\frac{1}{2}$ cups) self-raising flour
1 tsp smoked paprika
sea salt and freshly ground black pepper
185 ml (6 fl oz/$\frac{3}{4}$ cup) milk (full cream is best)
3 large eggs
125 g (4$\frac{1}{2}$ oz/$\frac{1}{2}$ cup) honey mustard
200 g (7 oz/1 cup) tinned corn kernels
120 g (4$\frac{1}{4}$ oz/1 cup) grated parmesan
65 g (2$\frac{1}{2}$ oz/$\frac{1}{2}$ cup) grated mozzarella
50 g (1$\frac{3}{4}$ oz/$\frac{1}{2}$ cup) grated cheddar
$\frac{1}{2}$ red onion, finely chopped
a small handful of coriander (cilantro) leaves, finely chopped

To serve

butter
green salad

Preheat the oven to 200°C (400°F/Gas 6). Grease a six-hole jumbo muffin tin and set aside. Line a baking tray with baking paper and set aside.

Spread the pancetta on the prepared tray and bake for 10 minutes, or until crispy. Allow to cool.

Combine the flour and paprika in a large bowl and season with salt and pepper.

Whisk the milk, eggs and mustard in a separate bowl and add the pancetta, corn, parmesan, red onion and coriander.

Stir into the flour mixture until just blended, being careful not to overwork. Spoon the batter into the prepared tin until three-quarters full. Sprinkle the remaining cheeses on the muffins and bake for 20 minutes, or until the muffins are golden and crunchy on top and cooked through.

Allow to cool slightly, then run a knife around the muffins to loosen.

Invert the muffins onto a tray and serve warm with some butter, a green salad and a glass of wine.

Serves 6

CORIANDER-CRUSTED CHICKEN WITH MISO BUTTER
A BIRD IN THE HAND ...

AN EASY CHICKEN DISH WITH THE VIRTUE OF ASSUMING YOU DON'T HAVE THE ENERGY TO DO MUCH ELSE THAN FLING A FRYING PAN OVER THE HEAT OF A STOVE.

INGREDIENTS

----

2 tsp coriander seeds, crushed

2 garlic cloves, finely chopped

2 tsp sesame oil

1 kg (2 lb 4 oz) free-range chicken portions

Miso butter

a small handful of coriander (cilantro) leaves, chopped, plus extra to garnish

35 g (1¼ oz) unsalted butter, melted

2 spring onions (scallions), chopped

2 tbsp rice vinegar

1 tbsp white miso paste

1 tbsp finely chopped fresh ginger

1 tsp soy sauce

2 tbsp sake

To serve

steamed greens

For the miso butter, mix the coriander, butter, spring onion, vinegar, miso, ginger, soy sauce and sake in small bowl and set aside.

Combine the coriander seeds, garlic and oil in a bowl to create a marinade. Rub the chicken with marinade.

03

Heat a barbecue to medium and cook the chicken, turning frequently, for 15 minutes, or until cooked through.

Place the miso butter in a saucepan over low heat and cook until heated through.

05

Plate the chicken with some steamed greens and pour on the miso butter. Sprinkle with the extra coriander and serve.

Serves 4

STEAK DIANE SALAD
AND THE BEEF GOES ON

I'm not sure why steak Diane went by the wayside. It seems to garner the same sort of 'do not mention the war' reputation as the Queen's coronation chicken. So to give it some cachet here, it's been incorporated into a salad.

INGREDIENTS

----

60 ml (2 fl oz/¼ cup) olive oil

3 x 150 g (5½ oz) scotch
  fillet steaks

Salad

750 g (1 lb 10 oz) new
  potatoes, halved

5 slices of prosciutto, chopped

3 garlic cloves, roughly
  chopped

2 tbsp olive oil

sea salt and freshly ground
  black pepper

80 g (2¾ oz/2 cups) mixed
  salad leaves

1 red onion, thinly sliced

250 g (9 oz) cherry tomatoes,
  halved

35 g (1¼ oz/¼ cup) crumbled
  Persian feta, or any
  creamy feta

Diane sauce

100 g (3½ oz) butter

125 ml (4 fl oz/½ cup)
  thickened cream

2 tsp bottled or fresh
  horseradish

2 tbsp tomato sauce (ketchup)

1 tbsp worcestershire sauce

salt and freshly ground
  black pepper

Preheat the oven to 180°C (350°F/Gas 4).

02

For the salad, cook the potatoes in a large saucepan of boiling salted water for 15 minutes, or until just tender. Drain well and return to the pan. Add the prosciutto, garlic and oil, season with the salt and pepper and toss to coat. Spread the mixture on a large baking tray and roast for 30 minutes, or until the potatoes are golden and tender. Set aside to cool. Combine the remaining salad ingredients in another bowl and add the potatoes once slightly cooled so they don't wilt the salad leaves.

03

Heat the oil in a frying pan over high heat, add the steaks and cook, in batches if necessary, for 2 minutes on each side. To ensure the steaks form a good seal on each side, don't move them around while cooking. Place the steaks on a plate, loosely cover with foil and set aside.

04

For the Diane sauce, combine all the ingredients in a small saucepan over low heat and simmer for 1–2 minutes until thickened slightly and warmed through. Season with salt and pepper.

Thinly slice the steaks and toss with the salad. Heap onto serving plates, drizzle on the Diane sauce to taste and serve.

Serves 4

PUMPKIN AND BURNT-BUTTER
SAGE RAVIOLI BAKE

* BAKED GOODNESS *

THIS IS THE ULTIMATE MID-WEEK, GENERALLY CAN'T-BE-ARSED COOKING SOLUTION.
THERE IS NO INGREDIENTS LIST 30 PRODUCTS LONG, NOR DOES IT INVOLVE
DIFFICULT PROCESSES. HAND ON HEART THIS IS ACTUALLY A RECIPE FOR PEOPLE
WHO COOK WITHOUT THE AID OF A COUPLE OF SOUS CHEFS AND A KITCHENHAND
FOR THE WASHING UP.

INGREDIENTS

60 g (2¼ oz) butter
a small handful of sage leaves,
   plus extra to garnish
1½ tsp freshly grated nutmeg
230 g (8¼ oz/1 cup) ricotta
900 g (2 lb) fresh pumpkin
   (squash) ravioli
75 g (2¾ oz/½ cup) shredded mozzarella
60 g (2¼ oz/½ cup) grated parmesan
80 g (2¾ oz/1⅓ cups) fresh breadcrumbs

Preheat the oven to 210°C (415°F/Gas 6–7).

Melt the butter in a large saucepan over medium heat, stirring until it starts to darken.

Add the sage leaves and nutmeg and cook until the sage leaves begin to crisp and shrink (under a minute).

Remove from the heat and combine in a bowl with the ricotta.

Cook the ravioli in a large saucepan of boiling water until the pasta floats to the top.

Add the pasta and ricotta mixture and half the mozzarella back into the pan and gently toss.

Tip the pasta into a large gratin dish or ovenproof dish and sprinkle on the remaining mozzarella, the parmesan, breadcrumbs and additional sage leaves if using.

Bake for 20–25 minutes, or until golden.

Cool slightly before serving.

Serves 4–6

BLACK FOREST
DESSERT

FABLE

I WONDER IF ALL THE CHILDHOOD STORIES THAT TOLD US NOT TO WANDER
INTO THE FOREST WERE FOR A REASON?

INGREDIENTS
250 g (9 oz) cream cheese, softened
30 g (1 oz/¼ cup) icing (confectioners') sugar
2 tbsp unsweetened cocoa powder
100 g (3½ oz) plain chocolate biscuits
   (cookies), roughly broken
100 g (3½ oz) white chocolate, shaved
200 g (7 oz/1 cup) morello cherries

Combine the cream cheese, sugar and cocoa in a bowl and mix well.

Dollop some of the cream cheese mixture into serving glasses, top with some biscuit shards, white chocolate shavings and cherries. Repeat, layering the remaining ingredients in the glasses. Refrigerate for 5 minutes, or until chilled, and serve immediately.

Serves 4

Get me a bowl. I'm involved

You want to eat well. You just don't want dinner to be labour intensive.

Got it. Now cook it.

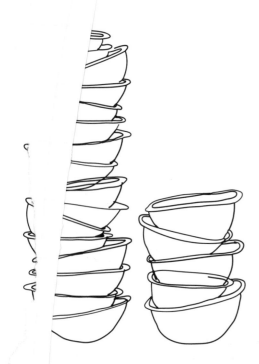

Menu

Panthay khowse

–

Baked eggs with yoghurt, chorizo and chilli

–

Bream with balsamic and basil

–

Tuna meatballs with olives and parsley pasta

–

Plum, soy and maple chicken sausage rolls

–

One-pot three-shot chicken

–

Pear cakes

–

Strawberries 'n' cream

–

Flourless white chocolate cake

–

Honey cakes with honey jumble meringue cream

PANTHAY KHOWSE

NEW YORK STATE OF MIND

MY MUM AND DAD FELL IN LOVE WHEN THEY WERE VERY YOUNG. BOTH OF THEM FROM A SMALL COUNTRY TOWN, MUM COULD HAVE MARRIED HIM AND NEVER LEFT. INSTEAD SHE JUMPED ON A PLANE, LEFT HIM PINING FOR HER MADLY NO DOUBT, AND TRAIPSED AROUND THE UNITED STATES FOR A YEAR.

MY FATHER IS HARDLY THE SHRINKING VIOLET, BUT MUM IS STRONG AND INDEPENDENT IN A SPECIAL UNASSUMING WAY. AND THE BEST BIT — SHE KEPT THAT INDEPENDENT SPIRIT. WHEN EVERYONE ELSE WAS HAVING BABIES, MUM AND DAD SPENT THEIR LAST CENTS ON A CAMPERVAN AND ENJOYED TWO YEARS TRAVELLING THROUGH CENTRAL AMERICA, INCLUDING MEXICO WHERE THEY WERE HELD AT KNIFEPOINT.

KUDOS.

SO EVERY TIME I EAT THIS CURRY I THINK OF MY MUM, HER QUIET INDEPENDENCE, AND THE FACT THAT GOOD FOOD REALLY DOES TRAVEL (SHE LEARNT THIS BURMESE CURRY RECIPE WHILE LIVING IN UPSTATE NEW YORK).

NOW I JUST WISH I COULD LEARN HOW TO DO IT — THE INDEPENDENCE THING THAT IS — A LOT MORE QUIETLY.

INGREDIENTS

1 large barbecued chicken (or you can roast a chook at home)
60 ml (2 fl oz/¼ cup) sesame oil
2 small onions, thinly sliced
3 garlic cloves, finely chopped
1 tsp grated fresh ginger
1 tbsp Indian-style curry paste
250 ml (9 fl oz/1 cup) coconut milk
250 ml (9 fl oz/1 cup) coconut cream
125 ml (4 fl oz/½ cup) boiling water
1 x 375 g (13 oz) packet of egg noodles

To garnish

1 small red red chilli, deseeded and finely sliced
3 hard-boiled eggs, peeled and roughly chopped
3 French shallots, finely chopped
lime juice, to taste
2 limes, quartered

Shred the chicken meat into a bowl, discarding bones, and set aside.

Heat the oil in a large frying pan over medium heat and fry the onion, garlic and ginger for 10 minutes, or until softened. Stir in the curry paste and cook for 2 minutes, or until fragrant. Add the chicken, stirring to coat, then pour in the coconut milk and cream and water. Turn the heat to low, cover, and cook for 15–20 minutes, or until the sauce has thickened slightly.

While the chicken is simmering, cook the egg noodles according to the packet instructions.

Arrange the egg noodles in bowls, add the chicken mixture and garnish with the chilli, egg and shallots and a generous squeeze of lime juice. Serve with the lime wedges.

Serves 6

BAKED EGGS WITH YOGHURT, CHORIZO AND CHILLI
FOOD AND WHINE

THIS IS BASED ON ÇILBIR, A TURKISH DISH OF POACHED EGGS WITH YOGURT. RATHER THAN HAVING YOU TROLLOPING AROUND YOUR LOCAL SPICE BAZAAR LOOKING FOR KIRMIZI BIBER, HERE I'VE JUST USED CHILLI AND PAPRIKA, AND ADDED CHORIZO FOR A LITTLE EXTRA GRUNT.

INGREDIENTS
2 chorizo sausages, casings discarded and filling finely chopped
600 g (1 lb 5 oz) baby rocket (arugula)
sea salt and freshly ground black pepper
8 eggs
2 garlic cloves, finely chopped
300 g (10½ oz) Greek yoghurt
100 g (3½ oz) unsalted butter
1 tsp paprika
1 tsp dried chilli flakes
10 sage leaves

To serve
crusty bread

Preheat the oven to 150°C (300°F/Gas 2).

Place the chorizo filling in a large frying pan and fry over medium heat for 5 minutes, or until cooked through. Using a slotted spoon, transfer the chorizo to a plate, reserving the juices in the pan. Return the pan to the heat, add the rocket and a pinch of salt and sauté over medium heat for 3 minutes, or until the rocket has wilted and most of the liquid has been absorbed. Place in a 25 x 25 x 5 cm (10 x 10 x 2 inch) gratin dish and make eight indentations in the rocket. Carefully break an egg and gently pour into a crater, trying not to break the yolk. Repeat with remaining eggs in the other indentations. Gently sprinkle on the chorizo and bake for 10-12 minutes, or until the eggs are set.

While the eggs are cooking, combine the garlic and yoghurt in a small bowl, season with salt and pepper and set aside.

Melt the butter in a small saucepan over medium heat, add the spices and cook until a foam appears and the butter takes on a reddish hue. Add the sage and cook for another 30 seconds.

Dollop the garlic yoghurt on the eggs, then drizzle over the spiced sage butter. Serve immediately with crusty bread.

Serves 4

BREAM WITH BALSAMIC AND BASIL

THE PROGENY OF RESTAURANT NON-ROYALS

THIS RECIPE IS BASED ON ONE I DISCOVERED FROM THE UK *OBSERVER FOOD MONTHLY* — BRILLIANTLY SIMPLE AND TASTY AS HELL.

INGREDIENTS

2 small whole bream, cleaned
  (about 300 g/10½ oz)
1–2 tbsp olive oil
2 garlic cloves, peeled and smashed
a large handful of basil leaves,
  roughly torn
125 ml (4 fl oz/½ cup) balsamic vinegar

To serve
fresh lemon halves

Preheat the oven to 190°C (375°F/Gas 5).

Score both sides of the bream to the bone. Rub the oil into the bream.

Combine the garlic, basil and balsamic in a mortar and pestle and smash to a rough paste.

Pack the cuts in the fish with the roughly pounded herb mixture and a few extra whole basil leaves. As a guide it is about 3 tablespoons of mixture per fish.

Place the fish in a roasting tin and roast for 20 minutes, or until flaking off the bone.

Serves 2

TUNA MEATBALLS WITH OLIVES AND PARSLEY PASTA

FASTA PASTA

THESE LITTLE BALLS OF GLORY ARE HEARTY ENOUGH TO MAKE YOU FEEL WARM INSIDE AND OUT — THE STUFF OF LEGENDS.

INGREDIENTS

Meatballs
600 g (1 lb 5 oz) tuna fillets, finely chopped
1 red onion, finely chopped
1 garlic clove, finely chopped
1 egg
sea salt and freshly ground black pepper
2 tsp olive oil

Pasta
450g (1 lb) angel hair pasta
1 tbsp finely grated lemon zest
250 g (9 oz) green Sicilian olives, pitted and halved
100 g (3½ oz/1 cup) shaved parmesan
1 red onion, thinly sliced
a handful of flat-leaf parsley, roughly chopped
80 g (2¾ oz) baby rocket (arugula)
juice of 1 lemon
1 tbsp olive oil

For the meatballs, combine the tuna, onion, garlic and egg in a bowl, mix gently and season with salt and pepper.

Mould into meatballs about the size of a large walnut, cover with plastic wrap and refrigerate for 20 minutes.

Heat a large frying pan over high heat, add the oil and cook the meatballs for 3 minutes on one side, turn and cook for 1 minute on the other side, or until brown and just cooked through.

While the meatballs are cooking, cook the angel hair pasta according to the packet instructions. Drain well and tip into a large bowl.

Add the remaining ingredients and the tuna meatballs and toss gently. Serve immediately.

Serves 4–6

PLUM, SOY AND MAPLE
CHICKEN SAUSAGE ROLLS

***************************** SAUSAGE ENVY *****************************

IN THESE HEALTH-CONSCIOUS TIMES, SAUSAGE ROLLS HAVE A BAD REPUTATION. GONE
ARE THE DAYS WHEN YOU COULD SIT AT A BUS STOP, AFTER THE NIGHT BEFORE, AND
CHEERFULLY CHOW DOWN A SAUSAGE ROLL. TRY THAT NOW AND PEOPLE WILL STARE
AT YOU LIKE YOU'RE SELLING NARCOTICS TO SCHOOLCHILDREN.

I THINK IF THERE WERE MORE SAUSAGE ROLLS AROUND, CHILDREN WOULD BE SAFELY
STANDING IN THE TUCKSHOP LINE AT SCHOOL RATHER THAN TALKING TO STRANGE
PEOPLE AT BUS STOPS.

INGREDIENTS
1¹/₂ tbsp olive oil
6 garlic cloves, finely chopped
1 red onion, finely chopped
1.25 kg (2 lb 12 oz) chicken mince (ground)
40 g (1¹/₂ oz/¹/₃ cup) dry breadcrumbs
sea salt and freshly ground black pepper
125 ml (4 fl oz/¹/₂ cup) plum sauce
60 ml (2 fl oz/¹/₄ cup) soy sauce
60 ml (2 fl oz/¹/₄ cup) maple syrup
2 x 375 g (13 oz) sheets of ready-made
    puff pastry

Egg wash
1 egg
100 ml (3¹/₂ fl oz) milk
a pinch of salt

To serve
soy sauce and plum sauce, for dipping

Preheat the oven to 200°C (400°F/Gas 6). Line two baking trays with baking paper and set aside.

Heat the oil in a frying pan over medium heat, add the garlic and onion and cook for 5 minutes, or until the onion is softened.

Place the chicken in a large bowl. Add the garlic and onion mixture and breadcrumbs, then season with salt and pepper. Pour in the plum sauce, soy sauce and maple syrup and, using your hands, mix until well combined.

On a lightly floured surface, roll out each pastry sheet to form a 30 x 45 cm (12 x 18 inch) rectangle. Cut each into three 15 x 30 cm (6 x 12 inch) rectangles.

For the egg wash, lightly whisk the egg, milk and salt in a small bowl and set aside.

Divide the chicken filling into six portions. On a clean surface, roll each portion of filling into a log shape approximately 3 x 30 cm (1¹/₄ x 12 inches) in size. Place each log in the centre of a pastry rectangle and brush one long edge with the egg wash. Leaving the ends open, firmly fold the pastry over the filling, pressing to enclose tightly. Cut each roll in half and place, seam side down, on the prepared trays. Brush the top with the egg wash and bake for 35–40 minutes until golden.

Makes 12

ONE-POT THREE-SHOT CHICKEN
SCHOOL OF WOK

THIS IS MY PEDESTRIAN VERSION OF NEIL PERRY'S THREE-SHOT CHICKEN.

INGREDIENTS

----

1 kg (2 lb 4 oz) chicken
   thigh fillets, fat and sinew
   removed, quartered

1 tbsp grapeseed oil

2 garlic cloves, crushed

2 tsp finely grated ginger

125 ml (4¼ fl oz/½ cup) bean
   paste

125 ml (4¼ fl oz/½ cup) mirin

500 ml (17 fl oz/2 cups)
   chicken stock

20 ml (½ fl oz) chilli oil

125 ml (4¼ fl oz/½ cup) light
   soy sauce

250 ml (8½ fl oz/1 cup) beer
   (try and aim for a dry malt
   style beer such as Asahi)

200 g (7 oz) fresh shitake
   mushrooms

To serve

steamed rice

fresh shallots

01

Preheat the oven to 180°C (350°F/Gas 4).

02

Heat the oil in a large heavy-based casserole dish over medium–high heat and sear the chicken in batches until browned all over but not cooked through. Remove the chicken and add the garlic and ginger, stirring until fragrant. Turn the heat to low, add the bean paste, mirin, chicken stock, chilli oil, soy sauce and beer. Stir until all the lumps of bean paste have dissolved.

03

Add the shitake mushrooms and simmer for 10 minutes until the mushrooms look plump and have absorbed some of the liquid.

04

Return the chicken to the pot and cover with a piece of silicon paper that fits within the pot, then cover with the lid.

05

Braise in the oven for 1 hour and serve hot with steamed rice and topped with shallots.

Serves 6 (great for freezing)

PEAR CAKES
WHERE THERE'S CAKE
THERE'S CALM

MAKE THESE AHEAD AND FREEZE THEM FOR THOSE DAYS WHEN COOKING IS TOTALLY BEYOND YOU.

INGREDIENTS

70 g (2½ oz) butter, chopped
2 egg whites
125 g (4½ oz/1 cup) icing (confectioners')
    sugar, sifted
1 tsp rosewater
50 g (1¾ oz/⅓ cup) plain
    (all-purpose) flour
40 g (1½ oz) ground almonds
1 tsp ground cinnamon
1 pear, halved, stoned and thinly sliced

Preheat the oven to 160°C (315°F/Gas 2–3). Grease a six-hole giant muffin tin or 12 dariole moulds.

Melt the butter in a small saucepan over medium heat and cook until foamy and dark golden in colour.

Meanwhile, whisk the egg whites in a bowl to soft peaks, then add the sugar, a tablespoon at a time, and whisk until thick and glossy. Fold in the rosewater, flour, ground almonds and cinnamon.

Mix in the melted butter and spoon the mixture into the baking mould.

Top each muffin with a slice of pear and bake for 15 minutes until firm to touch.

Makes 6 large or 12 small

STRAWBERRIES 'N' CREAM
BERRY GOOD

FIVE MINUTES OF YOUR TIME = PASTRY, CREAM AND STRAWBERRY RELISH

INGREDIENTS

2 tbsp sifted icing (confectioners') sugar, plus extra for dusting
2 tbsp aged balsamic vinegar
250 g (9 oz) strawberries, hulled and halved

Pastry cream

100 ml (3½ fl oz) cream
150 ml (5 fl oz) sweetened condensed milk
1 tsp natural vanilla extract

Pastry

1 sheet puff pastry
1 egg white, lightly beaten
2 tbsp caster (superfine) sugar

Preheat the oven to 200°C (400°F/Gas 6). Line a baking tray with baking paper and set aside.

Puree the sugar, vinegar and half the strawberries in a food processor. Toss the remaining strawberries in the puree and refrigerate until ready to serve.

For the pastry cream, pour the cream into a bowl and whisk until soft peaks form. Gently fold in the condensed milk and vanilla. Cover with plastic wrap and refrigerate until serving.

Working quickly on a lightly floured surface, roll out the pastry to form a thin 30 cm (12 inch) square, then cut into thirds. Brush the egg white over the surface of the pastry rectangles, leaving a 1 cm (½ inch) border and taking care not to let any run over the edges. Sprinkle the sugar evenly over each piece of pastry and bake for 20 minutes, or until risen and golden. Remove from the oven and place another baking tray on top to gently flatten the pastry. Transfer to a wire rack to cool.

Place one piece of pastry on a platter, spread with half the pastry cream and half the strawberry mixture. Repeat with the remaining pastry, pastry cream and strawberry mixture, then top with the final piece of pastry. Dust with the extra icing sugar and serve.

Serves 4–6

FLOURLESS
WHITE CHOCOLATE CAKE

CAKE THAT

THIS CAKE IS LIKE A LITTLE BLACK DRESS —
IT SUITS EVERY OCCASION.

INGREDIENTS

150 g (5½ oz) white chocolate, chopped
150 g (5½ oz) unsalted butter, softened
100 g (3½ oz) caster (superfine) sugar
5 eggs, separated
1 tsp natural vanilla extract
140 g (5 oz) hazelnut meal

To serve

whipped cream
hazelnuts

Preheat the oven to 200°C (400°F/Gas 6).
Grease and line the base of a 22 cm
(8½ inch) springform cake tin.

Melt the chocolate in a heatproof bowl over
a saucepan of gently simmering water.
Set aside to cool.

Cream the butter and sugar until pale
and fluffy, add the egg yolks, beating well,
then stir in the melted chocolate, vanilla
and hazelnut meal.

Whisk the egg whites in a separate bowl
until stiff peaks form. Fold a little of the
egg whites into the cake mixture, then
carefully fold in the remaining egg whites.
Spoon into the prepared tin and bake for
10 minutes.

Reduce the temperature to 170°C (325°F/
Gas 3) and bake for another 10 minutes,
for a soft centre. For a firmer cake, cook
for an additional 5–10 minutes. Serve with
whipped cream and hazelnuts.

Serves 6–8

HONEY CAKES WITH HONEY JUMBLE MERINGUE CREAM
SUGAR BEATS

A CAKE VERSION OF THE ULTIMATE BISCUIT CONFECTION OF MY CHILDHOOD — THE HONEY JUMBLE. THIS APPEALS TO THE FOODIE AND THE KID INSIDE.

INGREDIENTS
Cakes
75 g (2¾ oz) butter
175 g (6 oz/½ cup) honey
220 g (7¾ oz/1 cup) caster (superfine) sugar
3 eggs
150 g (5½ oz/1 cup) plain (all-purpose) flour
1 tsp bicarbonate of soda
1½ tsp ground ginger
1½ tsp mixed spice
½ tsp ground cloves
60 ml (2 fl oz/¼ cup) milk

Meringue icing
165 g (5¾ oz/¾ cup) caster (superfine) sugar
90 g (3¼ oz/¼ cup) honey
60 ml (2 fl oz/¼ cup) water
¼ tsp cream of tartar
3 egg whites
a few drops of red food colouring

Preheat the oven to 160°C (315°F/Gas 2–3). Lightly grease four 10 cm (4 inch) round cake tins and line the base and sides with baking paper.

For the cakes, melt the butter and honey in a small saucepan over low heat, stirring until smooth. Set aside to cool. Beat the sugar, eggs and the butter mixture in a bowl using electric beaters until pale and thick. Sift the flour, bicarbonate of soda and ground spices into a separate bowl. Incorporate half the flour, then half the milk into the egg mixture and repeat with the remaining flour and milk until just combined. Pour the batter into the prepared tins and bake for 20 minutes, or until the cakes are springy to touch and come away from the sides of the tins. Turn out onto wire racks to cool completely.

For the meringue icing, place the sugar, honey, water and cream of tartar in a saucepan over high heat and bring to the boil, stirring to dissolve the sugar. Reduce the heat to low and cook, without stirring, for 3 minutes. Whisk the egg whites in a large bowl with electric beaters until soft peaks form. Gradually whisk in the sugar syrup and continue to whisk until thick and glossy. Divide the icing between two bowls. Add the red food colouring to one bowl and stir to combine.

Cut the cooled cakes into 8 halves. Spread the pink icing over two halves and the white icing on two halves. Top each iced cake with another cake half and press gently to make a sandwich.

Makes 4

ACKNOWLEDGEMENTS

I owe you a pie. Know this. It is an unwavering fact.
Cook someone a pie and you have a friend for life.
The following people helped me to get this book off the ground
and I owe each of you a truly magnificent pie.

TOM

For never saying 'if' but 'when' and for providing the
kind of support for which a million 'thank yous' will
never suffice. I will always cook for you.

My Family
For their eternal encouragement in every endeavour.

BARBARA *Meynink*

My beautiful, beautiful
grandma who taught me a love
of cooking and the wonder
of words, long before I knew
these two things would become
my raison d'être. I miss you
desperately. If only it took a pie
to have you, and our chats about
books and the ins and outs
of the perfect meringue,
back in my life.

Sue Hines

and her spectacular team
at Allen & Unwin —
You are proof that
opportunity for emerging
writers still exists and
that professionalism in
the publishing industry
is alive and well.

THE GIRLS

For your late night
reading, recipe testing,
and patiently listening
to my rants.

Andrew Hoyne

For capturing and
creating a unique vision
and running with it.

Roald Dahl

For creating fantastical universes in
words that I wished were mine. A pie
would go down a treat with a cucumber
fizz, served by oompa loompas in a
land of giant peaches ...

JASON LOUCAS

For your beautiful
photographs and
architectural precision
when it comes to building
a salad.

And to those other people, suppliers and photographers the world over who by sheer random acts of kindness
took a leap of faith and provided some images on their own back and their own time for this book. I cannot wait
to meet you: David Lanthan Reamer; Ryan Kenny; Jason Weeding; and Natalie McComas. Also thanks to
Elaine Adams, Heather Barnsen, Huey Lau, Mud Homewares, No Chintz, the James Beard Foundation and
the International Culinary Institute.

INDEX

CONVERSION CHARTS

TEMPERATURE

Gas Mark	Fahrenheit	Celsius	Description
1/4	225	110	Very slow
1/2	250	130	Very slow
1	275	140	Slow
2	300	150	Slow
3	315/325	160/170	Very moderate
4	350	180	Moderate
5	375	190	Moderately hot
6	400	200	Moderately hot
7	425	220	Hot
8	450	230	Hot
9	475	240	Very hot

LIQUIDS

Metric	Imperial	Cups
1.25 ml	0.04 fl oz	1/4 tsp (teaspoon)
2.5 ml	0.08 fl oz	1/2 tsp
5 ml	0.16 fl oz	1 tsp
20 ml	2/3 fl oz	1 tbsp (tablespoon)
30 ml	1 fl oz	2 tbsp
60 ml	2 fl oz	1/4 cup
125 ml	4 fl oz	1/2 cup
150 ml	1/4 pint	2/3 cup
175 ml	6 fl oz	3/4 cup
250 ml	8 fl oz	1 cup (1/2 US pint)
300 ml	1/2 pint	1 1/4 cup
375 ml	12 fl oz	1 1/2 cup
500 ml	16 fl oz	2 cups (1 US pint)
600 ml	1 pint	2 1/2 cup
1.25 litres	2 pints	1 quart

Please be aware that in countries other than Australia, the metric tablespoon is 15 ml (1/2 fl oz). The Australian cup measure (used in the book) is 250 ml, but in the UK it is 285 ml and in the USA it is 236 ml.

First published in 2011

Allen & Unwin
Sydney, Melbourne, Auckland, London

83 Alexander Street
Crows Nest NSW 2065
Australia
Phone: (61 2) 8425 0100
Fax: (61 2) 9906 2218
Email: info@allenandunwin.com
www.allenandunwin.com

Cataloguing-in-Publication details are available
from the National Library of Australia
www.trove.nla.gov.au

ISBN 978 1 74237 681 3

Design by Hoyne
Art direction by Andrew Hoyne
Illustrations by Huey Lau and Lauren Wyllie
Index by Jo Rudd
Photography credits:
Jason Loucas: pp. 15, 17, 26, 38, 43, 58–9, 79, 91, 97,
125, 126, 160, 165, 169, 179, 185, 215, 219, 222, 227,
231, 233, 235, 245, 261
Ryan Kenny: p. 142
David Lanthan Reamer: pp. 51, 73, 103, 116, 236
Natalie McComas: pp. 22, 54, 157
Jason Weeding: pp. 19, 85, 210
Other photos by author: pp. 12, 25, 29, 35, 37, 53, 57,
67, 71, 82, 89, 106, 123, 129, 132, 139, 151, 159, 167,
170, 172, 175, 189, 205, 206, 213, 221, 250, 253, 257,
262, 264

Printed in China by C&C Offset Printing Co., Ltd

10 9 8 7 6 5 4 3 2